OVER LAND AND SEA

OVER LAND AND SEA

A History of West Ham United in Europe

MIKE MILES

pitch

First published by Pitch Publishing, 2024

Pitch Publishing
9 Donnington Park,
85 Birdham Road,
Chichester, West Sussex,
PO20 7AJ
www.pitchpublishing.co.uk
info@pitchpublishing.co.uk

A CIP catalogue record is available for this book from the British Library.

ISBN 978 1 80150 748 6

MIX
Paper | Supporting responsible forestry
FSC® C013604

Printed and bound in the UK on FSC® certified paper in line with our continuing commitment to ethical business practices, sustainability and the environment.

Typesetting and origination by Pitch Publishing

Printed and bound by CPI Anthony Rowe, UK

Contents

Introduction

WHEN I mentioned to a Chelsea-supporting friend of mine that I was writing a history of West Ham United in Europe, his all-to-predictable response was that it would be a pretty thin book!

I had to concede that West Ham have yet to trouble the organisers of the Champions League and that what success they have had in Europe (the Cup Winners' Cup in 1965, the Intertoto Cup in 1999) had been in competitions which no longer exist. Thankfully, that would change in 2023, when the club won the UEFA Conference League.

Nevertheless, West Ham have a rich tradition of playing against continental opposition. They travelled into Europe as long ago as 1921, when manager Syd King took his team to Spain.

West Ham United are one of the most successful teams in the history of European club competitions … yes, it's true. Prior to the end of the 20th century, they had played in the now deceased European Cup Winners'

Cup on four occasions. In each campaign, they reached at least the quarter-finals. They reached the final twice, losing to Anderlecht in Brussels in 1976 and, of course, winning the trophy at Wembley against TSV 1860 Munich in 1965.

In 2000, they became the first British winners of the much-derided UEFA Intertoto Cup and, in the process, qualified for the UEFA Cup. They managed to overcome a tricky first-round game in Croatia before being eliminated by Steaua Bucharești, thus sending their UEFA ranking plunging, although they still retained a win ratio of 50 per cent of all European games.

And when Ronnie Boyce scored West Ham's first European competitive goal against La Gantoise in September 1964, he launched a 27-game record run for the number of consecutive European competition matches in which a club has scored. The scoring sequence ended on Guy Fawkes Night in 1980, when the Hammers lost 1-0 away to Politehnica Timișoara in Romania.

If you include the three Cup Winners' Cup matches played after the consecutive scoring sequence ended, then the Hammers scored in 29 of their 30 games in the competition.

The 27-game record lasted 31 years until, on 6 December 2011 in the Champions League, Barcelona beat BATE Borisov of Belarus 4-1 to score in their 28th consecutive European match.

But the Hammers still hold the consecutive scoring record for a British club.

So there, Chelsea, Liverpool, Manchester City et al.

Probably every football supporter believes their team has a monopoly on misery. But I really believe West Ham would be near the top of any misery league.

Just to give a few examples:

West Ham had their best-ever First Division (pre-Premier League) finish of third under John Lyall in 1986, but missed out on Europe because of the post-Heysel ban.

Under the late Glenn Roeder in 2002/03, the Hammers – having staged a revival after managing to go until late January without a Premier League home win – were relegated with 42 points, a record high for a relegated team. Having already lost Rio Ferdinand and Frank Lampard, the club ended up selling several other rising England stars in Joe Cole, Glen Johnson, Jermain Defoe and Michael Carrick, all of whom they had nurtured from their youth set-up.

Alan Pardew achieved promotion via the play-offs in 2005 and, after a creditable ninth-place finish in the Premier League, reached the 2006 FA Cup Final. After 90 minutes, the East Londoners were 3-2 up against Liverpool. Surely this was the moment our trophy drought would end. Then a certain Steven Gerrard dispatched a missile into Shaka Hislop's net. Inevitably, West Ham lost on penalties. It was small consolation that it was one of the greatest finals.

We signed Argentinian superstars Carlos Tevez and Javier Mascherano, but 'forgot' they were owned by a third party. Somehow the club was only fined, rather than relegated, much to Sheffield United's disgust.

The club was bought by Icelandic millionaire Björgólfur Guðmundsson, aided by biscuit baron chairman Eggert Magnússon. Guðmundsson would then lose his fortune in the 2008 credit crunch.

West Ham were then purchased by David Sullivan and David Gold, two men who had made their fortune in the porn industry. For some reason, they appointed Avram Grant as manager, who got the club relegated after his one and only season. At our last game at Wigan, we went 2-0 up, only to lose 3-2. The misery was rounded off by a plane overhead carrying a banner reading 'Avram Grant: Millwall Legend'. Only West Ham could have a player (Scott Parker) voted PFA Player of the Year from a team that got relegated.

'Big Sam' Allardyce was the necessary shock medicine. He got the club back into the Premier League, winning the 2012 play-off final and established the Hammers in the top flight but struggled to win over the fans. Echoes of David Moyes.

Slaven Bilić was the right manager to celebrate the final season at the Boleyn Ground and he signed the brilliant Dimitri Payet. In 2016, the club moved to the London Stadium, an arena which was great for athletics but not football. Payet became homesick and left.

Having made the Europa League qualifiers in 2015 and 2016, West Ham somehow found a bogey side no-one had heard of, losing in successive seasons to Romanian club Astra Giurgiu.

Things got so bad at the London Stadium that during David Moyes'ss first spell in charge, a 3-0 home defeat by Burnley was interrupted by pitch invaders and fans trying to storm the boardroom. Mark Noble had to act as an impromptu bouncer, carrying one invader off the pitch.

The reign of Manuel Pellegrini ended after he signed our worst-ever keeper in Roberto and the crocked Jack Wilshere. Sullivan and Gold did a volte-face and back came Moyes. Then lockdown arrived. And then something changed. Playing behind closed doors, West Ham finished sixth.

In the Europa League in 2021/22, an epic win against Sevilla proved the London Stadium could be a cauldron of noise, though we then lost the semi-final to Eintracht Frankfurt in a very West Ham way, conceding in the first minute of the home leg and having Aaron Cresswell sent off early in the away leg. Still, the Irons finished seventh in the Premier League and were back in Europe.

It went back to being flaky in 2022/23. Moyes spent £160m but a relegation struggle ensued. West Ham beat Nottingham Forest 4-0 one week and lost 4-0 at Brighton the next, a defeat accompanied by chants of 'You don't know what you're doing'. But West Ham continued to win in Europe. The board stuck with Moyes, who won the must-win league games. The European journey led to Prague, where, in what would prove to be his last game for the club, Declan Rice became the first Hammers captain since Bobby Moore and Billy Bonds all those years ago to lift a trophy.

I am a West Ham fan. Why am I a West Ham fan? I have no known family connection with the East End and if I knew the grief and anguish West Ham would cause me over the years, I might have gone for a safer option.

I was born and grew up in Hereford and cut my football teeth watching the local team, Hereford United (who would, of course, play their own distinctive part in Hammers history), play in the Southern League at their Edgar Street ground. The 1964 FA Cup Final came along at just the right time. If that was the aperitif, then the Cup Winners' Cup Final a year later was the main course. And West Ham winning the World Cup that memorable summer of 1966 made an indelible impression on this 14-year-old.

I saw my first live West Ham match in September 1967. We didn't have a car and somehow I must have persuaded my father to undertake the long, tedious coach journey from Hereford to London. They were playing bottom club Wolves at Upton Park. West Ham had won their previous two matches 5-1 away from home. So, of course, they lost that day (2-1 if you're interested). But by then it was too late … I was hooked.

'It's hard to explain what the club is, but I do know that it's *my* club. I've been brought up with it all my life. One thing's for sure; it's something that has always been there. You can't explain it.' Colin Green, a West Ham supporter, quoted in Charles Korr's *West Ham United*.

As Brian Williams put it in *Nearly Reach the Sky*: 'There are people who consider football to be a religion, but I don't see it that way. Religious faith offers certainty, salvation and, in some cases, virgins. I've never found any of these while watching West Ham United and I've been following them for 50 years.

'If it's not a religion, it's certainly an addiction. I've seen all the great players who have turned out in claret and blue since the late 60s and rather too many of the not-so-great as well. I've been there when we've triumphed and when we've been humiliated. I've rejoiced at cup final wins, despaired at relegation, celebrated promotion, savoured the sweet and sour pleasure of unlikely escapes and looked on powerlessly as the club has been taken to the brink of financial disaster more than once. Who in their right mind would willingly become a football supporter and choose to support a club like mine?'

Now, if I knew the answer to that …

Mike Miles
London, May 2024

Chapter One

Early Days: West Ham Pioneer European Friendlies

IN THEIR official handbook for the 1976/77 season, West Ham listed 'matches against foreign clubs'. It boasted that: 'The Hammers have played over 200 matches under this heading. We do not claim this is a record, as several clubs which have consistently played in European competitions since the inception of the European Champions Cup in 1955/56 have also amassed impressive totals.

'Nevertheless, our continental tours of the pre-World War Two era were occasions somewhat out of the ordinary and we can lay claim to being the first British club to re-commence fixtures against teams from the central European powers after World War One.'

In *They Nearly Reached The Sky*, published in 2017, Brian Belton reckoned that: 'In the history of the club, West Ham have played more than 350 games against

European opposition right across the continent, some from countries that no longer exist.'

West Ham had first travelled into Europe in 1921 when manager Syd King took the team to Spain, a trip which included four matches against Athletic Bilbao which were won 6-0, 4-1, 3-1 and 1-0.

And, in the summer of 1923, as a reward for their prodigious efforts in reaching the FA Cup Final and the exalted heights of the First Division, the players were taken on tour to Hungary and Austria.

The following summer, the club visited Germany for the first time, playing five matches in that country, followed by two in Switzerland.

During a pre-season tour of Holland in 1925, West Ham even played a cricket match against a Dutch team.

However, there was one trip that unsettled the morale of the players. Touring Spain in 1926, their hosts seemed convinced that soccer was rather like bull fighting.

In one match, George Kay had his nose broken, later enduring considerable pain as the team trundled across the Spanish plain for their next match. Crossing the mountains on the way to Vigo, George made a near-fatal mistake – he pulled out the plugs stopping his nose from haemorrhaging and, in doing so, caught a severe chill. Kay's welfare now became the responsibility of trainer Charlie Paynter, a kindly male nurse who saw his centre-half through his ordeal while the team had to go home without their captain and trainer. Kay was not well enough to return to England for a month and when he and Paynter did arrive back at Liverpool docks, they had a halfpenny between them. Paynter had to wire Upton Park for funds for their rail journey home.

During the 1920s, West Ham had become avid travellers to the continent. These goodwill visits – to Austria, Hungary, Germany, Czechoslovakia, Switzerland, France, Spain, Holland, Denmark and Norway – involved long hours of travel by boat and train, but the West Ham squad presumably enjoyed these breaks away from the routine of training in dockland.

The Hammers' last trip to the continent before the outbreak of war was to play Kladno in Czechoslovakia in the summer of 1938. Come the end of the war, they were immediately on their travels again, playing seven friendlies in Switzerland in 1946.

A little over a month after the Hungarians' famous appearance at Wembley in November 1953, West Ham entertained some special visitors of their own in an early floodlit friendly at Upton Park – AC Milan. Boasting five internationals of different nationalities in their forward line, the Italian giants handed the academy scholars a lesson in the finer points of the game as they won 6-0.

The next day, there was a special meeting in the West Ham players' unofficial headquarters and, in a heated inquest, sauce bottles, cups and saucers, knives, forks, spoons and anything else that could be moved supplemented the salt and pepper pots as makeshift Subbuteo players in an attempt to unravel the events of the debacle.

Malcolm Allison wore the number six shirt that night, with centre-half Ken Brown delegated the responsibility of marking the great Swedish forward Gunnar Nordahll. When Nordahl bulldozed his way past Brown on one occasion, Brown croaked at Allison: 'What a bloody giant!' Milan had overwhelmed West Ham so thoroughly that Allison went home to his digs in Ilford on the trolley bus 'feeling very low … it was a painful experience'. But good often comes out of catastrophe and the West Ham team, through endless discussion, began to put things together.

Future Chelsea manager Dave Sexton, who was a player at Upton Park for nearly four years in the early 1950s, felt the same enthusiasm for experiment. 'We were all motivated by the performance of the Hungarians in beating England 6-3 at Wembley. So, when floodlighting was introduced at Upton Park, Ted Fenton made it his responsibility to bring more and more continental opposition to play us and we appreciated the experience.'

Indeed, manager Fenton used any variety of methods to get publicity for West Ham. Each spring, he would approach the board with a list of possible European tours and matches that could be arranged with sides visiting England. He even took it upon himself to make contacts and arrange matches.

Come the Ron Greenwood era, as a reward for their efforts in the 1961/62 season, the team were taken on a close season tour of Africa and everything went well until the final Ghana leg of the trip. As Greenwood recalled in his autobiography, *Yours Sincerely*: 'Nobody met us at the airport at Accra. The excuse given later was they thought we were on another plane. By this time, though, we knew there was only one flight a day from Johannesburg to Accra. We then found ourselves being shown into a hotel that was nothing more than a doss house. The blankets almost crawled. Nobody slept, except Johnny Dick, who could sleep anywhere. The tour had a hidden bonus for us, however. Through all its adversity our team spirit grew stronger. The problems we shared welded us together. It also taught me a lot about the character of my players. I noted all those who had a good sense of humour, those I could count on, those who looked for problems and those who were idle. And on my first tour as manager, I discovered much about myself.'

In the summer of 1963, West Ham were invited to compete in the prestigious International Soccer League in the United States. The Hammers were pitted against a truly international mixture of top-class opposition and went on to win their group, which included Kilmarnock

(3-3), Mantova (Italy 2-4), Oro (Mexico 3-1). Munster (West Germany 2-0) and Recife (Brazil 1-1).

The Hammers returned to the States to play the winners of the other group, Górnik Zabrze of Poland, over two legs at Randalls Island in New York. Johnny 'Budgie' Byrne hit the goal that earned his team a 1-1 draw in the first match. In the second game, Geoff Hurst got the only goal. The final against Dukla Prague of Czechoslovakia was again a two-legged affair, with the first match staged at the 110,000-capacity Soldier Field in Chicago, where the Czechs won 1-0. Tony Scott put the Hammers level in the second game back in New York, but captain Josef Masopust got the decisive goal.

Masopust predicted that 'West Ham would win a major European tournament within two years' and manager Greenwood later reflected: 'We learned more that summer than we would have done in five European campaigns about how the game was evolving around the world. It could have taken two or three years at home to gain the experience we achieved on our American adventure. Every one of our ten games was a lesson in itself and our reward came in the form of increased confidence, understanding and team spirit.' Two years later, the football world found out how right he was.

Finally, a word about Upton Park Football Club. Situated on the eastern borders of London and Essex, Upton Park Football Club preceded Thames Ironworks, much less West Ham United, as the first significant football outfit in the area. The club had developed during the initial decades of the Football Association and established itself as the top London club when the side won the first FA (Senior) Cup in 1882/83. The club retained the trophy the following season and went on to achieve several impressive results in the FA Cup itself.

Upton Park FC was even to make an international impact when the club was selected to represent Great Britain in the Paris Olympics of 1900. As all Olympic athletes needed to have amateur status, British league clubs would not have been allowed to compete in Paris, as they were professional outfits. With none of the remaining staunch Corinthian clubs stepping into the breach, Upton Park agreed to travel to Paris.

The matches in Paris were a haplessly organised and almost invisible sideshow to the Universal Exhibition to which they had been attached. Upton Park FC defeated the French representatives, Club Français de Paris, 4-0 in what has come to be taken as the final of the tournament, although the official records indicate that Upton Park played just that one game. There was a suggestion that they played a group of Belgian students 'somewhere in the Bois de Boulogne'. However, no medals were awarded. On a hot day, it would seem the fitness of the London players was the difference between the two sides.

From their East London home in West Ham Park – but a 20-minute walk from the London Stadium – the Parkers produced some of the first England internationals. Upton Park would fade into history after 1911, but the Upton Park Trophy, an annual play-off between the league champions of Guernsey and Jersey, still exists. First contested in 1907, the trophy was donated to the Guernsey FA by Upton Park to celebrate their tenth annual Easter tour of the islands in 1906.

Chapter Two

European Winners: The 1964/65 European Cup Winners' Cup Campaign

A PARAGRAPH in the 1964/65 FA Year Book gave a reminder of the fickle achievements of Ron Greenwood's team in the First Division, in which they had finished only 14th in 1964: 'West Ham were inconsistency itself, with a double win against the champions, Liverpool, wins against Manchester United, Everton and Spurs, and losing three points [in the days of two points for a win] to Ipswich Town and Bolton Wanderers, and two points to Birmingham City.' Amid this topsy-turvy season came an astonishing 8-2 defeat to Blackburn Rovers at Upton Park on Boxing Day, 1963 – with the Hammers winning 3-1 at Ewood Park two days later.

In the FA Cup, though, West Ham reached the final and, in May 1964, Ronnie Boyce headed the winning goal in the final minute of an enthralling 3-2

Wembley win over Second Division Preston and it was the following season, in competition with their fellow cup winners from all over the continent, that the technical niceties of Greenwood's playing philosophy were to be displayed to best advantage. In Europe, they were not so likely to be bludgeoned out of their elegant stride. The European Cup Winners' Cup was more a contest of skill and science than league football was and West Ham were perfectly equipped for the challenge. Even so, they had to overcome the insular belief of the English that continental clubs were second rate.

For Greenwood, the challenge of European football now lay ahead and he really enjoyed these opening rounds across the Channel, his football brain geared to the more sophisticated tactics prevalent on the continent. He made his team aware of the calibre of the competition by sending players of the ability of Boyce and Geoff Hurst to spy on their opponents. At that time, Greenwood was a believer in compiling dossiers on opponents, a method Leeds and England's Don Revie would famously use. Greenwood drew up what he called 12 'lessons', which he handed to his team to be studied as homework.

Greenwood wrote in his autobiography, *Yours Sincerely*: 'Now we were into Europe and this, for me, was the real prize, the test for which I had worked and waited. The prospect excited me but it did not frighten me, because I had never felt surer of anything than the ability of my players to cope with the continent. I did not care who we played. I was convinced that at our best we could be more than a match for their best. I wanted to do something for English football. I watched each opposing club as soon as I could after every draw, so that I could give each player of mine a vivid word-picture of his likely immediate opponent. To do this I related every opposition player to a British player my men would know.'

When Greenwood arrived at West Ham in April 1961 from Arsenal, where he had been assistant manager, the East London club were completing their third unspectacular season in the First Division since promotion in 1958. Greenwood inherited some fine players from Ted Fenton and also persevered with his youth policy, but he also brought with him two immeasurable assets; a deep understanding of the game and the ability to impart his knowledge to others.

West Ham's players were taught when to hold and when to part with the ball; the value of fluid formations; of moving into open spaces; of running off the ball as decoys; of playing constructive football from their own penalty area; of drawing defenders to create real chances to score. The old uncontrolled pace and power was abandoned in favour of flair and finesse. It may have needed an extra spark of resilience and consistency to bring success in the league, but in cup ties it was spectacularly effective. Greenwood had the patience and perseverance to put over his concept of play to the West Ham youngsters – a policy which paid rich dividends in Bobby Moore, Hurst, Martin Peters and Johnny Sissons. Greenwood strengthened his team with one expensive acquisition, signing Johnny Byrne from Crystal Palace for £65,000 in March 1962, and a handful of bargain purchases, including goalkeeper Jim Standen and winger Peter Brabrook.

The FA Charity Shield match against league champions Liverpool kicked off the 1964/65 season. A 38,858 crowd at Anfield were treated to a wonderful match, which finished 2-2. With no penalty shoot-outs in those days, the clubs were allowed to keep the trophy for six months each. The first home league game was a sell-out fixture against Manchester United. It, too, proved a great match, with the Hammers winning 3-1. These were indeed good times at Upton Park. Wolves were beaten 5-0, with Hurst scoring two. Against Tottenham, Byrne scored a hat-trick in a 3-2 win which marked the Hammers' first appearance on the new BBC football highlights programme *Match Of The Day* on 12 September 1964.

The League Cup took West Ham to Sunderland, where they found themselves 4-0 down after 38 minutes. Brabrook pulled a goal back, but Sunderland proved worthy winners.

West Ham started their defence of the FA Cup at home to Birmingham City. They were given a shock when Birmingham raced into a 2-0 lead. However, roared on by a 31,000 crowd, goals from Byrne, Sissons and Hurst (2) gave West Ham a 4-2 victory. The fourth-round tie, on January 30, was against London neighbours Chelsea and an all-ticket crowd of 37,000 were packed into Upton Park. In a hard-fought tie, an early goal by Tambling for Chelsea proved to be the only one of the game.

The Hammers' league form was also on the decline and there were only two wins in January and February, though the league season actually finished with West Ham in a respectable ninth position. But by the end of January, only Europe offered any chance of a trophy. There was the additional incentive that the final would be held only a few miles from Upton Park at Wembley Stadium. Beginning their campaign in September 1964, West Ham went into Europe unknown and inexperienced.

First round:
La Gantoise 1-0 (A), 1-1 (H)
Aggregate 2-1

Just 144 days after they had lifted the FA Cup at Wembley, West Ham began their first European campaign. Their challenge for the Cup Winners' Cup began in the Belgian city of Ghent against La Gantoise, a team of part-timers who usually only trained on three evenings a week.

Among the playing staff were an accountant, a teacher, a draughtsman and several clerks. Like the Hammers, they had also won their domestic knockout competition for the first time the previous season.

For West Ham, nine of the players who had started the FA Cup Final at Wembley the previous May were in Greenwood's starting XI, with Alan Sealey replacing Brabrook on the right wing and the teenage Peters starting in an unaccustomed left-back role.

Greenwood had been based in Ghent with the RAF during the Second World War and so quite enjoyed the idea of going back. He and his team made their way by coach down to Dover and took the ferry to Ostend. Then it was back on the coach to Ghent. Not everyone in the side was used to going abroad and two of them turned up without passports.

West Ham's opening match of their ultimately glorious run was settled by a goalkeeping error rather than an outrageous piece of skill or intricate team play. After 52 minutes, Sealey delivered a corner that was met by the head of Boyce, whose header looped past Belgium international goalkeeper Armand Seghers into the net.

The club programme for the following home league game, against Sheffield United, reported in its usual low-key way: 'Our first XI made its entry into continental competitive soccer last Wednesday evening and we take the opportunity to thank those who made the journey to Ghent to support the Hammers ... nearly 500 Hammers fans travelled to Belgium and the encouragement these and others gave our team was greatly appreciated. The one-goal margin which we gained was a most welcome result and will encourage our team for the second leg ... the system which we adopted served our purpose well and in general we could feel comfortably satisfied with the outcome that gives us an excellent chance of further progress in the tournament.'

While West Ham's Cup Winners' Cup success involved many glorious moments, history will not recall the second leg home draw with La Gantoise as one of them. The headline in *The Times* the next morning told the story: 'West Ham scrape through on aggregate – Belgian amateurs take the honours in inefficient match.'

Greenwood made two changes from the first leg, replacing injured goalkeeper Jim Standen with 20-year-old Alan Dickie and winger Sealey with Brabrook. It was one of Dickie's rare first-team outings and he only found out about his inclusion late in the day, later recalling: 'I didn't think I was in the team ... I got held up in Blackwall Tunnel. It was murder in those days. We were told to get to the ground by 6.30 at the latest. I didn't get there until 7.10 pm, to be told I would be playing. The kick-off was only 20 minutes away, so I had no time for butterflies.'

Described as 'distinctly below par' in the report in *The Times*, West Ham 'tried to play at a breakneck speed as if trying to catch the last train' as they went in search of an early goal to effectively end the hopes of their part-time opponents. Sissons rattled the post with an early shot but, despite incessant pressure, an early goal did not materialise. Unable to score for themselves, West Ham did so for the Belgians on 32 minutes, when Peters knocked the ball past Dickie for an own goal. Thankfully for the home side, their superiority was rewarded three minutes before half-time when Sissons crossed for Byrne to convert.

The club also felt they had to respond to criticism about increased ticket prices for the La Gantoise game; they had taken record receipts of £9,700 from an attendance of 24,300.

The programme for the Sheffield United league match broke down the various extra costs of European football – including £250 for travelling expenses for the three Norwegian officials.

Second round: Sparta Prague 2-0 (H), 1-2 (A) Aggregate 3-2

Before the second round against Sparta Prague, the club announced that captain Bobby Moore would be out of action for three months after undergoing a 'groin operation', although it is now clear that his absence was caused by the first brush with the deadly cancer that would tragically kill him three decades later.

For the home leg on November 25, Greenwood made two changes from the previous European outing. With Moore a rare absentee from the team sheet, the versatile Peters took his place at wing-half and Jack Burkett came into the team at left-back. Further forward, Sealey was recalled on the right wing for Brabrook.

Considered to be one of the strongest sides in the competition, Sparta Prague had thrashed Anorthosis Famagusta of Cyprus 16-0 on aggregate in the first round.

Described in one newspaper report as 'a match of intellect to satisfy the chess players', the first leg at Upton Park pitted West Ham's attacking flair against Sparta's organised defence and tactical nous. The Czechs were a typically dour, well-drilled Iron Curtain side and the same soubriquet could be used to describe their defence, as the Hammers were to discover in that first leg.

The East Europeans packed their defence with nine or ten men and did not stand on ceremony, inflicting a catalogue of gruesome fouls on Byrne, Sissons, Peters and Hurst, in particular. In the first half, the Hammers were unsuccessful in breaching the massed ranks of white shirts. And so, at half-time Greenwood switched John Bond from right to left-back, playing behind a more advanced Burkett.

Future Hammers manager John Lyall, who at the time was managing the youth team, recalled: 'Our plans weren't working. It seemed like one of those nights when everything you try won't work; you'd have bet on the game being a goalless stalemate. Continental teams could do that well, kill the heart of a game. It was done in a way you didn't really come across in English football then.'

Then, out on the right, Sparta conceded one of a string of free kicks. Sealey curled the ball into the goalmouth, where it was beaten out by a defender and landed at the feet of Bond. From about 25 yards out, the Hammers defender let fly. Bond remembered it as 'a rocket that banged straight into the roof of the net … I hit with my "wrong" left foot'. Bond had picked his moment. He had not scored for three and a half years, though his effort against Sparta was his 34th for the club.

Then, eight minutes from time, Byrne crossed and Sealey hit the post before burying the rebound to send West Ham behind the Iron Curtain with a two-goal advantage.

An unchanged West Ham United took to the pitch on a bright afternoon at Prague's Letna Stadium a fortnight later, still without Moore. While they were on the defensive for much of the game, the Hammers did escape early on to take the lead through left-winger Sissons on 14 minutes. Byrne eluded two challenges before finding his young team-mate, who fired high into the net.

From then on, the odd counter-attack aside, it was all Sparta. Goalkeeper Jim Standen took centre stage, saving shot after shot, including a penalty from Ivan Mráz. Standen's afternoon then turned sour on 73 minutes as he allowed a Vladimír Táborský shot through his hands, the ball hitting the crossbar before Mráz reacted quickest to finish. Then, with two minutes remaining, the same player converted a Tadeusz Kraus cross to set up a nervous finish. West Ham survived, however, to edge their way into the last eight.

Forty-five thousand Czech fans were silenced by the discipline, determination and, above all, bravery of the Hammers' all-English team, who triumphed over some savage tackling and indifferent decisions by the Bulgarian referee to reach the quarter-finals. Relief only came at the final whistle and their bruised bodies and torn legs bore testimony to the battering they had taken. Sissons was manhandled off the field by the referee and Sealey needed seven stitches in a shin gash.

Quarter-final: Lausanne-Sport 2-1 (A), 4-3 (H) Aggregate 6-4

Three months after edging out Spartak Prague, West Ham returned to European action in Switzerland in mid-

March 1965 at the picturesque Stade Olympique de la Pontaise, overlooked by the Alps.

By then, they had lost their hold on the FA Cup at the hands of Chelsea and their league form was indifferent. There had been only four league victories, alongside nine defeats. Typical of their inconsistent form was a 2-3 home loss to Sunderland three days before they met Lausanne-Sport.

The Swiss were managed by the legendary Karl Rappan, a manager with 40 years' experience at the top level. From 1960 to 1963, Rappan coached the Swiss national side before joining Lausanne, who he would guide to the league title in 1965. Under him, the national team had qualified for the World Cups of 1938, 1954 (automatically, as hosts) and 1962. Lausanne was more or less the Swiss national side. In the Cup Winners' Cup, they had already accounted for the Hungarian side Honvéd, 2-1 on aggregate, as well as Slavia Sofia, 5-3 overall.

Interviewed in the programme for the Rapid Vienna match in September 2021, Brian Dear recalled: '"Have you got a passport Stag?" Ron asked as I sat in the Boleyn Ground bath, having just marked my return to the Hammers first team with two goals against Sunderland in March 1965. "Yes, I've got one," I replied, knowing West Ham were flying to Switzerland for Tuesday's European Cup Winners' Cup quarter-final against

Lausanne. "But I'm not going all that way unless I'm playing!" Ron sighed. "Just get yourself back in time for the coach."'

Captain Moore was back from injury, with Peters resuming his early-season role at left-back. Elsewhere, Joe Kirkup made his first appearance of the season at right-back, while Hurst played alongside 21-year-old inside-forward Brian Dear in attack.

The opening stages were a cat and mouse affair, with both sides jostling for domination without taking overall control. Switzerland striker Robert Hosp rattled the crossbar before Dear opened the scoring on 21 minutes with a close-range finish. Eight minutes into the second half, quick thinking from Moore doubled the Hammers' advantage as he intercepted a free kick and sparked a counter-attack, finished with aplomb by Byrne. Lausanne, with nine full internationals in their ranks, edged the remainder of the game and were rewarded when a rare Moore error allowed Hosp to halve the arrears ahead of the return leg.

West Ham welcomed Lausanne-Sport to East London following a humbling 4-0 defeat at Blackburn Rovers the previous Saturday and the Hammers needed any energy they had saved at Ewood Park to stave off a determined Swiss side. A capacity crowd were treated to a thrilling tie that produced seven goals and was only ultimately settled by Brian Dear's 89th-minute strike.

Chance after chance was created and it was astounding that it took until eight minutes before half-time for the first goal to arrive, courtesy of Lausanne's Netherlands international forward Pierre Kerkhoffs. Amazingly, West Ham were two goals clear again by the break. Sealey created both in the space of 60 seconds, the first an own goal by Ely Tacchella and the second scored by Dear. At 4-2 up on aggregate, the tie should have been won, but Lausanne scored twice more, through Charly Hertig and Norbert Eschmann, either side of a Martin Peters header. As the final whistle approached, nerves were fraying all around the Boleyn Ground before Dear's decisive late goal completed a 6-4 aggregate win.

Semi-final: Real Zaragoza 2-1 (H), 1-1 (A) Aggregate 3-2

'In every way, this was a first-class match of first-class entertainment.' *The Times*' report of this breathless semi-final first leg at Upton Park was effusive in its praise of both combatants. 'A game of attack from start to finish, the visitors refused to sink into the defensive mindset that so often afflicts teams when they play away in European competition – then and now. The result was a fantastic match that ebbed and flowed.'

West Ham struck first when the prolific Dear headed in a Sissons cross. Just after the midway point of the first half, it was 2-0. Moore found centre-half Ken Brown on the right wing and his cross picked out Sissons, who lifted the ball for Byrne to volley home.

Any thoughts that Zaragoza would shrivel were put to the back of West Ham minds, however, as the Inter-Cities Fairs Cup holders refused to give up. With their 'Magnificent Five' forward line, the Spaniards poured forward with great intent. Eleuterio Santos hit the crossbar and Marcelino the post before Canário struck ten minutes after half-time. At 2-1 to the Hammers, the return leg was set up perfectly.

West Ham's run to the 1965 Cup Winners' Cup Final was based, in the main, on expansive flowing football and moments of individual and collective brilliance. At the Estadio de La Romareda, it was centred on sheer grit, determination and organisation, led by captain Moore.

Ken Jones of the *Daily Mirror* told how, on the eve of the game, he came across Moore in a bar at around 1am. The captain was having a quiet drink as his persistent insomnia gripped him. 'Christ Bobby, there's fans in here. You'd best get to bed,' Jones told him. It did not affect Moore's performance.

However, it seemed as if all the hard work would go to waste as early as the 24th minute when Zaragoza's Spanish international winger Carlos Lapetra hooked in the loose ball after his initial effort had been clawed out by goalkeeper Standen. The same player had an outstanding chance to put Zaragoza ahead on aggregate shortly before half-time, but he blazed over when it appeared easier to score.

Having spent the opening 45 minutes camped inside their own half, West Ham came out with more attacking intent following Greenwood's half-time team talk. The resulting improvement first saw Dear denied by goalkeeper Enrique Yarza before Sissons silenced the hitherto vociferous home support by latching on to Dear's pass, racing clear and slotting calmly into the net. It would not be long before the Spaniards resumed their onslaught, but Sissons's goal had given West Ham renewed energy and belief – and an all-important lead to cling on to.

When Dutch referee Leo Horn blew the final whistle, the shattered Hammers hardly had the energy to congratulate one another, but they had done it. For the second season in succession West Ham were going to Wembley.

Thousands of fans at home, tuning into the radio commentary, joined the tiny band of Hammers fans in Spain in celebrating as their heroes held on for an historic victory.

Brian Moore was doing the BBC radio commentary from an open position and he said later that he could hardly make himself heard because the din was so deafening.

In the Stoke City programme of 11 April 2015, Ken Dyer spoke to Brian Dear about his memories of that game in Spain. Dear recalled: 'At the reception on the Tuesday before the game we each got a bottle of sherry and a silver ashtray. Nice, but maybe they wanted us to have a good smoke and drink before the game. They had what they called "Los Magnificos", a celebrated five-man attack, one of the best in Europe at that time. I can still remember their names – Canario, Santos, Marcelino, Villa and Lapetra.

'They were quite a tough side, I remember, a sterner challenge to be honest than TSV Munich, who we played in the final. I scored early on in the first leg at home. It was a diving header, a rarity for me. I was just in the middle of one of those purple patches at the time, so much so that from the middle of March until the end of the season, I scored 14 goals in 15 games.

'The second leg in Spain was three weeks later and it was a tough trip. I remember we flew into a military airport because it was nearer and I can recall arriving at the stadium early for the match and it was already nearly full. It was a bit daunting, I can tell you!

'Lapetra scored in the first half to put them 1-0 up and level on aggregate but then early in the second half, I threaded a through ball to Johnny Sissons, who took the ball on and scored. That certainly wasn't one of my usual strengths but, just for a few seconds, I turned into Johnny

Haynes! The ironic thing was that if we had drawn on aggregate that night there was no extra-time planned and both teams would have had to travel directly to Nice in the South of France for a replay two days later.

'The last ten minutes of that match was horrendous really, so nerve-racking, but what joy and relief at the final whistle because we were through to the final – to be played at our own Wembley Stadium. I can still see our chairman Reg Pratt, coming into the dressing room afterwards and he was so happy. "Come on," he said. "Let's go out and celebrate." I had never seen him like that before. It was a wonderful time to be a West Ham player. We were all good mates, there were no big-time Charlies.'

The 1964/65 League season finished with the Hammers in ninth position. Between them, Hurst and Byrne scored 42 league goals out of the team's total of 82.

However, the most eye-catching individual goalscoring performance was Dear's five in a 20-minute spell against West Bromwich Albion on Good Friday morning. West Ham won 6-1.

Final:
TSV 1860 Munich 2-0 (Wembley)

The date was 19 May 1965 and it will probably go down as the greatest night in West Ham's history. They faced TSV 1860 Munich from West Germany in the final of the European Cup Winners' Cup.

Wembley was packed with 100,000 spectators. As you would expect, by far the largest proportion of the crowd were supporting West Ham, but around 20,000 German fans travelled to London and they would form an extremely vociferous part of the huge crowd with their Bavarian hats and flags.

Unusually, at a time when live football was a rarity on UK television, the BBC screened the whole game live. It was later estimated that 30 million viewers throughout the UK and the rest of Europe watched the match. The final match-up was a mouth-watering prospect, with the Germans' athleticism, power and unimpeachable self-belief pitted against West Ham's superior skill, quality and artistry.

As Brian Dear remembered in 2021: 'The final was amazing. Ending up with 14 goals in 15 games, I'd suffered reactions to inoculations needed for our upcoming tour to the United States. Seeing my plaster the day before, Ron asked: "How's your neck? Can you play?" I reckoned he was looking for excuses to change the team. "I'm fine," I insisted. On the coach to Wembley no-one seemed affected by the occasion. Ron had prepared us well, a brilliant Hungarian referee was taking charge and, like us, our West German opponents were here for football – not fighting. Allocated the biggest dressing room, we were so relaxed and Bobby Moore joked: "Stag, when we go outside grab yourself a ball and walk behind me – you'll get your photo taken!"'

As the *Daily Mirror's* Ken Jones pointed out in his preview of the final, the club's achievements were regarded as a one-off by people outside of East London, but he thought their football was right for European success. He predicted: 'West Ham will win it ... and convince the doubters of their greatness.'

In the pre-match build-up, many of the press previews were of the opinion that the two teams were evenly matched with the Hammers installed as slight favourites, if only because the game was being played at Wembley and the majority of fans would be supporting them. These were the days before penalty shoot-outs decided drawn matches and UEFA had decreed that, if the teams were level at the end of extra-time, a replay would be held 48 hours later at Feyenoord's stadium in Rotterdam. Hundreds of intuitive Hammers' fans were already getting prepared for such an event by announcing to their employers that fictitious grannies had suddenly died and that they would need time off work to attend the funerals!

West Ham's opponents were managed by former Austrian international Max Merkel. In the mid-1960s, TSV were the dominant team from Munich, not Bayern. They had won the South German Championship in 1962/63 – qualifying for the new national league, the Bundesliga – and lifted the German Cup in 1963/64. They would go on to finish the 1964/65 season in third place in the Bundesliga. Merkel had assembled a powerful, talented attack which included club captain Rudi Brunnenmeier, a forceful striker in the Uwe Seeler mould, Alfred Heiß, a two-footed sprinter with magnetic ball control and a fierce shot who was equally at home on either wing, and Hans Küppers, a time and motion study in himself. Two Yugoslavs added skill to the defence; Stevan Bena from Vojvodina, expert at creating space for his forwards, and Petar Radenković, the second Lev Yashin, a black-garbed goalkeeper with long reach and unbelievably fast reactions.

TSV 1860 had a simple passage through the first round of the Cup Winners' Cup, beating Union Luxembourg, with Brunnenmeier scoring twice in each leg. They then won in Porto, although the Portuguese played strongly in Munich in the second leg to gain a draw. The West Germans' poor home form continued in the quarter-finals, where they were held to a goalless draw by Legia Warsaw after winning 4-0 away. Their semi-final opponents were present under false pretences; the Italian Cup Final was so long delayed that Torino won a toss to decide who should enter Europe, but Roma eventually took the trophy. Both Munich and Torino opened strongly at home, taking two-goal leads before half-time. The tie went to a play-off, a match turned in TSV's favour by some astonishing saves from Radenkovic.

On the evening of the final, it was warm and humid. The atmosphere inside Wembley was quite extraordinary. Unlike the FA Cup Final, when so many people in the crowd were invariably neutral supporters, the stadium was packed with true football fans, with the majority fervently supporting West Ham.

Before the game, a telegram was delivered to the Hammers' dressing room. It was a message from their North London rivals, Spurs, who had dominated English football to such a huge extent in the early 1960s. The somewhat wistful telegram merely said: 'Those were the days. Hope they are yours too.' It was a nice sentiment from a club who had a touch of class about them in that era, both on and off the field.

The atmosphere at Wembley was electric, with thousands of Germans waving banners and shouting 'München! München!' The Hammers fans replied with melodious verses of *I'm Forever Blowing Bubbles*, greatly enhanced by the acoustics of the new roof built around the Wembley stands.

There were four differences in the West Ham team that had beaten Preston in the FA Cup Final a year earlier. The stylish Joe Kirkup had regained the right-back spot from the veteran John Bond, while Martin Peters was at right-half after the unfortunate Eddie Bovington broke a kneecap playing against Sunderland in March. Alan Sealey had taken over the right-wing spot from Peter Brabrook.

West Ham dominated the match with inspired, flowing football. It was wonderful to watch. Only some prodigious saves from Radenković and some equally prodigious misses at close range prevented Munich's complete annihilation. The Germans, pinned back in defence, waited like vultures ready to pounce on a weakening prey. Jim Standen made three memorable, if unorthodox, saves to prevent an injustice. But not even Radenković could keep out the waves of pressure. In the 69th minute, Ronnie Boyce seized on a partial clearance and Seeley, on the right wing, shot with unstoppable velocity. Barely had the roaring crescendo paused for breath when he scored again, converting a perfect cross from Bobby Moore at close range. In a stroke of good fortune, Martin Peters had miscontrolled the ball, but it turned into a perfect pass for Sealey five yards out.

This is how Brian Moore described the second goal on BBC Radio: 'Here comes Hurst, runs over the ball, it goes to Boyce. To Bobby Moore [who] clips it forward … it's a goal! Another goal for West Ham! Alan Sealey the scorer again.'

Sissons twice hit the woodwork after elusive dribbles as West Ham ran out worthy winners. Captain Moore, master of the occasion, made what was becoming his now annual walk up the Wembley steps to collect a trophy and manager Greenwood claimed after the final: 'This was Bobby Moore's greatest game for West Ham.'

This is how the West Ham fanzine *Fortune's Always Hiding*, described the battle for ascendancy when reassessing the final many years later: 'Munich began to get more into the game, after Hurst and Sissons had also gone close to giving West Ham the lead, but Moore twice intercepted with immaculate timing. With the West Ham captain now in command, carrying the ball forward, and passing accurately with both feet, West Ham swept forward as the first choruses of *Bubbles* swept the stadium.

'The first half ended as it had begun, with West Ham's flowing football causing the German rearguard tremendous problems. Hurst, who began his career in midfield, showed what a great footballer he was by winning the ball and passing it intelligently, slowing the game down then stepping up the tempo. Boyce and Peters worked equally hard in midfield, whilst up front the pace of Sealey on the right and the constant interchanging of Dear and Sissons often left the Munich defence bewildered. If West Ham were good in the first half, they were simply magnificent in the second. Moore began to move upfield more frequently and the whole team played with inspired self-belief.'

Alan Sealey, with his two goals inside three second-half minutes, was an unlikely hero. He had managed only three other goals that season. He broke his leg that summer in a freak accident playing cricket and missed the whole of the 1965/66 campaign. He played only four more league games for the Hammers before moving to Plymouth Argyle.

The European triumph was a unique achievement for the team from the East End. However, despite the euphoria on the pitch that night, other matters proved to be something of an anticlimax for the men in claret and blue. Wembley had laid on a buffet in the restaurant afterwards, but it was only for the players, officials and directors of both clubs, with no provision made for wives and girlfriends, who presumably were not best pleased. To add insult to injury, the players' cars were still at Upton Park, where they had left them before going to the hotel on the night before the match. It meant that, instead of heading off to celebrate at a nightclub in London's West End, everybody went back to Upton Park on a coach and arrived around midnight at a totally deserted ground which was in complete darkness.

After the Hammers' victory, the whole of Europe applauded their performance and messages of congratulation poured into Upton Park. One even came from their West London rivals, Chelsea, which said: 'Well done, you East End lot. A real West End show.' Another came from Liverpool manager Bill Shankly, whose injury-hit team had been beaten by Inter Milan in the semi-final of the European Cup the previous week. Shankly's typically aggressive message said: 'Well done.

I feel that British teams are more than ready for these European people.'

Even Prime Minister Harold Wilson – a genuine football fan – sent a telegram of congratulations from Downing Street after watching the match on television. 'Splendid match and a wonderful victory,' it read.

Dr Luiz Murgel, part of the Brazil backroom team when they won the World Cup three years earlier, was at Wembley to see the Hammers' victory. After the match, he prophetically vouchsafed: 'If the football of the England team is like this display by West Ham, then England will be a real danger in the World Cup next year. West Ham's football was brilliant – so clever and so quick.'

The praise for West Ham's performance in the following day's newspapers was almost overwhelming. The sports pages across Europe were magnanimous as they heralded the winners. The leading French sports newspaper, *L'Equipe*, ran a headline stating: 'West Ham have discovered a new football formula.' Similarly, the Fleet Street press boys went into raptures. The *Daily Express* carried a banner headline on the front page saying: 'Forever Blowing Bubbles – Night of Glory.' One match report announced: 'There could have been no greater match to place before the greatest night audience in English football history.'

The highly-respected reporter Bryon Butler graphically wrote: 'Moore and company used Wembley's green carpet as an artist uses his canvas. Their movements were precise, their designs bold and imaginative. They were a credit to themselves and English football.'

The esteemed J.L. Manning described it as 'the best football match I have seen at Wembley since the stadium opened 42 years ago'.

A report in another newspaper announced: 'West Ham lifted the roof off super Wembley when they won the European Cup Winners' Cup in probably the greatest night of soccer splendour England had ever seen.'

Another soccer scribe wrote: 'West Ham's display was so majestic that, at times, it seemed they were touched by the gods. They are going to be greater than Bill Nicholson's double-winning Spurs and greater than the pre-Munich Manchester United.'

It was praise indeed and, given the exultation rightly being accorded to West Ham, it was difficult to disagree with such a proud sentiment. After all, never before had the club experienced such euphoria and success. It was not unreasonable to assume that winning the FA Cup and European Cup Winners' Cup in successive seasons would be the beginning of a long period of unbroken success.

Manager Greenwood had drummed in this message to his players before the start: 'Getting to Wembley means nothing in this competition or any other. Nobody is interested in losers. You are here to show millions of people what West Ham can do.' And speaking after the match, he had a gratified smile as he said: 'It was the way we won.'

Geoffrey Green of *The Times* gave his blessing: 'That was the night when Wembley for the first time was available to the genuine supporter of the club, the man who lives on the terraces through the winter. No longer did the majority of seats go to "outsiders". The true blue fan at last took his rightful place in the national theatre of the game to cheer his own side. That was one agreeable sidelight. Another was the memorable way Wembley cheered the losers from the field; the way the Munich banners also saluted West Ham in their lap of honour; and how Olympic Way itself was lined by cheering thousands waving farewell to the German supporters in their coaches going home. The East End that night was aglow with bonfires and singing and dancing in the streets until dawn's early light.'

West Ham's 2-0 victory, which made them only the second British club to win a European trophy (Spurs having won the same competition two years earlier), produced, in the words of their captain 'probably one of the greatest nights for a celebration the East End had known since VE Night … everybody seemed to think it had been one of the finest games of football they had ever seen'.

Sipping tea in the dressing room after the famous victory, Greenwood said: 'This was our greatest game … a tremendous advertisement for football.'

Two-goal hero Sealey said: 'I've got to thank Ronnie Boyce for the first one. I just had to beat their goalkeeper, who was so fantastic. The second was the result of a planned free kick.'

Captain Moore added: 'We felt we let the fans down last year against Preston and we didn't do ourselves justice. Now we have come back and achieved all we set out to do.'

Geoff Hurst wrote in his 1970 autobiography *The World Game*: 'It wasn't so much HOW West Ham played that night that thrilled me but WHY. What happened at Wembley simply was that three years of dammed hard work in training suddenly brought its reward. It may have been the occasion or the pitch, or our own mood of determined confidence, or the adventurous skill of the German opposition, or even a combination of all these factors. But suddenly that night, everything went right. I cherish my medal, the solid token of our achievement. But more, I can feel warm and pleased every time I dig out the memories of that match … 90 minutes when 22 professional footballers, half of whom couldn't speak to the other half, found a common language in the love of the game and the pleasure of playing it the best they knew how.'

Hurst also described the unusual role he played in those European matches. 'Although I had knocked in a few goals over the previous seasons, Mr Greenwood decided that my strength was better employed in midfield as a first line of defence. This kept down my shooting chances considerably, but I didn't mind, as this was another stage in my development as an all-round player.'

West Ham are not the only all-English team to triumph in Europe – Manchester City repeated the achievement in 1970 – but they were certainly the most local. Nine were Londoners (the exceptions were the Geordie Joe Kirkup and Geoff Hurst, from Ashton-Under-Lyme) and six were even born within a mile or two of Upton Park.

Leslie Page wrote in the *Soccer Star* magazine a few weeks after the final: 'West Ham were something of an enigma in league and cup, always promising so much and yet somehow finding themselves beaten by teams who were not truly their equals. Maybe they saved something for this European competition and if they did, then Ron Greenwood and the West Ham board deserve all the praise we can give them, for not only was the match a magnificent game of football resulting in a brilliant win for West Ham, but it was also the biggest, best and brightest boost that the game has had for many a year.'

In the same publication, Eric Batty had this to say: 'Many people have suggested that West Ham's success was further proof that England's game is on the upgrade but, in my view, nothing could be further from the truth. West Ham are so outstandingly "continental" in their method and skill that only a halfwit would accuse them of playing typical English football.'

Later that year, the club's players and officials were invited to attend the BBC's prestigious Sports Personality of the Year awards in recognition of winning the Cup Winners' Cup. The event, which was screened live to a huge television audience, took place at the BBC Television Centre in London on 16 December. The 'great and good' of British sport were in attendance, including the victorious Hammers team and their manager, Ron Greenwood.

There was a specific reason why they had been asked to attend. It was a proud moment for all at Upton Park and their thousands of watching fans when it was announced that West Ham had won the Team of the Year award as a result of their spectacular display at Wembley. Moore received the trophy and expressed his thanks on behalf of everyone at the club. Fittingly, it was Rudi Brunnenmeier, the captain of TSV, who presented the award. West Ham also became the first football team to win sport's world fair play trophy.

The first home programme of the 1965/66 season for the game against Sunderland heaped suitable praise on the cup winners. The standard 16-page issue devoted four pages to the events at Wembley the previous May and noted that two of West Ham's opponents had won their respective leagues (Sparta Prague and Lausanne-

Sport), testimony to the strength of the opposition the Hammers had had to face. You could also buy an 8mm film of the final, although the 90-minute sound version would set you back £52 – an awful lot more than a ticket to the final itself!

The final word must go to Ron Greenwood, who had masterminded the whole European campaign: 'I was just a player when I saw the 1953 Hungarians and I never imagined for a moment that one day I would see a side of my own applying so many of the same principles. But when West Ham beat Munich 1860 in that Cup Winners' Cup Final, they played in a way very different from the standard English game. They moved on and off the ball in a way similar to the Hungarians – not exactly, of course, because our overall methods were adapted to the players we had, but the basics were the same. 'That West Ham side proved a point for me. The match exceeded my wildest hopes. We won with two second-half goals by Sealey, but it was the manner of the victory that counted most of all. I said to my players before the start "Here's our chance to show the world what we can do'. And that is precisely what we did. Three years of hard work and faith went into our win. Our principles were justified; we proved that football at its best is a game of beauty and intelligence. Players and ball were in happy harmony, while skill and method had flourished together. Ideas and passes flowed. For me, it was fulfilment.'

Chapter Three

European Semi-Finalists: The 1965/66 European Cup Winners' Cup Campaign

AT THE start of the 1965/66 campaign, West Ham seemed to find it difficult to wriggle free from the euphoria that followed their springtime Wembley triumph. Complacency nourished carelessness in league and cup football.

Bobby Moore was fully preoccupied with Alf Ramsey's plans for his international team for the World Cup finals in England that summer. The England captain's listlessness while wearing his West Ham shirt worried his club manager, but if Moore sometimes performed without his usual authority, his leadership was still strong enough to see the team out of a number of embarrassing scrapes.

West Ham had warmed up for the season with a three-match mini-tour of West Germany, where they lost 0-1 to FVB Stuttgart, beat Eintracht Frankfurt 2-1 and drew 1-1 with by now familiar opponents TSV 1860 Munich.

The Hammers slumped to a 0-3 defeat at West Bromwich Albion on the opening day. Four successive defeats during the first 11 days of September, when the defence haemorrhaged 17 goals at Sunderland (1-2) and Sheffield United (3-5), and at home to Leicester (2-5) and Liverpool (1-5), quickly put paid to any notions of winning the First Division championship and it became apparent that any success would once again have to come via cup competitions.

Indeed, the Hammers were destined to play almost the equivalent of half a league programme in cup ties as they reached the League Cup Final, the FA Cup fourth round and the semi-finals of the Cup Winners' Cup – 20 cup games in all. Combined with league fixtures, the 62-match total remains the most ever contested by West Ham in a single season. Martin Peters and Moore played 63 first-class matches, and Geoff Hurst 62 that season. And that was before the World Cup that summer.

Substitutes were allowed in league football for the first time in 1965/66 and when Jack Burkett was injured against Leeds United on August 28, his replacement Peter Bennett became the club's first ever league substitute.

West Ham hovered around the foot of the table for most of the season, although they managed to improve near the end of the campaign to finish 12th. Four teams took both points from Upton Park and five goals were conceded at Nottingham Forest, Leeds and Sheffield United. Chelsea managed six at Stamford Bridge.

A 10-3 semi-final aggregate win over Cardiff City gave West Ham a League Cup Final spot against West Bromwich Albion. A year on and this would have been a Wembley final but in the last of the two-legged versions, West Ham won 2-1 at home, only for a 4-1 drubbing at the Hawthorns to put the trophy well beyond the Londoners' reach.

The club played four FA Cup ties, but only in two rounds. In the third round, Oldham Athletic were defeated 2-1 in an Upton Park replay, but a 4-1 fourth-round replay defeat at Blackburn ended that particular dream.

The 1965/66 European Cup Winners' Cup

First round:
Bye

Second round:
Olympiacos: 4-0 (H), 2-2 (A)
Aggregate 6-2

West Ham had finished ninth in the league in 1964/65, so their European ambitions were confined to the defence of the trophy they had won at Wembley.

Receiving a first-round bye as holders, the Hammers were paired with Greek cup winners Olympiacos Piraeus in the second round, the first time they had met a Greek side in senior football.

As if by magic, West Ham suddenly rediscovered much of the old flair and inventiveness that had led to their success in winning the trophy the previous year but had so far deserted them in the bread-and-butter quest for league points.

In the first leg at Upton Park, Moore's men were 2-0 ahead at half-time through typical strikes from Hurst and only the brilliance of the Greeks' goalkeeper Giannis Fronimidis and a host of missed chances kept the final score down to 4-0 as Johnny Byrne and the recalled Peter Brabrook added further goals for what looked like an unassailable lead to take to Piraeus.

When Martin Peters scored his and the Hammers' second goal in the 53rd minute of the return leg to silence the 40,000 partisan Greek fans, the holders' lead was impregnable. Only an own goal by Bovington and a scandalous penalty allowed the home side to save face in front of their fanatical support.

The referee in that second leg was Tofiq Bahramov. The following summer, the moustachioed Soviet official would become famous – or infamous if you were German – when he was the linesman who allowed Geoff Hurst's controversial second – and England's third – goal in the

1966 World Cup Final at Wembley. So confident were the Hammers about the second leg that, according to captain Moore, there was a right old knees up on the flights to and from Greece, and there is a story of one player waking up on the pitch and wondering what the time was.

In his 1970 autobiography, *The World Game*, Hurst expressed his awe of the Greek crowd. 'We met them [Olympiacos] during our second year in Europe and, having beaten the Greeks 4-0 at home, we went out to Athens fancying we had little left to do to get through. How little we knew of the reception waiting for us.

'The Greeks were absolute fanatics. The crowd was less than 40,000, but I have never in my life heard a noise such as they made. For an hour before the game they were roaring and when we came out to meet their favourites, we were greeted by a jeer that made the din of 100,000 at Wembley seem just a whisper. We came out to a shower of fruit, stones and fireworks aimed at our heads, and the barrage started up again any time in the match when things looked like getting dull. The Greek team took their tone from the crowd. They flew into us, shouting and screaming like madmen. They came into every tackle like a horde of dervishes, their eyes and mouths open with rage.

'Yet, somehow, we survived to draw 2-2 and Bobby Moore proved himself a great captain that day. Not only was he everywhere in defence as a player, but he was also everywhere on the pitch as a diplomat and trouble-stopper. Had Bobby not been so quick to step in, I am sure one West Ham player or another would finally have been goaded into thumping out … in which case none of us might have left the field alive! And incredibly in the last five minutes, the crowd suddenly sensed the match and the tie was lost and they swung right round to give us a terrific ovation at the end.'

Quarter-final:
Magdeburg 1-0 (H), 1-1 (A)
Aggregate 2-1

West Ham faced a crowded March fixture list: two Cup Winners' Cup quarter-final games, a two-legged League Cup Final and four league games – eight games in three weeks.

By the time the Irons were due to face Magdeburg of East Germany in the quarter-finals in March 1966, they were playing two games a week. The leg-weary Londoners managed only a slender 1-0 lead to take behind the Iron Curtain following Byrne's vital first-leg strike at the Boleyn. They failed to secure the big lead they had hoped to take to East Germany. The Hammers always seemed hurried and allowed themselves to be hassled into mistakes. The long-ball game West Ham played resulted in too much possession being gifted to their opponents. West Ham did not get their noses in front until a minute after the interval when Byrne hammered a cross from Peters into the net. Thereafter, the Irons launched raid after raid, but few were carefully built and none was accurately finished. They squandered their chances of building a tie-winning lead by trying to batter their way through the wall their visitors had erected.

In East Germany, Hammers supporters were obliged to have an armed police escort after being stuck on the East-West Germany border for four hours. Officials seemed concerned that the five West Ham coaches might harbour West German stowaways!

Their team achieved a noble end by harshly efficient means. Despite being forced to defend almost from start to finish, West Ham drew 1-1 with Magdeburg before 35,000 spectators at the Ernst Grube Stadium to qualify for the semi-finals. There was no denying the spirit of the English team. When, after yet another spell of heavy pressure, they eventually broke through to score in the 77th minute through Joachim Walter, West Ham sprang into life to shatter the Germans. Less than 60 seconds later, the Hammers were level, a brilliant move involving Hurst, Brabrook and Peters ending with John Sissons – who seemed to specialise in breakaways in Europe – scoring another precious away goal from close range. It meant the Germans had to score twice in the last 12 minutes, which was an unlikely task against a well-organised West Ham side.

Semi-final:
Borussia Dortmund 1-2 (H), 1-3(A)
Aggregate 2-5

West Ham faced the club's second European semi-final and their potential opponents were Liverpool, Celtic or Borussia Dortmund.

Their next 21 days would be crammed with that semi-final, six First Division matches and the second leg of the League Cup Final. Tired legs were being sapped by too many games. The league form would plummet and, after the disappointment of the league cup, they were left with disappointment.

On the eve of the club's semi-final with Borussia Dortmund came the bombshell news that Moore wanted to quit West Ham and wouldn't be renewing his contract. The timing of his announcement was particularly unfortunate and Greenwood promptly stripped the player regarded as his right-hand man of the captaincy and handed it to Johnny Byrne. Moore did still play against the Germans. Such was the mood, Greenwood was even quoted as saying: 'Let's face it, we shall probably be murdered.'

Greenwood not only stripped Moore of the captaincy, he went to a newspaper with a remarkable public attack on his deposed skipper. The outburst was untypical of a measured man and very oddly timed, coming just a week before the first leg of the semi-final against Borussia Dortmund, the biggest match of West Ham's season. But Greenwood evidently felt a need to pour out his frustration.

Brian Scovell of the *Daily Sketch* was the reporter handed the exclusive. The article on Monday, 4 April was headlined: 'West Ham sack Moore'. If the headline was eye-catching, the quotes from Greenwood were even more extraordinary. From the high of Wembley, West Ham had spent much of the winter in distress in the relegation zone. Was Moore one of the reasons for the decline? 'I am absolutely sure of it,' Greenwood told Scovell. 'Moore has not been really playing for us for eight months. We got into the big time with that cup final win at Wembley and some of the players think they are still playing at Wembley.'

After the glories of the previous two seasons, West Ham had not lived up to their reputation as England's coming force. They had done well enough in the cups, reaching the League Cup Final and the European semi-final. But the league campaign had been disastrous, with long months spent perilously close to the relegation zone.

The West Ham bubble was set to burst. Moore's restlessness was irritating Greenwood, Peters was sadly out of touch for most of the season and Hurst was far from his sharpest. In contrast, Borussia Dortmund seemed at their most formidable. They had a prodigious new discovery, Sigi Held, a miniature whirlwind at centre-forward, and an impassable centre-half in Wolfgang Paul. Lothar Emmerich, a left-winger with little more than phenomenal shooting power, proved a match-winner for Dortmund at Upton Park.

West Ham started the match as if their lives depended on it and, putting their off-field problems to one side, played some of their best football of the season to put the Borussia defence under immense pressure, much to the delight of their fans, who created a constant barrage of sound in support of their claret and blue heroes. Deposed captain Moore was superb in defence while Byrne was a revelation under his new responsibilities in attack, but somehow Dortmund managed to go in at half-time without conceding a goal. Then, seven minutes after the interval, Peters got the goal his team deserved when, taking a pass from Jimmy Bloomfield, he ran at the heart of the German defence before hammering a low shot past Hans Tilkowski's left hand, scoring in front of the North Bank.

With four minutes left and the West Ham fans wondering if one goal was enough to take to Germany, they realised it wasn't even enough for the night as Emmerich plundered a shock equaliser. Two minutes later, the same player – who scored 43 goals that season

– got on the end of a cross from Held and prodded home the winner. West Ham had tried to play football on the night to win, but succeeded only in playing football.

Only two days later, on Good Friday, West Ham went to White Hart Lane and thrashed Spurs 4-1 – without Moore. A day later, they went to Chelsea with Moore reinstated and lost 2-6.

In the *London Evening News*, Moore was quoted as saying: 'Only two people, Mr Greenwood and myself, knew I was not going to renew my contract at the end of the season. We agreed that it would be kept secret until the end of the heavy Easter programme. I kept my end of the bargain.'

Greenwood admitted: 'If the picture has been presented wrongly, I am to blame. After a talk with the board, I decided it was time the public knew what was happening. They have a right to know.'

For the second leg in Germany, Greenwood made five changes from the team that was so heavily defeated at Stamford Bridge. West Ham embarked on their eighth European adventure in 18 months, comforted by the knowledge that they'd never failed to score away from home in the competition. The man who barred their way to the final was once again left-winger Emmerich, who increased Dortmund's aggregate lead to 4-1 with his second goal of the match to delight the flag-waving, klaxon-hooting 35,000 crowd at the Westfalenstadion.

Just before half-time, Byrne gave the small band of fans who had made the trip a glimmer of hope when he headed past Tilkowski. But the task was beyond a team that had previously risen to every European challenge. Full-back Gerhard Cyliax's goal five minutes from time tied it up for the Germans, but at least Greenwood's team had the consolation of knowing they had been defeated by the best side in the competition, as was proved when Dortmund went on to defeat Liverpool in the Hampden Park final.

In his autobiography, *Sincerely Yours*, Greenwood maintained: 'I was happy enough when we were paired with the West Germans, Borussia Dortmund. Peters put us ahead just after half-time in the first leg at Upton Park and we might well have scored at least a couple more. But we overstretched ourselves going for another goal, a familiar story, and we were cruelly punished in the last five minutes when Lothar Emmerich turned in two goals.It was magnificent match but, realistically, we were now in trouble.

'Borussia were unbeaten at home that season and on all the evidence they were one of the best sides in Europe. A little voice inside me kept insisting we had no chance in the second leg but what manager ever admits private thoughts like that? I talked about courage and composure and looked confident. I did feel we might stand a chance if we could hold steady for half an hour and perhaps steal a goal ourselves. So much for hope. Borussia scored with their first movement of the game. Sigi Held centred, Emmerich headed the ball against the crossbar and then pushed home the rebound. We played well enough for the next 89 minutes, and Byrne even managed a goal, but there was no real way back for us. Borussia won 3-1, and then went on to beat Liverpool in the final. We had gone down to a better side, so there were no complaints.'

In the programme for the following game against Arsenal on 16 April 1966, the following lament appeared: 'After two years of campaigning on the continent we regretfully said farewell to European competitive football in Dortmund. It would be better to use the German expression of "auf wiedersehen" rather than "farewell", this being in keeping with the language of the country where we made our exit and of a less definite nature than its English counterpart, as we must hope that this reverse is temporary rather than final.'

West Ham travelled sadly home, no longer holders of the European Cup Winners' Cup. It would be nine long years before they were invited to participate again.

Like My Dreams They Fade And Die

In June 1965, a few weeks after the Wembley triumph, Eric Batty had written in *Soccer Star*: "For West Ham, this is probably just the beginning. If things go well for them, they can rise to the heights, and I wish them well … for West Ham are clearly a power in the world game.'

In a newspaper column, Billy Wright, the former England captain, predicted a great future for that youthful West Ham team, with its slick passing game, intellectual coach, imperious captain and core of internationals. 'West Ham have the potential to dominate the English game for years to come. They are a young team and there are no limits to the heights that they can attain.'

It was a magnificent compliment from one of England's most respected and esteemed players. Unfortunately, it is an eternal paradox of sport that the most expert practitioners tend to be the least reliable pundits. This is especially true of football and, sadly, Wright's words ultimately proved to be way off the mark.

West Ham were about to drift into years of decline and mediocrity. It would be exactly ten years before they won another trophy, by which time virtually all of the successful team from the mid-60s had departed the club. The sole exception was Ronnie Boyce, who became a member of the club's coaching staff.

It would prove to be a spectacular fall from grace and the resultant pain for the Hammers' disbelieving fans would be insuperable. Just like one of the lines from their famous theme song, West Ham's dreams were about to 'fade and die'.

After 1965, West Ham always seemed to be asking themselves: 'What's gone wrong?' Ron Greenwood, the great enigma of English soccer, was enmeshed in the fine strands of a complex West Ham philosophy which was straining to produce football of stunning simplicity.

In his biography of Bobby Moore, *The Life And Times Of A Sporting Hero*, Jeff Powell described the mid-60s West Ham as 'like a delicate cobweb glistening in the sunlight, West Ham were beautiful to behold but inspired no feeling of permanence. On so many days they spun a silken web of delightful football, only to be blown into tatters by a storm of old-fashioned British sporting aggression'.

Bobby Moore, quoted in the same book, said: 'It was well known that everyone enjoyed playing against West Ham as much as they enjoyed watching them. We had endless discussions about what went wrong but nobody seemed able to put their finger on it.

'Maybe it was a question of emphasis in the minds of the management. Ron Greenwood and John Lyall shied away when you mentioned putting some stick about. The emphasis was on skill.'

What bothered Moore most was that when he looked through the West Ham team, he, like the fans, could find no glaring weakness, no excuse for repeated failure. 'You looked at a few of the individuals and felt there might have been room for improvement. But the

11 pieces of the jigsaw fitted when we won the cups. They'd put the ingredients in the cocktail shaker and the team had come out right. It's like a drink [and this was a subject he understood]. Sometimes a cocktail is fabulous, sometimes it's diabolical. But when you get it right it's a crime to let it go.'

West Ham's most successful player and his manager did not enjoy a happy relationship, certainly not in the way Billy Bonds did with John Lyall a decade later. Moore's frustration led to a belief that Greenwood simply did not have the man-management skills necessary to be a successful league-winning manager as well as a principled one.

When Martin Peters left the club in 1970 after a fundamental disagreement with Greenwood over his future, it can be viewed as further evidence of the latter's inability to deal with international footballers. Moore and Peters, in their differing ways, were criticising their manager's lack of ambition and poor man-management.

Perhaps even Greenwood's famous football brain could not adjust to the game's increasing demands for more direct tactics at the cost of his passing philosophy. And he could, or would not, compromise.

In *Sincerely Yours*, Greenwood admitted to wondering, as early as 1963, if West Ham weren't already a side better suited to cup football than league. 'We were sprinters rather than marathon men. The blame was partly mine, of course. I began to wonder – not for the last time – if I had put enough concrete into the mixture. Was the team hard enough? Was I being too idealistic? Questions like this are easier to ask than answer but one thing never wavered: my faith in good, intelligent, football.'

Another West Ham hero, Billy Bonds, tried to put his finger on the Greenwood enigma in his own biography, *Bonzo*, published in 1988. 'England manager was his proper level. With players of international ability, Ron did not need to waste his energies upon the motivation that is necessary in the bread-and-butter stuff of club competition. Motivation was definitely not one of his strengths as a manager. When he took over with England, he worked with a squad of the best players who needed no gee-up. He could concentrate upon tactics – collective and individual – and at that he is the best.

'Hammers learned this playing in Europe. Ron's assessment of the opposition was always spot on. When the action started you felt as if you'd been playing them for years instead of for the first time.

'So why, with such an excellent manager and three of England's 1966 World Cup-winning side, did West Ham not achieve more? Perhaps part of the answer is that Ron was, at times, too much of an intellectual.'

Chapter Four

European Finalists Again: The 1975/76 European Cup Winners' Cup Campaign

PRIOR TO the start of the 1975/76 season, West Ham United returned to Wembley to play Derby County in the Charity Shield. The league champions beat them 2-0 but when the league season kicked off, West Ham made their best ever start and were undefeated until their tenth game.

Alan Taylor picked up where he had left off the previous May, scoring in each of the first three matches. This included two at Anfield in a 2-2 draw. After a brilliant recovery at Leicester, where a 3-0 deficit was cut back to 3-3, West Ham were second. On 8 November, West Ham drew 1-1 at home to Coventry City – enough to put them on top of the First Division.

League-wise that was as good as it got. The next 14 matches yielded only a miserable two points. Alan

Taylor's goal against Queens Park Rangers on 24 January provided the Hammers with their only post-Christmas league win as they finished 18th.

The domestic cups offered no solace. Their FA Cup defence ended at the first time of asking as Liverpool won 2-0 at Upton Park and in the League Cup, Spurs won a fourth-round replay 2-0 at the Boleyn.

Anglo-Italian League Cup

West Ham United were one of dozens of English and Italian clubs who competed with and against one another in two now-defunct competitions.

Set up in 1969, the Anglo-Italian League Cup was a short-lived two-legged 'final' which pitted the English League Cup or FA Cup winners against the Coppa Italia holders. It was held five times between 1969 and 1976.

It was organised initially to compensate Swindon Town, who won the League Cup in 1969 but were barred from competing in the Inter-Cities Fairs Cup because they were a third tier club. The Robins took on Coppa Italia winners AS Roma and won 5-2 on aggregate.

In 1970, Bologna defeated Manchester City, then Tottenham Hotspur beat Torino in 1971 before the tournament took a three-year break.

Despite being involved in another Cup Winners' Cup campaign, West Ham also participated in the Anglo-Italian League Cup. Only two games were played, both against Fiorentina of Italy, with West Ham losing both legs 1-0. The format was a simple one, a home and away leg between the winners of the Italian Cup and the FA Cup. AC Fiorentina had defeated AC Milan 3-2 in the 1975 final of the Italian Cup. At the time, Fiorentina were an excellent side and were regarded as one of the favourites for that season's Serie A title. Moreover, they had serious European pedigree in that they had previously been beaten finalists in the European Cup and had been victorious in the European Cup Winners' Cup.

On 3 September 1975, in a rain-soaked Florence, the Hammers took the field with Billy Bonds playing his first senior game of the season after a long lay-off with a serious groin injury. Unlike some of the previous Anglo-Italian encounters, there was a good attendance of around 35,000, including 1,000 Hammers fans.

For the first 15 minutes, there was little more than sparring between the two sides, but in the 20th minute an innocuous 20-yard shot from midfielder Vincenzo Guerini slipped through keeper Mervyn Day's hands at his right-hand post. Although West Ham fought back and Billy Jennings had a late header superbly saved, they were unable to find an equaliser. It must be said that Fiorentina were well on top throughout and deserved more than their single goal victory. The game ended with the Londoners suffering their first defeat of the season.

There was a three-month gap between the two matches and the second leg was played on a cold Wednesday evening in December in front of a disappointing audience of fewer than 15,000. At that point, West Ham were enjoying a good season – sixth in the First Division and already through to the quarter-finals of the Cup Winners' Cup. Fiorentina were only the second Italian side to appear at Upton Park – AC Milan had won a friendly 6-0 back in the 1954/55 season.

Bonds was again suffering from a groin injury and missed out, while Johnny Ayris made his first start of the season to supply pace down the right wing. The two teams began by testing each other out although, as early as the fourth minute, a stunning volley from Italian striker Walter Speggiorin just cleared the bar. It was the same player who scored what proved to be the only goal of the evening. After being penned in their own half for much of the first 20 minutes, Fiorentina went ahead when full-back Giancarlo Galdiolo floated a 40-yard pass into the Hammers penalty area for Speggiorin to take in his stride and blast an unstoppable shot past Day.

The visitors then put more emphasis on their defensive qualities and, although Trevor Brooking put in a commanding performance in midfield, there proved to be no way through for the Londoners.

Kevin Moseley wrote in the *Daily Mirror*: 'For all their spirited enthusiasm, West Ham failed to break down Fiorentina's superbly organised defence. No one could doubt the Italians' ability.'

West Ham manager John Lyall lamented afterwards: 'We did what you must never do against an Italian team – let them score first. Then they defended so well and it was frustrating to play against.' West Ham winger Ayris recalled: 'I had never played against an Italian team before. Their defending was awesome. I never got a kick all night.'

European Cup Winners' Cup
First round:
Lahden Reipas 2-2 (A), 3-0 (H)
Aggregate 5-2

According to the programme for the second leg against Lahden Reipas of Finland: 'The match in Helsinki was an exciting affair, the home club twice holding the lead in a game of swaying fortunes that eventually ended at two goals each. The opening exchanges set the scene, each side in turn switching from defensive lines to fast attack.

'This brought an early success to Reipas, for they opened their account in the fourth minute during a goalmouth melee. It took us some time to recover from this shock reverse, but almost on the half hour a cross from our left wing eluded the outstretched feet of defenders and attackers alike until Trevor Brooking stroked it into the net.

'Having restored their equilibrium, the Hammers came out after the interval with renewed confidence, but only eight minutes into the second half were again in arrears. This time the finishing blow was a great drive that hit the rigging. West Ham continued to put pressure upon the Finns' rearguard and a one-two ended with a Billy Bonds shot that went just inside the post.'

After coming back from Helsinki with a 2-2 draw, West Ham had a hard job breaking down the resistance of their Finnish opponents in the Upton Park leg. Though the eventual margin was 3-0, two of those goals were netted in the closing minutes. West Ham were denied a goal until the 60th minute, when Keith Robson's power drive from close range penetrated a resolute defence. The Reipas team continued to make a spirited fight of it and came close to equalising before the two late goals, from Pat Holland and substitute Billy Jennings, settled it in the Londoners' favour.

According to captain Billy Bonds: 'We flew out to Helsinki [...] confident they would present us with few problems. But we soon found out the days were past when Scandinavian teams could be dismissed as 6-0 pushovers!'

Bonds believed his team had not done themselves justice, though he had the personal satisfaction of scoring his first European goal. But the experience had taught West Ham the value of returning from European trips with something tangible in the goals department.

In *Just Like My Dreams*, manager John Lyall had this to say: 'We faced Reipas Lahti [the name of the football team's parent sports club] of Finland in the first round, and everyone told us we would get through easily. We travelled to Finland for the first leg and just scraped a 2-2 draw. It was a big disappointment. I remember calling the players up to my hotel room after the match. They were very subdued, and I felt I needed to put it into perspective for them. "It hasn't gone the way we hoped," I said. "But we get another bite at them. Let's make sure we learn the lessons and do the job properly next time." A lot of them were youngsters and I think they felt they had let me down.'

By the time the Hammers headed out to the USSR to take on Ararat Yerevan in the latter part of October, they had returned to the giddy heights of the top of Division One, albeit for a week, having amassed 22 points from a possible 30.

Second round:
Ararat Yerevan 1-1 (A), 3-1 (H)
Aggregate 4-2

The programme for the home leg had this to say: 'There was no doubt that our 1-1 draw at the Rasdan Stadium was one of our best ever results in European competition. Ararat put on pressure directly from the kick-off, and it was during this opening period of 20 minutes that we gave early indication of our defensive propensities. Eleven minutes after the resumption a combined move downfield ended with the ball being pushed through by Billy Bonds to leave Alan Taylor in the clear with only the goalkeeper to beat.'

When the equaliser did arrive, it was to general astonishment. Goalkeeper Day was being harassed by Petrosian and the Armenian succeeded in dispossessing Day by heading the ball from between his hands and pushing it into the net. Despite the problems with travel, 47 Hammers fans had made the long trip to Armenia, a venue which caused much puzzlement among the players. They stayed in a hotel overlooked by Mount Ararat where, according to the Bible, Noah's Ark came to rest. Unfortunately, the hotel was a dive, with more cockroaches in the rooms than guests.

On the pitch, in a 66,000-seater stadium, Yerevan showed themselves a fair, technically accomplished team. They hit the post in a goalless first half, but Alan Taylor would put the Londoners ahead, before the controversial equaliser.

Tommy Taylor said he would 'always remember that trip because the place was so poor that all the kids were coming up to us asking for money for food. The hotel was shit and there was no food there either, so we had to bring our own. It was grim and I remember John McDowell sleeping in a bath because there were cockroaches in all the rooms. I tried to tell him they came through plug holes, too, but he said he felt safer in there!'

Despite the conditions and the obvious poverty, the travelling Hammers thought it was a lovely stadium and a big crowd made it a great atmosphere.

The return leg at Upton Park was played on Fireworks Night and captain Bonds felt the Armenians seemed intimidated by the atmosphere provided by 30,000 Cockneys and 'clearly did not fancy it'. The visitors sustained some early setbacks and by half-time, they were two goals in arrears. A goal shortly after the interval put them back in contention, but within 12 minutes the Hammers were 3-1 ahead. That's how it finished, with the Hammers going through 4-2 on aggregate to the quarter-finals.

Quarter-final:
Den Haag 2-4 (A), 3-1 (H)
Aggregate 5-5 (West Ham won on away goals)

Billy Jennings scored a hat-trick against Stoke on 20 December but there was not much else to be pleased about in the league over the next few months. It was the absence of Bonds that perhaps hit the Hammers the most. The skipper was ruled out for three months after damaging his groin in November and by the time he returned on 28 February – for the 0-4 defeat at Manchester United – the Hammers' slide down the First Division table was well under way. Liverpool had also ripped the Eastenders' grip off the FA Cup, winning 0-2 at Upton Park in the third round. The collapse at Old Trafford – the team's sixth match without a win – was hardly the best way to prepare for the Cup Winners' Cup quarter-final first leg against Den Haag on 3 March.

For the second European round running, the Hammers found themselves victims of a German official's incompetence. With the Dutch side already one goal ahead, referee Rudi Glöckner erroneously deemed Mick McGiven to have handled in the penalty area. Captain Aad Mansveld duly scored from the spot to claim his second of a game that was barely 15 minutes old. Glöckner then decided to award another penalty for a foul by defender Kevin Lock on Simon van Vliet which clearly took place outside the box – with Mansveld completing his hat-trick – before curiously awarding a drop ball to the Dutchmen, who netted a fourth goal through Lex Schoenmaker just before half-time as the Hammers stood around in confusion.

Captain Bonds, recalling what he described as 'an utter calamity' in the first leg, said: 'Our dressing room was not exactly the liveliest place during the interval, as we all tried to take in a 4-0 deficit. But John Lyall would not let the heads drop. "All right, we're losing 4-0. But it's not over. Go back out there and get at them. We'll beat them at Upton Park no trouble, so if you can pull a goal or two back, we will still be in with a shout. Go out there and attack".'

The Hammers somehow hit back with two goals from Billy Jennings to offer some hope for the return leg. And it was those two goals in Holland that ultimately made the difference as a 3-1 win at Upton Park on 17 March – thanks to a machine-gun burst of three strikes in eight first-half minutes from Alan Taylor, Frank Lampard and Bonds – saw the East Londoners through on the away goals rule with the aggregate score level at 5-5.

In the programme for the Manchester United match on 8 February 2015, the club included the home leg against Den Haag as one of their 50 greatest games.

The equation was simple: West Ham needed to win by two clear goals to go through on away goals, so long as the second leg finished 2-0 or 3-1 in their favour. While the task was simple to explain, it was far harder to achieve against a Den Haag side managed by the legendary Serb Vujadin Boškov, who would go on to win the same competition with Italian side Sampdoria 14 years later.

What West Ham needed was a fast start and an early goal, but the Dutch, playing a high line to catch the Hammers' speedy attackers offside, held out their hosts in the early going. It took 28 minutes for Lyall's men to break the deadlock, doing so when Brooking's low shot came back off goalkeeper Ton

Thie and Alan Taylor poked the ball through the mud and into the net.

Five minutes later and West Ham were level on aggregate. Brooking was again the catalyst, rolling the ball to his left for full-back Lampard, who had earlier been ordered to pull up his trademark rolled down socks by Hungarian referee Karoly Palotai.

Lampard latched on to Brooking's pass and thumped an unstoppable 30-yard shot past Thie and into the top right-hand corner.

With noise levels inside the Boleyn Ground growing with every passing second, West Ham won a throw-in down the right flank. The ball was hurled into the penalty area, Alan Taylor got goal-side of left-back Joop Korevaar and the referee pointed to the spot. Billy Bonds stepped up and sent Thie the wrong way from 12 yards to make it 3-0 on the night and 5-4 to West Ham on aggregate.

The Hammers lost some of their fluency after the half-time break when Paddon and Tommy Taylor had to be replaced. Fourteen minutes into the second half, Day parried Mansveld's free kick and Schoenmaker expertly steered the ball into the net from six yards, levelling the aggregate score. Boskov's men had half an hour to find a goal that would send them through.

The game became increasingly fraught, with three players being booked as challenges continued to fly in from both sides. With just a few minutes to go, Den Haag had the ball in the net for a second time, only for the goal to be ruled out for offside. The final whistle was greeted by a mixture of joy and relief by the home fans.

Manager Lyall was rightly praiseworthy of his players' achievement. 'It is brilliant, terrific and tremendous. It's not easy to pull two goals back against a side as good as this one. You want all your players to hit form at the same time and tonight they did.'

Although Bonds, in his autobiography, credited Lyall with the half-time team talk which helped salvage the first leg, the manager himself remembered it a little differently in his *Just Like My Dreams* book. He wrote: 'In the quarter-finals we were drawn to meet Den Haag of Holland. I had a virus and a temperature of 103 degrees and was told it would be unwise to go to the match. Ron Greenwood took over. At half-time we were 4-0 down. Ron Greenwood knew exactly what to do. He knew we had to attack in the second half to have any chance in the return leg. Ron's tactical changes helped Billy Jennings score two goals. We lost 4-2 but it could have been far worse. I knew the Dutch would find the atmosphere in our cramped little ground difficult to cope with in the second leg and I think they found the occasion intimidating.'

Three days later, Lyall's side capitulated 6-1 at Arsenal. The contrast in spirit between the two games accurately reflected the fortunes of the team in the respective competitions. The last league win had been against QPR back on 24 January and not one more domestic victory would be claimed that season as the club slumped to 18th.

Semi-final
Eintracht Frankfurt 1-2 (A), 3-1 (H)
Aggregate 4-3

The Sun reported after the Hammers' narrow 1-2 semi-final first-leg defeat at Eintracht Frankfurt: 'West Ham tamed the shrew of West German football with a performance of steely determination and gritty purpose.' Graham Paddon had hit a 30-yard screamer past goalkeeper Kunter to score a vital away goal and give the Hammers an early lead, but the Germans then hit back through Neuberger and Kraus. Urged on by a season-best crowd of 39,202 in the second leg, West Ham scored three second-half goals, through Brooking (twice) and Keith Robson, to Frankfurt's one, to win 3-1 on the night and 4-3 on aggregate.

West Ham had performed really well in their semi-final against Eintracht Frankfurt and the normally unemotional John Lyall beamed like a Cheshire cat afterwards: 'This was the best display in the club's history,' he remarked in the bedlam of the dressing room afterwards. 'Everything I hoped for when I took the job came true tonight.'

When fans reminisce about great nights under the Upton Park lights, chances are they will recall the 3-1 victory over the Germans that took the Irons to Heysel. They don't come any better than the thrills served up on that magnificent rain-lashed evening, when the silky skills of Brooking, who glided across the sodden turf to score twice, and Robbo's rocket from long-distance put the Boleyn crowd on cloud nine.

Fan Graham Martin Johnson, in his book *Any Old Iron*, described the atmosphere at Upton Park that wet but memorable evening. For him, the Frankfurt semi-final 'must be said as a definite when it comes to one of my West Ham at home all-time high points'. He recalled: 'The British Legion band did the one thing I'd not seen them do before and that was to come out and do again at half-time the long-extended version of *Bubbles*. It was the most atmospheric game I had ever been to or been to since.' He had to rub his eyes that night just to check that Brooking was not walking on water.

If ever a goal encapsulated the quality of Keith Robson's cultured left foot, it was that glorious moment when he ran diagonally towards the West Stand, turned his marker and struck the sweetest shot high into the roof of the net in front of the jam-packed South Bank terracing. He recalled that 'even though I scored in the final, my greatest memory is of the goal against Eintracht Frankfurt in the semi-final, second leg'.

Skipper Bonds would nominate the game as one in which his mate Trevor Brooking put in one of his finest club performances, not only running the game but also scoring twice. Bonds said Brooking 'mesmerised' the German side.

Final:
Anderlecht 2-4 (Heysel Stadium, Brussels)

And so, to the European Cup Winners' Cup Final at the Heysel Stadium, Brussels on 5 May 1976. The opposition were the Belgian side Anderlecht.

There were 58,000 spectators at the Heysel Stadium, with West Ham's followers outnumbered by a strong Belgian following. For Anderlecht, this was virtually a home game, playing the final in their home city.

Pat Holland's 29th-minute goal was a fitting reward for his side's enterprising play and it seemed that one hand had been placed on the trophy. But three minutes before half-time, Frank Lampard's attempted backpass to Mervyn Day was intercepted by Peter Ressel, who squared for Robbie Rensenbrink to equalise. 'I felt a twinge in my stomach as I turned to pass, with the result that I only half hit the ball,' explained Lampard afterwards. He failed to appear for the second half because of the injury, which would ultimately require surgery.

That moment proved to be the turning point and, with the Hammers still adjusting after bringing on Alan

Taylor as substitute and moving John McDowell to left-back, François Van der Elst sped into the penalty box to put Anderlecht into the lead. Even though Keith Robson levelled with just over 20 minutes remaining, heading a Brooking curler in off a post, West Ham succumbed as Holland fouled Rensenbrink to concede a penalty, which he scored himself before setting up Van der Elst for his second to seal the victory.

'Europe has been a marvellous experience but perhaps we have allowed those games to distract us from the domestic programme,' said manager Lyall in the aftermath of defeat.

Robert Banks wrote in *An Irrational Hatred Of Luton*: 'I remember the final – or the night of the final – quite well. It was played in Anderlecht's Heysel Stadium in Brussels, a fact I thought was rather unfair, as Anderlecht was the opposition. Dad pointed out that the stadium to hold the final was picked before the tournament began, and there was no fiddling involved. Also, he said that when West Ham got to the final before in 1965, they had played at Wembley, which was nearly home advantage.

'Two vivid memories remain from that night. The first was West Ham's disgusting new strip. It was an Admiral strip with a blue yoke and huge collars with Admiral badges on. The West Ham badge was right in the centre and looked truly awful.

'The second was the unfairness of it all. Anderlecht were by far the better side and, despite going 1-0 up, we didn't stand a chance. François Van der Elst [later to join the Hammers] rounded Mervyn Day to slot home the fourth. I think it was Coleman who shouted "Fooooooooouuuurr-two!" It was only a few years later that I learned that the West Ham side had nearly all been playing on through considerable discomfort.'

Hammers skipper Billy Bonds was full of praise for the fans and their part in helping West Ham reach another European final. He also pointed out how, though travelling could be gruelling, it was nonetheless a change from the ordinary routine of league games.

However, there was personal sadness attached to this particular game. His mother-in-law had been taken seriously ill three weeks before the final. It meant he did not fly to Brussels with the team, instead travelling later, with the fans.

He got home after the game to find she had died while he was away. 'Instead of showing Lyn [Bonds's wife] my medal, I quietly put it away in a cupboard and it was months later before she even saw it,' he wrote in his autobiography.

Bonds recalled that the match ' began as if we were at home, not the Belgians' and that 'for around 40 minutes it looked very much as if the trophy was going to have Hammers' name on it for a second time'. However, he admitted, 'everything changed' with Anderlecht's equaliser and that 'they came out after the interval to slaughter us'.

Lampard's under-hit back pass in the final and relegation from the top flight in May 1978 mark the low points in his otherwise impeccable career.

Lampard reflected: 'People often think that the backpass against Anderlecht was a mistake but as I went to play the ball my groin gave way and I hardly touched the ball, which was intercepted and led to their equalising goal.

'I had struggled with a groin injury for about six months and it finally gave out in that game. I stayed on the pitch for a few more minutes, but I was finished.

'I remember the physio, Rob Jenkins, who is a big mate of mine, taking me to see the club medic, Dr Roper, the next day and he said "We'll have to operate. If it doesn't work, you'll never play again. Or we can forget the operation and you can stop playing now."

'It was a bad night for me but if it had been a poor backpass, it would have been even worse. The fact that it was caused by an injury makes it easier to cope with in a way. I ended up having my pelvis fused with a piece of bone from my hip.'

John Lyall had guided West Ham to their second European final. In *Just Like My Dreams*, he had this to say: 'We lost the final 4-2, but it was a wonderful game of football and I felt we had upheld the nation's reputation in our first European final since 1965.'

When Lampard left the game injured at half-time, Lyall made four positional changes to accommodate substitute Alan Taylor and a couple of players in claret and blue shirts that night have subsequently questioned those changes.

It was John McDowell who spoke out most strongly. He would continue to maintain that West Ham could have won the game in the second half if Lyall hadn't made so many changes.

McDowell felt Lyall should simply have put Kevin Lock on to replace Lampard, but his was a lone voice in the dressing room.

Lock was upset by the way he had been treated that season. He had played in all the games up until the semi-final against Eintracht Frankfurt. He was fit to play in the first leg, but Lyall dropped him. He told him he wasn't going to play him and that he was going to tell the press that Lock wasn't in the right frame of mind. It still rankles with Lock that he didn't get a medal, whereas reserve goalkeeper Bobby Ferguson got one and he hadn't played in any of the games.

West Ham would play Eintracht Frankfurt in another European semi-final in April 2022. In a look-back feature, both McDowell and Lock would show that time had not healed the wounds of 1976.

According to McDowell: 'Anderlecht had struggled down our flank until Frank's unfortunate injury enabled Robbie Rensenbrink to equalise on half-time. Everything then started to unravel. Instead of bringing on defender Kevin Lock, John [Lyall] unbalanced us by introducing substitute Alan Taylor up front.'

Lock said: 'Despite featuring in both quarter-finals against Den Haag, I never played another game in that European campaign. Missing out against Anderlecht was one of the biggest disappointments of my career.'

In the programme for the KAA Gent Europa Conference League semi-final on 20 April 2023, goalkeeper Mervyn Day reflected: 'Nearly 50 years on, I now realise what a massive deal it is to play in Europe. Those opportunities don't come around too often, especially at a club like West Ham, and back then you needed either to finish in the top four or win the FA Cup or League Cup to qualify.'

Remembering the trip to Ararat Yerevan, he said: 'Flying from Stansted, we endured a three-hour plus journey behind the Iron Curtain into Moscow. Once there, we had to wait through two hours of document checks before boarding our connecting flight for the final 1,500 miles to Yerevan. After that horrendous journey, we then discovered cockroaches in our hotel, forcing Mick McGiven and Keith Coleman to escape into the room I was sharing with Alan Taylor. Keith found a bit of space on Alan's bed but there was no room for Mick on mine and he had to grab his sleep in a chair.

'Anticipating what 1970s Soviet Union would be like, the club had, fortunately, brought its own food to Armenia, keeping everything as English as possible. We were all given an allowance, too, but with the authorities limiting us to around £15 worth of Russian roubles, we couldn't find anything to spend it on.'

Of the dramatic semi-final second leg win over Eintracht Frankfurt, Day said: 'I have no idea just how that second leg was played. There'd been torrential downpours in the East End throughout the day and when we arrived at Upton Park a couple of hours before kick-off, the ground staff were frantically forking the pitch in a desperate bid to drain all the surface water. The boggy surface made the night even more difficult for Eintracht, who now found the Hammers crowd almost on top of them, too. In an intimidating atmosphere, we could see that the West Germans were scared. Running out of the tunnel, the roar that greeted us was just unreal.'

Day still struggles to explain the contrast in the team's form in Europe compared to their domestic struggles. He said: 'Having been in that top spot in early November, I really can't put my finger on why we finished down in 18th, just two places above the relegation spots, with only one league win after Christmas. Each time we played after a European game we were really poor. Perhaps it was the travelling. Perhaps it was the lack of time we had to prepare for our next match. Perhaps it was just down to the fact that, with our small squad and no ability to rotate, we had tired legs out there after putting in so much effort on those muddy midweek pitches.'

It was the European nights that were to prove most memorable that season. And, as their league form crumbled, these European nights took on extra importance. As *Hammer* put it: 'Our eventual position in the table was incontrovertible evidence of the general decline which befell us in the latter half of the campaign ['Programmese' for "we were playing like a bunch of toerags"].'

But terrible league form could be forgotten on marvellous nights like those against Den Haag and Eintracht Frankfurt. West Ham needed to win at Upton Park and did so in thrilling style.

Chapter Five

Back Into Europe: The 1980/81 European Cup Winners' Cup Campaign

WEST HAM'S previous Cup Winners' Cup campaigns had been played out against poor league form in the First Division. Now, having been relegated at the end of the 1977/78 season, the Hammers were starting their third season in the Second Division. But they had beaten Arsenal 1-0 in the FA Cup Final the previous May, qualifying for their fourth European Cup Winners' Cup adventure, and manager John Lyall prepared his team assiduously for the 1980/81 season, sensing that this time promotion was just the other side of Green Street.

The season started with a 0-1 Charity Shield defeat by Liverpool but by the time the two clubs met again at Wembley the following March, in the League Cup Final, the Londoners were as good as promoted.

The Hammers machine may have coughed and spluttered initially, losing 1-2 at home to Luton Town and drawing at Bristol City and Preston. But a 4-0 home win against Notts County at the end of August effectively commenced the race and by the time the chequered flag was waved the following May, West Ham had left the rest of the pack trailing distantly in their wake. An incredible 16 home league games were won in succession between August and March, a sequence halted only when the exhausted Hammers returned from Cup Winners' Cup action in Tbilisi and scraped a 1-1 draw against Oldham Athletic. Nevertheless, they won all their remaining home matches to make it 19 victories in 21 league fixtures at Upton Park.

The Hammers were almost as convincing on their travels, winning more away games than any other Second Division side, losing on just three occasions. They claimed the championship trophy, setting a post-war Second Division record of 66 points in the final season before the introduction of three points for a win.

The European Cup Winners' Cup
First round:
Castilla CF 1-3 (A), 5-1 aet (H)
Aggregate 6-4

Castilla CF were an interesting side. Officially, they were an affiliated junior club to Real Madrid and under

Spanish League rules (which still apply) a filial cannot play in the same division as the parent club.

But in the 1979/80 season, Castilla reached the final of the Spanish Cup where they met … Real Madrid. They lost 6-1 but, since Real had also won the league, they entered the European Cup and Castilla were included in the Cup Winners' Cup.

The Hammers lost the first leg of the first round tie 3-1 at the famous Santiago Bernabéu Stadium in Madrid, but it was events on the terraces and in the streets that dominated the following morning's headlines.

Though you might not have known it from the coverage in the programme for the return leg: 'It was a result over which the Hammers could hardly enthuse … That first meeting was another of those matches of two halves. A goal in the 18th minute and an overall superiority gave Hammers supporters a satisfying feeling at the interval – although a second counter would not have been undeserved and could have stemmed the Spaniards' subsequent enthusiasm. For the Hammers, the second half was a tragedy; for Castilla it was patently the fulfilment of many of their hopes. They took their chances and will undoubtedly face the return with additional confidence.'

The match was an exasperating one for the Irons. After David Cross headed home the opening goal from a Brooking centre, the visitors dominated the first part of the game. Four clear opportunities were squandered. They clung to their one-goal advantage for more than an hour before a juddering dozen minutes, in which they conceded three goals, did for them. And this from a team who had kept a clean sheet in the previous six games.

Manager John Lyall would refer to a 'nightmare 15 minutes during the second half. We gave away the second goal with a mistake that happens only once in a blue moon. To do it again for the third goal was unbelievable'. He was referring to two horrendous backpasses by Billy Bonds and Geoff Pike, both of which had cost West Ham dearly.

Although both Alan Devonshire and Nicky Morgan were booked, the match itself was not remotely vicious. But something infected the travelling West Ham fans; Spanish police ejected around 50 of them from the stadium in the face of a fracas. Frank Sait, an 18-year-old West Ham fan, was run over by a bus as the ruckus continued outside the stadium.

The next day, the British newspapers had a field day with headlines like 'Shame night', 'Hammers fans in police battle' and 'Hammers Europe bid turns sour – 3-1 defeat as fans go on the rampage'. One hack told the world: 'West Ham's hopes of an all-conquering return to European football look a long way off following the sad events at Madrid's magnificent Bernabéu Stadium.' West Ham captain Billy Bonds was quoted as saying:

'Deep down, I wonder if one day UEFA will say "That's it, we've had enough" and ban British clubs.' Less than five years later, after the Heysel riots, they would.

Bonds admitted that the Madrid game was the one time in his Upton Park career that he fell out with the West Ham supporters. Bonds said that the people who had caused trouble in and around the stadium were 'scum'. The fans turned on him, for the first and only time, over his comments.

In his testimonial brochure, Hammers stalwart Alvin Martin wrote of that campaign and of how the fans could turn on such a crowd favourite as Bonds: 'Our cup final victory the previous May meant the chance of European football and what a new experience that proved to be. We were drawn against Castilla of Spain in the first round and I'm sure Bonzo won't remember the away leg with any affection. Before the game he struggled to pass a fitness test after a stomach bug laid him low. After the game, which we lost 3-1, he found himself at the centre of big controversy surrounding the behaviour of our fans at the Bernabéu.

'Basically, Bill's comments to a reporter were taken out of context. The subsequent newspaper reports virtually quoted him as saying our fans were a "bunch of animals". Bill realised he could never repair the damage that was caused by one irresponsible journalist's misinterpretation of events. Obviously, many of us believe what we read in the press and, understandably, our supporters were hurt by the alleged comments.

'They made their feelings clear in the early minutes of our next home game, when they jeered him every time he touched the ball. There were banners up demanding an apology from the captain. None of us had seen anything like it where Bill was concerned. He was the fans' idol. Bill's response was to make as many full bloodied tackles as was humanly possible in the first, frantic minutes of the game. And, sure enough, he soon turned the jeers to cheers.'

The fans complained of police brutality. An angry John Lyall called for jail sentences of 'at least three years' for the hooligans. As the dust settled, it was confirmed that around 20 fans had been injured and a handful arrested. It was also clear that West Ham would likely be punished for the behaviour of their travelling support. At first, UEFA decided that the Hammers would have to play the second leg – in which they had to try and overturn a two-goal deficit – at least 187 miles away from Upton Park. After a four-man delegation had attended an appeal hearing in Zurich, however, it was subsequently announced that the game could indeed take place at the Boleyn Ground – but behind closed doors.

At 7.30pm on Wednesday, 1 October 1980, the second leg kicked off at the Boleyn Ground. For almost two hours, the stadium echoed to some of the strangest noises ever to accompany an important match. Individual voices could be heard throughout the ground and a single cheer or casual comment achieved the same level as the lusty sound that usually came from the North and South Banks. As the match progressed, an unaccustomed sound was the repeated thud of boot on ball. One reporter remarked that it was the first time in his career that he had heard that sound so consistently at a big match.

This was no ordinary evening, even by the standards of international football. The big story was the crowd: it was not there. The attendance was listed officially as 140 plus 122 reporters, commentators, ball boys and others considered necessary to stage the match.

There were those who felt UEFA had overreacted to what the West Ham chairman later called 'the disturbing and disorderly conduct of a very few who disgraced themselves' and that the club had been singled out for punishment as an example to other clubs and their supporters. If that was the case, the events of the next five years showed, sadly, that the lesson was not brought home with enough severity to dampen the excesses of crowds, either at home or abroad.

But there was a game of football to be played that night. As a subsequent West Ham programme reported: 'The Hammers set the tone with a gloriously struck 25-yard shot from Geoff Pike after Pat Holland beat three men on the run. On the half-hour Trevor Brooking was fouled on the edge of the penalty area and his free kick was headed home by David Cross to level the aggregate. Cross knocked back the ball for Paul Goddard to crash in the third five minutes before the interval, and most present appeared to consider the contest as ended.

'Castilla had other ideas, especially as they had twice been foiled by good saves from Phil Parkes in the first half. Skipper Bernal hit a wonderful shot from 30 yards 11 minutes after the resumption to level the aggregate again and his team survived a bar-rattling header from Cross to take the tie to extra time.

'Substitute Nicky Morgan began the move that ended with Cross heading in again; and the seal was set on a great night (on the pitch at least) as Cross completed his hat-trick in the last minute.' Surely professional football's most quietly celebrated hat-trick.

The official attendance of 262 was the lowest ever for a first-team fixture at Upton Park. They had witnessed a match played in the most bizarre of environments. Robert Oxby of the *Daily Telegraph* described the circumstances in which the match was played: 'When the day of the second leg against Castilla arrived, there were fears that some of the West Ham supporters who had caused trouble in Madrid might materialise and stage a protest or attempt to gatecrash the stadium. So, there was a considerable police presence to check on the bona fides of the journalists, officials and even ball boys who had been especially recruited to field the ball from the deserted terraces.

'In the event, everyone stayed at home except the 140-odd privileged customers who huddled in the cold main stand. The atmosphere was unreal, with the only noise coming from a record player in the neighbouring flats and the babble of English and Spanish voices.'

Manager Lyall puzzled over how to prepare his team for a European game in an empty stadium. He decided to play two full-scale practice matches at Chadwell Heath. In both games, he asked the reserve lads to tackle, chase and harry the first-team players as if it was a competitive match. 'I wanted them to get some idea of what it was going to be like playing a fiercely competitive match without an audience.

'Usually before a big match you can hear the murmur of the crowd outside and fans clicking through the turnstiles. On this occasion there was only an inhibiting silence, which made the task of preparing the players more difficult than usual.

'When the referee blew his whistle to start the game, the noise echoed around the ground. From above me, high in the stand, I – and probably everyone else in East Ham – could hear Eddie Baily shout: "Get stuck into them". By the end of the match, he had lost his voice.'

In 2022, full-back Ray Stewart reflected on that campaign. 'Chasing that 1-3 first-leg deficit, goals from

Geoff Pike, David Cross and Paul Goddard looked to have put us through before Castilla pulled one back and sent us into extra time. As players, we could also hear everything and anything shouted from the directors' box, where our club medic – the Glaswegian Doc Brill – was clearly getting frustrated as we struggled to get our noses back in front. "Will you all just try to pass the ball to your own team-mates"? he roared in a loud Scottish accent that bellowed around the Boleyn Ground.'

West Ham had progressed to the second round in dramatic fashion, but the club's reputation had suffered badly – not withstanding UEFA's decision to rescind their original verdict. Moreover, the club had suffered a heavy financial loss, given the absence of gate receipts from the second leg.

Second round:
Politehnica Timişoara 4-0 (H), 0-1 (A)
Aggregate 4-1

West Ham were meeting Romanian opposition for the first time and, as was pointed out in the match programme (in the days before the break-up of the Soviet Union and Yugoslavia), the only continental countries from which the Hammers had not met teams were Albania and Turkey.

Hammers DJ Bill Remfry promised to find some Romanian music. If unsuccessful, he pledged to 'offer some music from countries with whom they enjoy similar backgrounds'.

In the Upton Park leg, West Ham put on one of their best displays of the season. Not many teams could survive the kind of performance eventually rewarded with three goals in a six-minute spell that rocked the Romanians on their heels. Billy Bonds started it by heading home Ray Stewart's free kick. Three minutes later, Paul Goddard crashed in the second after Geoff Pike's shot had been parried. Then, three minutes later, Stewart scored from the spot.

The Romanians then had their best spell of an eventful evening, but they failed to accept chances and were fortunate that their profligacy went unpunished when Stewart had his second spot kick of the night saved and a Cross shot bounced back off the bar. However, within a minute of his near miss, Cross capitalised on another rebound to add the fourth goal.

The return leg in Timişoara was full of incident. Prior to kick-off, the home fans in the 25,000 crowd were confident they could wipe out the 4-0 deficit. Within ten minutes, a player on each side had been booked. Among Italian referee Riccardo Lattanzi's collection was an unusual one in those days – a name in the book for diving in the penalty area.

Politehnica nearly cut their arrears when they hit the bar from a free kick, but the Hammers defence held firm, maintaining a blank scoresheet at half-time. However, the Romanians' pressure eventually paid off and, eight minutes after the interval, their captain Dan Păltinișanu shot in from the edge of the penalty area with Phil Parkes unsighted. Parkes was called upon to make a couple more saves within a short time, but the Romanians' hopes faded as the hands of the clock moved to the magic moment when the referee signalled the finale.

According to Alvin Martin: 'We had a more comfortable aggregate win over them, but our trip to Romania – apart from the football – wasn't very enjoyable. On the coach journey from the airport to our hotel, we were unfortunately held up by a funeral procession. We were playing cards when Dev [Alan Devonshire] happened to pause during a hand of poker and spotted, through the window, a topless coffin with a dead body inside. I don't know who had the paler complexion – Dev or the poor bloke in the coffin. And he lost the next hand!

'Seriously, the game in Romania was quite an intimidating experience. We were pleased to go there with a four-goal cushion from the first leg. The Romanian fans created an unbelievable noise and although I've seen our crowd intimidate the opposing team, this was something else. On the pitch, Timișoara were niggly and their aggressive approach added to the provocative atmosphere.'

The game was notable for being the first time in 28 Cup Winners' Cup outings that West Ham had failed to score.

Quarter-final: Dinamo Tbilisi 1-4 (H), 1-0 (A) Aggregate 2-4

The draw for the quarter-finals saw West Ham paired with Dinamo Tbilisi from the southern Soviet state of Georgia (birthplace of Joseph Stalin). The club had built a reputation as one of the most formidable sides in European football.

The West Ham management had always valued sound information about opposing teams they were soon to play but they encountered a problem with watching Dinamo Tbilisi.

The Soviet domestic season had only just resumed after its winter break and, although Tbilisi had arranged a couple of friendly matches, neither John Lyall nor Eddie Baily could get to the games. They had to settle for film clips. Tbilisi manager Nodar Akhalkatsi, meanwhile, was able to watch the Hammers play Cambridge United.

If having seen Tbilisi play beforehand would have made any difference to the eventual outcome, we will of course never know, but the Hammers might have been better prepared for what they faced at Upton Park on 4 March 1981.

West Ham continued to make their own small contribution to thawing the Cold War. Bill Remfry made a special effort in his *Off The Record* column in *Hammer*, mentioning Tchaikovsky, Shostakovich, Chekhov, Turgenev and Gogol (who were all good players!) and telling his readers: 'Western pop music is slowly becoming accepted in the USSR … I shall endeavour to play some Georgian or Armenian music this evening; if not, we will have to settle for *Georgia On My Mind*.'

Despite the 4-1 loss, the consensus was that the Georgians were not only the best team that had been seen at Upton Park all season but were also one of the finest combinations to visit Upton Park during the last couple of decades.

Robert Oxby of the *Daily Telegraph* reported: 'Their vibrant flowing football was all against the sterile defensive tradition that the visiting club on foreign soil should seek merely to contain the opposition. Unhinged by the thrust and perception of the brilliant Chivadze (the reigning Soviet Footballer of the Year) and Kipiani, United were harried into defensive errors and the Georgians went 4-0 ahead through goals by Chivadze, Gutsayev and Shengelia (2). Cross gave United small consolation with a goal just before the end and, at the final whistle, the crowd gave the visitors a standing ovation. The beaten West Ham players applauded Dinamo into the tunnel.'

Alvin Martin recalled: 'We were confident of beating Dinamo Tbilisi, bearing in mind they had just finished a three-month break in the Russian season when they visited Upton Park for the first leg in March. We were virtually unbeatable at home but unfortunately Tbilisi hadn't read the script. After taking an early lead, they gave us a footballing lesson that night. David Kipiani was in superb form and I can recall sitting in the bath afterwards feeling totally stunned. We had been brought back down to earth with a bump, as it must have been for our crowd.'

John Lyall reflected: 'We knew, of course, that Tbilisi had a glowing reputation for the quality of their football, and it was easy to see why after just a few minutes of our game at Upton Park. Technically they were a wonderful side, so comfortable and composed on the ball, so full of running off the ball. Their movement off the ball was breathtakingly simple, and it was their angled running across the pitch that made them so difficult to mark. It was an education to watch them, and they remain one of the finest European sides I have ever seen. At the end of the match our crowd of 35,000 gave the Russians a standing ovation. They obviously realised the task we faced, but they also wanted to acknowledge a team of the highest quality.'

Fan Graham Martin Johnson wrote in his book *Any Old Iron* that 'this was probably the finest away performance I can ever recall at Upton Park. Tbilisi were simply tremendous'.

West Ham's European trips did not all fit into the 'exotic' category. Their journey to Tbilisi was a classic case in point.

West Ham had travelled to the second leg with few expectations of overturning Dinamo's big lead. But Trevor Brooking described their journey as the most miserable since he began crossing frontiers. There was to be the obligatory stop in Moscow, although Tbilisi is more than 1,000 miles to the south. After the personal checks, the entire party had to suffer no fewer than four luggage inspections and the whole dreary business took four hours. Those who complained were told: 'Four hours? But that's a speed record for a British football club.'

In Tbilisi, there was bright sunshine and no customs or luggage checks greeted the party. West Ham were met by a battery of tired local officials who had been waiting all night at the airport. Moscow had forgotten to tell them of the overnight delay. Tbilisi was so different from Moscow. The party were given a tremendous welcome; a special lunch was laid on for the press, with each representative presented with a pottery gift.

In the second leg at the 80,000 all-seater Lenin Dinamo Stadium, West Ham played intelligently, holding on to the ball in the search for breaks. Stuart

Pearson, who was brought on in the 65th minute, scored the only goal of the game in front of about 2,000 West Ham supporters (for whom it was a 4,000-mile round trip, via Moscow). It was a tasty volley from a right-wing centre by Cross.

There was further frustration when the party arrived at Tbilisi airport after the match. The aircraft had returned to Moscow and there would be a three-hour delay before it returned. At last, the party set off for Moscow where, although it was 2am, bureaucracy was rife. More queues and much interrogation of Trevor Brooking, who had achieved the improbable feat of going home with more money than he had brought with him.

'How is it possible?' asked the soldier at passport control. 'You must give an explanation.' 'I beat the others at cards. We had lots of time to kill.' 'The English are mad,' said the soldier, probably not for the first time.

Tbilisi would show their win at West Ham was no fluke and go on to beat FC Carl Zeiss Jena in the final in Düsseldorf. West Ham had now competed in the European Cup Winners' Cup four times. They had won it once and on the other three occasions had been knocked out by the team who eventually won the competition. Some consolation, I suppose.

Postscript To Four European Cup Winners' Cup Campaigns

Spread over these four campaigns, the Hammers scored in each of their first 27 matches – a record that stood for 31 years.

Of those 27 matches, the club won 14, drew six and lost seven. Each game averaged more than three goals. West Ham scored 56 goals to average more than two a game, although in conceding 36 goals they leaked an average of more than one a match.

Only two managers, Ron Greenwood and John Lyall, were in charge between 1964 and 1981, the period spanning West Ham's involvement in the competition.

Twenty-one different Hammers hit the back of the net in those 27 games. Top contributors were Johnny Byrne with six, David Cross five and Brian Dear, Martin Peters and Keith Robson with four each. Geoff Hurst was limited to a couple of goals, both against Olympiacos.

David Cross' treble at home to Castilla was the only hat-trick. Ray Stewart converted the only penalty, at home to Politehnica Timisoara.

Forty-seven players donned the claret and blue shirt. Ken Brown, Geoff Hurst and Martin Peters had 15 appearances each, while Bobby Barnes Alan Dickie and Bobby Gould made only one each. (My thanks to Bob Hillier for this information).

Centre-forward Cross, interviewed in the match programme for the Europa League tie against Sevilla in March 2022, recalled: 'It was my first ever competitive match against overseas opposition [Castilla] and within 17 minutes of my European debut, I'd nodded home Alan Devonshire's cross to put us ahead. That'd been the only time I'd managed to escape the attentions of Castilla's Jose Espinosa. The Spanish centre-half was never more than two yards away and at half-time I asked John Lyall "What's he doing?" He replied "It's called man-to-man marking, David. They do that in Europe". I spent the second half taking their number five into the most ridiculous positions on the Bernabéu pitch, hoping to create space for others, but Castilla managed to reply with three goals to give the Spaniards a 3-1 victory.

'Playing the first leg against Politehnica Timișoara at home, I was taken aback by how friendly the Romanians were in the tunnel at Upton Park. Chatting, smiling, patting us on the back they seemed like really nice lads. "Why are they being like this?" I thought. The first leg [won 4-0] had gone off without incident, but standing in the Timișoara tunnel a fortnight later, the mood was so different. The Politehnica players were now swearing at us and one even kicked me before we'd even walked out. Now it clicked – they'd obviously expected us to do the same to them in London and that's why they'd been so friendly towards us.

'Two Celtic players had been sent off over there in the previous round but, bringing our four-goal lead into the second leg, we kept our cool in a really hostile atmosphere both on and off the pitch. Politehnica were just villainous. From being so timid at the Boleyn Ground, they were now so aggressive in their own back yard.

'Dinamo Tbilisi were the best team I encountered during my 179 games and five years at West Ham United. Their regimented, well-drilled football was typical of Iron Curtain teams in that era, but we were taken completely by surprise.'

Chapter Six

Into Europe Through the Back Door (one): The 1992/93 Anglo-Italian Cup

THE PREMIER League kicked off in August 1992, but West Ham were not invited to the party. Relegated the previous May (bottom for the first time since 1932), their main focus for the 1992/93 season had to be getting on the Premier League gravy train. Ironically, as the Eastenders dropped, former manager John Lyall was celebrating promotion to the Premier League with Ipswich Town. Typically, Lyall refused to gloat, offering sympathy towards his old stalwart Billy Bonds for the position he now found himself in as Hammers manager.

Hammers managing director Peter Storrie warned that the club was at 'an all-time low'. Harry Redknapp returned to Upton Park as assistant manager and several years later he recalled: 'What I first saw at Upton Park shook me to the core – the club was going nowhere.'

On 24 February, news emerged of Bobby Moore's death from cancer. Before the home game against Wolves, wreaths were laid around the pitch and there was a one-minute silence before kick-off.

Nonetheless, under Bonds, West Ham made a swift return to the top flight by gaining promotion as runners-up behind Newcastle United. Typically, promotion was secured only on the last day of the season with a 2-0 home win against Cambridge United.

Anglo-Italian Cup

A Wembley final and the chance to face Italian opposition in Italy – that was the prospect facing West Ham and all the other First Division clubs in that 1992/93 season following the relaunch of the Anglo-Italian Cup.

The campaign saw West Ham return to European competition for the first time since 1981. The Hammers were in group eight, with those 'European' teams Bristol Rovers and Southend United.

Preliminary round
Bristol Rovers 2-2 (H)

Two appalling defensive lapses by the Hammers on 2 September 1992 kept Rovers' hopes of a trip to Italy alive, as West Ham twice squandered the lead. Julian Dicks emerged as the Hammers' hero by scoring both goals – a volley and a header – in the 2-2 home draw against Bristol

Rovers in the Anglo-Italian Cup, a competition that he claimed was 'a waste of time'.

Preliminary round:
Southend United 3-0 (A)

Having convincingly overwhelmed Southend on 30 September, West Ham had to wait until after the game to collect their passport to Italy. With the Hammers and Bristol Rovers inseparable in their qualifying group on identical 5-2 goal tallies, it meant the toss of a coin and, for once, Lady Luck shone on Upton Park when Rovers wrongly called 'tails'.

International Group Phase

Cremonese 0-2 (A)
Reggiana 2-0 (H)
Cosenza 1-0 (A)
Pisa 0-0 (H)

West Ham were drawn in Group B in the main group stage. First up on 11 November were Cremonese, where the English side went down 2-0. Manager Billy Bonds commented: 'Cremonese were a bit niggly at times, but I was quite pleased how our players stayed cool.' According to Alvin Martin: 'Cremonese played the typical Italian way. They sucked us in and then hit us on the counter-attack twice to win the game.'

Despite serving a lengthy ban from domestic football, Dicks was allowed to compete in the Anglo-Italian Cup game at Cremonese. 'West Ham walked into an Italian dirty tricks war,' wrote *The Sun's* Lee Clayton after the Hammers' 2-0 defeat. 'Billy Bonds' team were elbowed, punched, kicked and stamped. Bonzo's boys have been criticised this season for their increasing disciplinary problems, but they deserve praise here for somehow keeping their cool. Hammers full-back Julian Dicks was Cremonese's number one target. He was kneed in the face, punched and clattered by crude challenges. But, to his credit, Dicks kept his cool and, on the whole, avoided confrontation.'

But Dicks denied being singled out for special treatment by the Italians, claiming it was Trevor Morley who took most of the punishment. 'Trevor was battered in that game, he got really hammered,' Dicks wrote in his autobiography.

West Ham's experience was not an isolated one. This bridge-building competition was rapidly turning into a bridge-burning exercise. In front of paltry crowds, the cynical tackles flew in, and red and yellow cards were being pulled from referees' pockets like confetti. It was being asked whether this tournament was worthwhile against a backdrop of around 50 domestic games.

The Hammers' Cremonese excursion saw no end of niggly behaviour, with five names being taken, and it was no different against Reggiana at Upton Park on 24 November. A further three yellow cards were brandished, while Trevor Morley got his marching orders. West Ham, reduced to ten men for 70 minutes, were no doubt pleased with the victory and, as Billy Bonds admitted afterwards, it was a good workmanlike performance, but it was victory at a price.

Ian Bishop, commenting afterwards on Morley's dismissal, said: 'Trevor said he thought the lad was going to headbutt him, so he defended himself first.'

Clive Allen's 44th-minute volley earned West Ham a win in their second visit to Italy, to Cosenza on 8 December. Just 800 fans braved the diabolical conditions to see Hammers win a game that, according to referee Roger Dilkes, would have been cancelled due to a waterlogged pitch had it been played in England.

Midfielder Martin Allen commented afterwards: 'Their number five was a lunatic. I don't know what planet he's from. He must be a member of my family.'

Derby County's 3-0 victory over Cremonese earlier in the evening effectively ended the Hammers' interest in the competition before they had even kicked off against Pisa at Upton Park on 16 December. West Ham needed a seven-goal margin to overall Derby, but it never remotely looked like happening.

Even so, both sides managed to turn a non-event into a busy evening for referee Cardona as the competition's appalling disciplinary record worsened. Matthew Rush and Giovanni Fasce were both shown the red card in the 56th minute. That double dismissal took the number of cards brandished in the Hammers' four international qualifying games to three red (coincidentally the same as the number of goals they managed to score) and eight yellow.

So, West Ham departed the Anglo-Italian Cup, probably with few regrets.

Chapter Seven

Into Europe Through the Back Door (two): From Intertoto to UEFA Cup 1999/2000

WEST HAM'S involvement in the Intertoto Cup meant that they would have the shortest close season in their history. Only 62 days had passed since the last game of the 1998/99 season before they took to the field against Jokerit of Finland. On the plus side, this meant the Hammers had already played four competitive games before the Premier League season began and the head start this gave them in terms of match sharpness would be reflected in them standing in third place after five games.

Three new names had been brought to Upton Park. At a cost of £1.75m, Paolo Di Canio was, in retrospect, a bargain, certainly compared to the club record fee of £4.5m that was needed to bring Cameroonian midfielder Marc-Vivien Foé, along with £1m Scott Minto, to East London.

The season's contribution to 'great West Ham cock-ups' took place on 15 December 1999. The Hammers played a League Cup quarter-final against Aston Villa and, with the game in extra time, Emmanuel Omoyinmi was brought on as a 113th-minute substitute. Unfortunately, Omoyinmi had previously played in the competition for Gillingham while on loan and thus was ineligible to play. This did not occur to him or manager Harry Redknapp or club officials. West Ham won the game on penalties, but the Football League ordered the game to be replayed after Villa complained. West Ham, naturally, lost the replay, going down 3-1.

West Ham finished ninth in the Premier League, putting them in the top nine for the third consecutive season. Highlights included a Di Canio goal against Wimbledon that was hailed as goal of the season. Barely a week later, appropriately on April Fool's Day, West Ham lost 7-1 at Manchester United.

Redknapp's take on all this was: 'It's been a good season again. People don't realise that West Ham have only finished in the top ten 14 times in its entire history and this is only the second time that we've done it three years running.'

Intertoto Cup

Following their fifth-place finish in the previous season's Premier League, West Ham entered the Intertoto Cup.

The competition kicked off on 19 June 1999 when 40 European minnows competed in two-legged ties. The subsequent 16 winners from the second round progressed to the third, when West Ham entered the competition as one of the eight top seeds.

Despite their bye into the third round, the mid-July start to competitive games meant that, at just eight weeks, it was the shortest close season since the Hammers moved to Green Street in 1904.

West Ham believed they should have gained automatic entry into the UEFA Cup by finishing fifth but according to the programme for the Jokerit game: 'The European rug was whipped from under our feet. Fifth place in any other season would have got us in.'

Once again, the Hammers would not get their due European reward after a high league finish (in 1986/87, having finished third, they had lost out on a UEFA Cup place due to the post-Heysel ban on English clubs). Nevertheless, it represented a return to European competition after an 18-year gap.

These days, you would assume a fifth-place finish would guarantee European football. But in 1999, this was not the case. The top three of Manchester United, Arsenal and Chelsea took the three Champions League spots and the UEFA Cup positions were assigned to Leeds, who finished fourth, and Tottenham and Newcastle, who, despite finishing only 11th and 13th respectively, qualified for the UEFA Cup by virtue of winning the League Cup and reaching the FA Cup Final. This left us all dressed up but uninvited to the European party.

We at least managed to find a side entrance in the form of the much-maligned and often-mocked Intertoto Cup. The competition was essentially a long-winded second chance for teams that just missed out on the UEFA Cup and, while it was often not taken seriously, with teams putting out severely weakened sides, we took the sensible decision of making the competition essentially our pre-season schedule with a view to eventually earning the UEFA Cup place our league season had deserved.

Third round:
Jokerit 1-0 (H), 1-1 (A)
Aggregate 2-1

West Ham kicked off the new season playing in 90-degree heat. Try as they might, the Hammers could not add to an 18th-minute goal scored by Paul Kitson. Paolo Di Canio created the goal, his turn and cross from the left edge of the penalty area giving Kitson the chance to head home at the far post.

The Hammers struggled to break down a well-organised defence and towards the end they began to suffer for having had only a fortnight's preparation for a match against a side who were already midway through their domestic campaign.

The Hammers were missing Joe Cole for the second leg in Helsinki and struggled at times on an uneven pitch. They did create most of the chances but had to rely on a 20-yard free kick from Frank Lampard in the 71st minute to earn a semi-final place.

About 500 Hammers fans were in Helsinki and they saw Michael Carrick come on as a late substitute to make his first-team debut.

Semi-final: Heerenveen 1-0 (H), 1-0 (A) Aggregate 2-0

Four days later, West Ham could only take the slenderest of leads to Holland after a frustrating display at Upton Park against a Heerenveen team who gave the home side a number of problems.

The Hammers took the lead as early as the seventh minute when Frank Lampard collected a misplaced pass in midfield, ran 20 yards and then hit a 25-yard rising right-foot shot which went in off the left-hand post. He also struck a post in the 80th minute.

Ultimately, it was a smooth enough passage into the Intertoto Cup Final. Once Paulo Wanchope had scored in the 25th minute, doubling the aggregate lead, the home side had to score three times to progress. Wanchope's second goal since his move from Derby County was a close-range strike into the roof of the net after a 35-yard drive from Lampard had been parried by Vonk. Then West Ham soaked up sporadic pressure and Heerenveen rarely looked like breaking through.

Final:
Metz 0-1 (H), 3-1 (A)
Aggregate 3-2

Apparently, Harry Redknapp persuaded chairman Terence Brown to cut admission prices for the final against French side Metz to tempt more fans to attend. Normal prices for the Jokerit and Heerenveen matches had produced less than a half-full stadium. Redknapp was rewarded with a 25,372 attendance.

Louis Saha headed the only goal at Upton Park, after 13 minutes, and despite West Ham exerting mounting pressure they were unable to capitalise. They even saw Lionel Letizi, the Metz goalkeeper, save a second-half penalty from Frank Lampard after a foul on Paolo Di Canio.

West Ham refused to let their heads drop and increased the intensity of their barrage of the Metz goal, which forced the visitors to pull ten players back for most of the time. Redknapp was his usual optimistic self afterwards, predicting: 'I still feel we can go there and score. We're capable of winning 1-0 or 2-1.'

Some 2,200 Hammers' supporters made the trip to France for the second leg of the final. Unfortunately, there was trouble on the terraces containing Hammers fans and a coin was thrown at Metz midfielder Frederic Meyrieu. According to *Hammer:* 'There's no denying there was some trouble in Metz. But contrary to press reports, there were no running battles with police, no tear gas thrown and no arrests. It was largely provoked by firework-throwing Metz fans and security men making gestures.' UEFA took a different view and fined the club 20,000 Swiss francs.

On the field, the Hammers produced a stunning display at Stade Saint-Symphorien, with Trevor Sinclair and Lampard both netting before half-time. In the second half, Metz, who had been outclassed in the first 45, were now comfortably the better team and West Ham were hanging on. Nenad Jestrović scored in the 68th minute to set up a tense finish but Wanchope delivered the killer blow six minutes later when he rounded goalkeeper Letizi to poke home. Many of the West Ham fans must have missed it, though, their view reportedly blocked by a mountain of fire extinguisher foam.

Harry Redknapp was in no doubt: 'That was a great performance and a great day for West Ham, to win the Intertoto Cup and to be in the UEFA Cup and turning in such an outstanding performance against a good French team, to go over there and play so well and win 3-1. We took great support over to France and they enjoyed their day. Yeah, I think that was special. That was a real good day for me and West Ham's history.'

West Ham were one of three Intertoto Cup winners, along with Montpellier and Juventus. Their reward was a diminutive trophy about the size of a table cigarette lighter. The real reward was qualification for the UEFA Cup – the Hammers' first exposure to that competition.

Perhaps surprisingly, Di Canio singled out this game as the greatest moment from his time at West Ham, because it meant so much to the club and fans after such a long absence from Europe.

He wrote in his autobiography: 'I know the Intertoto is not the Champions League – one newspaper even called it the "InterTwoBob Cup". I think that's silly. Prestige aside, it offered us a chance to play in the UEFA Cup, a goal we reached by winning the competition. They were all laughing when we entered the Intertoto, but I think they stopped once they saw we made it into Europe. Perhaps we didn't have a squad to go all the way in the UEFA Cup, but many of our youngsters gained experience playing against foreign clubs and, at their age, that can be invaluable.'

UEFA Cup

So, as one of the three winners of the 1999 Intertoto Cup, West Ham gained entry to the 1999/2000 UEFA Cup.

First round:
NK Osijek 3-0 (H), 3-1 (A)
Aggregate 6-1

After all the huffing and puffing to qualify for the UEFA Cup the hard way, West Ham carried on from where they had left off to establish a three-goal lead against Croatian side NK Osijek at Upton Park.

Once Steve Lomas gave the tie its first strike at goal, there was no stopping the home side. Most of West Ham's inventiveness stemmed from Di Canio. For the first goal, he floated the ball to the left where Javier Margas had stolen to the far post, his deft header presenting Wanchope with a tap-in.

Four minutes into the second half, Osijek goalkeeper Mario Galinović's clearance fell to Di Canio and he skipped past him to make it 2-0. Lampard added the third from a Sinclair pass.

After a comfortable victory in the return leg, with Kitson, Neil Ruddock and Foé on target in a 3-1 win, West Ham were given a bigger challenge in the shape of the Romanian side Steaua Bucharest.

However, it almost didn't happen. Igor Štimac, making only his second appearance for the club, had collected a booking in the second leg in Croatia. This brought to UEFA's attention that Stimac should not have been playing in European competition, as he had yet to serve a two-game ban picked up in his Hajduk Split days. It could have been another Omoyinmi scenario, but UEFA admitted culpability in not informing all parties of the suspension and Osijek's attempt to be reinstated was rejected.

Not for the first time in his West Ham history, reports on the first leg in Bucharest heavily featured Paolo Di Canio and his latest run-in with officialdom. He claimed referee Claus Bo Larsen had twice called him a 'bastard' during the game. The referee denied the allegation but said he had told the Italian to get up as he sat on the ground appealing for Steaua players to be cautioned.

Steaua Bucharest took control of the tie with goals from Laurentiu Roșu and Sabin Ilie either side of half-time, but the talking point afterwards was Di Canio's substitution. The volatile Italian was apparently given the final warning by Larsen: 'Get off before I send you off.' The message was transferred to manager Redknapp, who replaced the forward with Joe Cole after 55 minutes. It looked a mysterious decision at the time, with the Hammers a goal down, although Di Canio had been booked in the first half for throwing the ball away.

The second leg took place on Thursday, 4 November. An attendance of 24,514 turned up to see the Hammers attempt to overturn the two-goal deficit. With Cole pulling the strings in midfield, a host of chances were created but none were taken. Posts were hit and an open goal chance spurned and so the Romanians went through on a 2-0 aggregate.

According to Alyson Rudd in *The Guardian*: 'West Ham ran rings around Steaua for the first 75 minutes and even when the Romanians became less cautious there was no stopping West Ham. Not many goalless draws in European competition contain this much drama and had a mere fraction of the number of chances created by Harry Redknapp's side been taken, West Ham would by now be eagerly awaiting the draw for the next round.'

After going out to the Romanians, Redknapp joked: 'We're going into the Essex Senior Cup. We're dropping into that now and we'll keep going into cups until we finally win one.'

A reminder of good times past was an obituary in the Steaua programme for Johnny Byrne, who had recently died from a heart attack in South Africa at the age of 60. Fittingly, Johnny had requested that his ashes be scattered on the pitch at Upton Park, the scene of so many of his footballing triumphs.

In the programme for West Ham's Europa Conference League game against FCSB – previously Steaua Bucharest – former Hammers captain Lomas looked back on that Intertoto campaign. 'Ending up fifth in 1998/99 – the club's highest ever Premier League placing and the second-best finish in the history of West Ham United – we were totally underwhelmed to discover that our reward was a shortened summer break and an early return for pre-season training.

'Having missed out on UEFA Cup qualification, we'd now be playing in the third round of the much-maligned Intertoto Cup and none of the lads were happy that their holiday plans had been so disrupted for our 17 July kick-off. But we soon got our heads around the situation and all agreed we'd rather be playing games than going through gruelling pre-season training sessions at Chadwell Heath.'

Remembering the Intertoto final, Lomas said: 'At full time, having just beaten Metz 3-2 on aggregate, as West Ham captain they sent me over towards a group of dignitaries, who presented me with something that resembled an egg cup. "Oh, we're all going to get one of those instead of a medal," I thought. But it turned out to be the Intertoto Cup itself! I took the trophy back into the dressing room, where the players collectively stared at me in disbelief saying "So we came back early from our summer holidays just for that?"'

Moving on to the UEFA Cup, he said: 'I'm not sure who did the advance party reconnaissance for our visit to the Romanian capital but, just like Croatia, it proved to be another surreal trip abroad. Walking through our hotel, nobody could have failed to notice so many attractive young ladies in and around the lobby. In another one of those "only at West Ham moments" it turned out that the club's stay had clashed with the Romanian equivalent of a Playboy Club convention.

'We arrived at the stadium on a miserable late-October night of torrential rain, where saturated fans were jumping up and down in the puddles trying to keep warm. Just before kick-off a big delegation of dignitaries started walking across the waterlogged pitch. We thought it was the city mayor and other local VIPs but then John Moncur spotted a bloke in a Stetson hat. "That's J.R. Ewing out of Dallas!" he insisted, pointing towards American actor Larry Hagman. In my 226 matches for West Ham and almost 500 career appearances, I never saw anything as comical again.'

Chapter Eight

Blink and You Missed It: The UEFA Cup 2006/07

AT THE end of the 2004/05 season, the Hammers just about scraped into the top half dozen in the Championship, but somehow managed to achieve Premier League status by way of the play-offs. Survival seemed to be the most realistic target for the Irons the following season, but Alan Pardew's men exceeded expectations. Seven successive victories in January and February (including a 3-2 triumph at Arsenal, thus becoming the last team to defeat the Gunners at Highbury before they moved to the Emirates), pushed the club to a ninth-place finish.

Reaching the FA Cup final for the first time in a quarter of a century made it a pretty good season for the Londoners. West Ham would lose on penalties to Liverpool but, as the Merseyside club had already qualified for the Champions League because of their league position, West Ham somehow qualified for the UEFA Cup.

They were drawn to meet Italian side Palermo, who had only qualified for the tournament after a match-rigging scandal led to a number of clubs being penalised and the Sicilian club being promoted from eighth to fifth in Serie A.

Having finished their first season back in the Premier League in a credible ninth position and coming close to winning the 2006 FA Cup Final, West Ham were expected to push on during 2006/07. They started the campaign brightly but slipped down the table and found themselves dragged into the relegation zone.

An Icelandic consortium bought the club on 26 November 2006 and, with the side in 17th position, sacked manager Pardew, replacing him with former West Ham player Alan Curbishley. This being West Ham, the signings of Argentine internationals Javier Mascherano and Carlos Tevez at the end of August were subsequently investigated by the Premier League, who were concerned that their rules had been breached regarding third party ownership. On 27 April 2007, West Ham pleaded guilty and were handed a record £5.5m fine, but, crucially, avoided a points deduction.

On the field, West Ham ultimately escaped relegation by winning seven of their last nine games, including a 1-0 victory at Arsenal and, on the last day of the season, a 1-0 win away to newly crowned champions Manchester United (with Tevez, inevitably, scoring the only goal).

By then, the Hammers had long finished with their first European campaign since 2000. They only managed two games in the UEFA Cup, being eliminated 4-0 on aggregate by Palermo. Violence involving West Ham supporters was again in evidence. Twenty West Ham fans appeared in an Italian court following their arrest after fights with rival supporters in Sicily before and after the return match in Palermo.

UEFA Cup 2006/07
First round:
Palermo 0-1 (H), 0-3 (A)
Aggregate 0-4

More than 32,000 fans crowded into Upton Park for the first leg. Most of them would have gone home disappointed as the Italian side, who had reached the last 16 the previous season, flew back to Sicily with a one-goal lead.

The UEFA match report said: 'Palermo look on course to reach the UEFA Cup group stage for the second year running after an impressive victory at West Ham United FC. Palermo, who made the last 16 on their UEFA competition debut in 2005/06, were taking on a West Ham team high in confidence as for the first time they started with high-profile Argentinian signings Carlos Tevez and Javier Mascherano. But it was Palermo's Andrea Caracciolo who hit the target just before half-time against a club back in Europe after seven years away.

'Tevez's arrival in East London had caused a particular stir, and the striker was lively from the off. However, the Sicilian defence was holding firm, and it was not until after the half-hour mark that West Ham really went close, Paul Konchesky having a free kick deflected wide and Anton Ferdinand heading the resulting corner off target. Alberto Fontana in the Palermo goal then made a crucial save as Tevez looked to turn in Bobby Zamora's pass, and within a minute the visitors were ahead as Caracciolo broke free of his markers to turn a cross past Roy Carroll.

'Caracciolo nearly had another in the 59th minute but this time Carroll rushed to smother a through ball. Ferdinand then turned another West Ham corner over as he rose in the box, but Caracciolo had a shot deflected wide by Nigel Reo-Coker. Home substitute Marlon Harewood's shot then hit the post to the relief of the beaten Fontana, and the one-time UEFA Cup Winners' Cup winners were unable to force an equaliser, meaning they face a tough task in Sicily in two weeks' time.'

Manager Pardew was bullish in his post-match assessment, declaring: 'I think we have got a good chance in the second leg.' He insisted 'we have nothing to be frightened of' and went on: 'I thought we competed really well against a really good side. The breaks didn't go our way.'

The second leg in Sicily was two weeks later. In between the two legs, West Ham had lost 0-2 at home to Newcastle United and by the same score at Manchester City, so they did not land in Palermo in good form. It should, therefore, be of little surprise that the Hammers succumbed to their Italian hosts, even if 0-3 was not a true reflection of the evening.

However, it was events off the pitch that dominated the newspaper headlines. According to *The Guardian*: 'There was no shame in this young West Ham side succumbing here; that lay instead with the supporters who disgraced their club. West Ham's UEFA Cup campaign was extinguished last night. It will no doubt be to the relief of police authorities across Europe.'

There were numerous arrests on the eve of the match. Palermo fans had been angered by T-shirts worn in the first leg at Upton Park mocking the town's historical mafia links. In Palermo, some 500 fans gathered on the night before the match, many throwing bottles and chairs at each other, before the local Carabinieri stepped in to break up what they described as 'a huge battle'. At least 20 West Ham fans were arrested and another six injured.

The loutish behaviour continued on the day of the match when a throng of about 500 West Ham fans paraded down the city's main shopping street, skirmishing with locals. Just before kick-off, a large group of fans were escorted across the pitch into the away section, one pair being so insensitive to the locals' feelings as to unfurl an enormous England flag as they marched across the pitch.

When asked for his thoughts on the fans' behaviour, manager Pardew could only praise the hospitality! 'I am aggrieved to hear there was more trouble before the game, but I certainly don't know all the facts because I've been cooped up in a hotel, so I don't want to make a judgment on anything,' he said. 'All I will say is, our own experience was that the people in Palermo were brilliant to us when we were in the hotel and the police were very helpful. I hope our fans have experienced the same.'

Stuart Fuller, had this to say in his book *Passport To Football*: 'The West Ham fans had been given a corner, hemmed in by thick glass on two sides and a caged roof on the lower tier. With hours to go before kick-off we did the only thing we could to pass the time. Sing! After exhausting the traditional West Ham songs, we started on Duran Duran's greatest hits, followed by an Elvis and Sinatra medley before descending into the surreal with the Flintstones theme. The players came out to warm up and were greeted with great relief; the kick-off was approaching.

'At regular intervals West Ham fans, who had bought their tickets from Italian booking agencies, were seen being led from the home end and around the pitch to be deposited in our stand, giving the police plenty of opportunity to practise their golf swings using their batons on any who dared step out of line. A 3-0 defeat on the night was hard to swallow, but a lesson was learned on how far away from European football West Ham were in terms of technique and approach.'

At least, unlike in 1980 after similar scenes in Madrid, UEFA was not called to adjudicate on any punishment for West Ham.

But just so we don't forget, a football match did break out amidst the violence, which turned out to be 'physical but largely fair', according to *The Guardian*. Carlton Cole, in his first start for West Ham, was tackled late by Andrea Barzagli, which earned the Italian a booking, but Cole was himself cautioned for his own heavy and late challenge from behind on Cristian Zaccardo.

West Ham exerted the first-half pressure and it seemed sure to pay. But that was not to account for Alberto Fontana in Palermo's goal, seen when Marlon Harewood's overhead effort required an acrobatic stop, with Cole's powerful shot denied by a solid block.

Yet the Hammers' burst of supremacy could not last. Fábio Henrique Simplício, whose earlier long-distance shot had been thwarted, was given his second such chance from a free kick played short. His weak shot trickled past the unsighted Roy Carroll, doubling Palermo's lead in the tie.

Shortly after half-time, Mark Bresciano drew another good save from Carroll but Cole had more cause to berate his own failure to find the net when heading Jonathan Spector's cross against a post. Seized by cramp after the move, Cole's participation was ended. Two minutes later, West Ham's participation in this tournament went the same way. David Di Michele pulled Danny Gabbidon out of position and hoisted a cross into the path of Simplício. With Carroll advancing off his line and stranding himself, the Ghanaian's lob produced his second goal of the night.

West Ham's devastation was complete when Eugenio Corini played a sublimely weighted long pass for Di Michele. The West Ham defence walked forward as one, opening the gate for the Italy international, who scored at Carroll's near post.

Pardew argued: 'We gave them a real game but are not getting the breaks. There were not four goals between the sides.'

Alas, there were. But it was West Ham's deteriorating Premier League form which would push Pardew through the exit door two months later.

Chapter Nine

A (Brief) Return to Europe: Europa League 2015/16

ON THE evening of 2 July 2015, West Ham United took their first steps back into European competition after a gap of nine years.

West Ham had qualified by heading the Barclays Premier League Fair Play League (incidentally, the last occasion on which qualification by such a route would be possible). They began their campaign in the first qualifying round, one of 102 sides to debut at the height of summer, before the schools broke up and many clubs had not even started pre-season training.

West Ham were also under new management. Sam Allardyce had left the club in May by 'mutual consent' after four years in charge. For once, this reason had a ring of truth to it. Both he and the board felt he had taken the club as far as he could.

His successor was the Croat Slaven Bilić, an ex-West Ham player from the Harry Redknapp days, albeit only for one season. He had had his new squad together for a matter of days before it was time to play his first competitive game. To get to the final would involve 22 games played over 45 weeks. And with the move to the Olympic Stadium only a season away, staying in the Premier League was non-negotiable.

Their first opponents were FC Lusitanos of Andorra, who qualified by virtue of finishing second in the Andorra Primera Divisió and who were still searching for their first win in Europe. Andorra was ranked 48th in European footballing terms; only Gibraltar and Armenia were below them.

First qualifying round:
FC Lusitanos 3-0 (H), 1-0 (A)
Aggregate 4-0

Slaven Bilić decided to watch his first match in charge from the directors' box (and succeeded in drawing a strong rebuke from Xavi Roura, the Lusitanos coach, who accused him of a lack of respect). Academy manager Terry Westley was in the dugout and named a side that included seven players who had come through the ranks at Upton Park. That meant first-team debuts for Darren Randolph in goal, Lewis Page and Reece Oxford who, at 16 years and 198 days, was West Ham's youngest ever player.

The Times report described the Andorrans as a team who were 'agricultural in the tackle at times' and 'gradually lost their shape and stamina'. They had reportedly brought 82 fans, higher than their normal average gate.

On a warm, humid evening in East London, the Hammers, though well in control for most of the game, still took 40 minutes to convert their obvious superiority into goals. Mauro Zárate beat two men before chipping over an inviting cross for Diafra Sakho to head home the first goal of the new season from close range.

In the second minute of first-half injury time, Morgan Amalfitano combined with Zárate to pull the ball back for Sakho to score his second goal with ease.

The Hammers' third came from captain James Tomkins, who headed home a Matt Jarvis cross. West Ham should have extended that three-goal lead, with both Tomkins and Reece Burke going close from set pieces.

It's probably a fair bet that none of the other Europa League games that week came anywhere close to matching the near-35,000 attendance at the Boleyn Ground. Incredibly, all tickets had been snapped up in less than four days, even for a match against a team who were 411th in the UEFA rankings. That illustrates the magic of European football to a generation of West Ham fans who had been starved of it while having to watch

London rivals Chelsea, Spurs and Arsenal enjoy season after season of European trips.

In addition, this was the last season at the Boleyn and adult tickets were made available for a very reasonable £10.

West Ham's trip to the Pyrenees for the return leg gave the Andorran club a first ever opportunity to host an English side and, indeed, their chance to win their first game in a European competition.

The temperature reached 28°C and there were 1,300 people in the small stadium, with an estimated 500 of them Hammers fans.

According to *The Times* report: 'At an altitude of 3,356ft, Andorra la Vella is the highest capital city in Europe. Clearly the thin mountain air affected Diafra Sakho's judgment after the forward experienced a rush of blood that resulted in a sending-off after just 14 minutes. Sakho was involved in an off-the-ball altercation with Luigi San Nicolás, the Lusitanos defender.'

Despite this early setback, the visitors were in front seven minutes later as Elliot Lee (son of former Hammer Rob Lee) coolly converted Matt Jarvis's flick to score the only goal of the night. There were further chances for both sides. Lee came close to adding a second late on but his curling shot bent the wrong side of the post before Tomkins was on hand to clear Alfi Conteh-Lacalle's injury-time effort off the line.

Second qualifying round: Birkirkara 1-0 (H), 0-1 (A) Aggregate 1-1 (West Ham won 5-3 on penalties)

West Ham's Europa League qualifying campaign saw them welcome Birkirkara of Malta to the Boleyn Ground. Their opponents qualified for the competition by winning the Maltese Cup and booked their place in the second qualifying round with a 3-1 aggregate win over Armenian side Ulisses.

The Hammers were playing their 51st match in European competition. They had won 26, drawn nine and lost 15 of the previous 50. This was one of 33 ties being played in this round of the competition, with the winners to be joined by 25 other teams who were to enter at the next stage.

Another near-capacity crowd was in attendance for what was officially the first game of Slaven Bilić's tenure. West Ham continued their European adventure with a narrow 1-0 win. Despite the Hammers being in firm control throughout, the game looked as though it would remain goalless until Tomkins bundled home Zárate's inswinging corner from close range.

Statistics tell the story: 74 per cent possession for the home side and 14 shots to one.

The Guardian had an interesting take on the match: 'It was worth the wait in the end for Slaven Bilić, even though there was a brief moment when the West Ham United supporters seemed to mistake him for Sam Allardyce and offered a reminder of unhappier times with a few frustrated jeers midway through the second half of this sleepy game. July is an odd time to play football and an even odder time to boo your own team. Some people are never happy.'

The Maltese fans had chartered a plane to bring them to London for arguably the biggest game in their history and they brought a colour and noise to the away section that some Premier League clubs would be proud of.

Before the second leg in Malta, Bilić had urged his players to keep their cool and he probably wasn't referring to the temperatures that were hovering around 35°C. He had warned his players not to become involved in any situations similar to that which saw Sakho sent off against Lusitanos, which meant he missed three European games.

So the headline in *The Times* summed up the situation nicely: 'West Ham left sweating on their place in Europe.' It reported: 'It took just 15 minutes for the 1-0 first leg advantage to be embarrassingly chalked out. James Collins was too slow to react to the penetrative run of Liliu and the eventual delivery was swept home by Fabrizio Miccoli, the former Italy international, from six yards out.'

If that wasn't bad enough, things got even worse for the visitors just before half-time. Tomkins lost his head and his place on the pitch when, after some goading from Nikola Vukanac, he pushed the defender. The referee issued a straight red card and once again West Ham were playing with ten men away in Europe.

In the second half, there was hardly any attacking threat displayed by either side and, according to UEFA's own stats, not a single effort on target. The match meandered through extra time – the only issue of note being the expulsion of Mauricio Mazzetti for a second bookable offence.

And so, to penalties. The Hammers scored all five of their kicks to the Maltese side's three. Substitute Diego Poyet, son of Gus, stroked home the winning penalty after Mark Noble, Zárate, Aaron Cresswell and Joey O'Brien had all scored.

This set up a third qualifying round clash with Astra Giurgiu of Romania, the conquerors of the Scottish side Inverness Caledonian Thistle.

Third qualifying round: Astra Giurgiu 2-2 (H), 1-2 (A) Aggregate 3-4

Interviewed in the *London Evening Standard* on the eve of the match, defender James Collins was quoted as saying: 'We have to be streetwise. James Tomkins got sent off in Malta and Diafra Sakho the previous match. We must be more professional.'

Collins clearly forgot his own pre-match warning when he picked up a third West Ham red card in as many ties. He tugged at Constantin Budescu just four minutes after he had hacked at the Astra striker, leaving his team to play half an hour with ten men. By then, West Ham had built a two-goal advantage but they let that slip in the final 20 minutes after Collins was dismissed.

Enner Valencia had headed the first Hammers goal, but he was then taken off on a stretcher after appearing to twist a knee. Zárate scored a superb individual goal early in the second half to apparently put the Hammers firmly in control. Adrián clawed one effort off his line, but the goalkeeper had little chance as Fernando Boldrin swept in Astra's opener or when defender Angelo Ogbonna then turned the ball into his own net. To compound a miserable evening for the home side, manager Bilić was given his marching orders in injury time and was asked to leave the dugout by referee Adrien Jaccottet.

West Ham had qualified for the tournament through their Fair Play ranking. Now, after five matches, they had had three players and their new manager shown the red card. Whilst there may be irony in how West Ham got into the competition, there was nonetheless a lack awareness of how playing European opponents, despite how sub-standard they might appear on paper, differed from facing Premier League teams.

To progress to the play-off round, the Hammers knew they either had to win this game or secure a draw with a higher scoreline than 2-2. To add to the challenge, they had to do it with their manager forced to watch from the stands following his sending-off in the home leg. With 11 changes made to the side from the first leg and three players making their debuts, there was an obvious lack of experience on the field and an apparent lack of desperation to save the tie on a hot night in Romania. Despite Bilić insisting prior to the match that Europe was important to West Ham, he left a whole host of senior players at home, with Kevin Nolan and Carl Jenkinson the only first-team starters in the party. Perhaps he had that Sunday's Premier League opener at Arsenal in mind.

Manuel Lanzini, making his West Ham debut, scored after only two and a half minutes when his low shot squeezed in off a post. But two goals in four minutes from Astra skipper Constantin Budescu earned the Romanian side victory. Modibo Maïga missed a late chance to take the game into extra time but Astra created better chances at more regular intervals and twice hit the post.

So, West Ham were knocked out of the Europa League in the third qualifying round, 4-3 on aggregate, before their league campaign had even started. Hammers fans wanted European football. Three near full-house attendances against virtually unknown opposition proved that.

But they were entitled to wonder whether the European campaign was worth it after a July start and six matches without facing any big-name European teams. It ended before it even got interesting.

In his autobiography, *Boleyn Boy*, Mark Noble wrote: 'It was difficult for Slav to strike the right balance between getting us ready for the Premier League and making sure we could compete in Europe. He used a mix of first-team players and youngsters during the Europa League qualifiers, and we didn't have much of a flow. We were playing competitive fixtures while we were still in pre-season mode and although we cruised past Lusitanos, we had a scare in the next round, almost crashing out when we travelled to Malta to face Birkirkara in testing conditions.

'The pitch was awful, it was roasting hot and we were up against it when Tonks got sent off in the first half.

'We needed penalties to go through, but it was becoming a grind. Slav wasn't fussed about Europe. He knew that we weren't ready to play at that level. The squad wasn't deep enough, and he was right to prioritise the league. We didn't need the distraction and nobody cared when our reserves lost to Astra Giurgiu in the third qualifying round.'

Manager Bilić, who led former club Besiktas to the last 16 in the previous season's Europa League, said of his team selection: 'You can't be sorry. I said it was tempting, but when you make a decision, you stand by it and you know the consequences. When the Premier League starts, we have a game and, of course, we are looking to get a positive result.'

Three days later, West Ham pulled off the surprise Premier League result of the weekend by beating Arsenal 2-0 at the Emirates. Bilić would probably claim that this justified his selection in Romania.

West Ham then lost their first two home matches, to future champions Leicester City and promoted Bournemouth. But they then went and won 3-0 at Liverpool, their first victory at Anfield since 1963.

It looked like being one of those seasons, but only two more league games were lost before Christmas, including a 1-4 reverse at Tottenham, and positive results included a 2-1 victory at Manchester City.

Progress in the League Cup was halted at the first hurdle by a 1-2 defeat at Leicester.

After the Hammers drew 1-1 at Aston Villa on Boxing Day, they were tenth. This would prove to be their lowest league position of the whole campaign.

After a 2-2 draw at Chelsea on March 19 they were fifth. When West Ham had last played at Stamford Bridge – on Boxing Day 2014 – they were fourth but played poorly and lost 0-2, going on to fall away in the second half of the season. This time around, even a draw was seen as a poor result, a reflection of the real progress under Bilić.

West Ham's FA Cup campaign offered a tantalising glimpse of Wembley after victories over Wolves (1-0), Liverpool 2-1 in a replay (a game won in the 121st minute by an Ogbonna goal) and Blackburn Rovers (5-1). In the quarter-finals, the Hammers then held Manchester United 1-1 at Old Trafford. Unfortunately, they lost 1-2 back at the Boleyn Ground.

By the time of their penultimate home league match on 7 May, West Ham were still in with a chance of Champions League football. But Swansea City didn't cooperate and ran out 4-1 winners. Three days later came the final home league match for 2015/16. Manchester United were the visitors for what was the last ever fixture at Upton Park, or the Boleyn Ground if you prefer. A night of high emotion ended in a 3-2 win for West Ham.

So, on to the Britannia Stadium, with a victory over Stoke City needed for automatic entry into the group stages of the Europa League. Naturally, the Hammers lost, despite taking the lead.

Bilić was, by all accounts, not the first choice when the two Davids considered the options to replace Sam Allardyce, but he managed to bring the entertainment which had gone missing under his predecessor back to the club. This was epitomised by Dimitri Payet. The French midfielder had been a revelation since his £11.25m signing from Marseille.

Bilić took a team that, after their disastrous Europa League exploits, could have been in a relegation fight to a seventh-place finish that even felt disappointing at the final reckoning. Though they lost momentum in the final weeks of the season there was a real feeling of progress around the East London club and they could head down the road to the Olympic Stadium with a sense of purpose and the belief they could compete with the best.

But then, similar sentiments were being expressed as West Ham paraded the Cup Winners Cup around Wembley in May 1965.

Chapter Ten

Back Into Europe (For Four Matches): 2016/17

Sunday, 15 May 2016
The Britannia Stadium, Stoke

West Ham went into their final match of the 2015/16 Premiership season in sixth place, with a Premier League era-record points total of 62. The 38th and final game was against Stoke City at the Britannia Stadium. Win that and they would guarantee themselves at least sixth place and another run at the Europa League. But West Ham do not do such things easily.

It was a familiar enough story. West Ham dominated for long spells and should have killed off Stoke after Michail Antonio's 23rd-minute opener. Then, shortly after Diafra Sakho spurned a glorious chance to make it 2-0 early in the second half, Giannelli Imbula hauled Stoke level. West Ham then threw it away. Mame Biram Diouf's header from a corner in the 88th minute meant that they slipped to seventh in the final rankings and would have to rely on Manchester United winning the FA Cup Final to enter the Europa League at the third qualifying round stage. 'I will be a Manchester United fan,' said Slaven Bilić. 'We really deserve to be in Europe. We are desperate.'

Saturday, 21 May 2016
The FA Cup Final at Wembley Stadium

In the 78th minute, Crystal Palace substitute Jason Puncheon scored the goal which threatened not only to win the trophy but to secure his team a place in the following season's Europa League. But just three minutes later, Juan Mata grabbed an equaliser and, despite Chris Smalling getting himself sent off for a tackle more appropriate to the egg-shaped ball game, Manchester United won the FA Cup with a brilliant volley from Jesse Lingard in the 20th minute of extra time.

United's win meant West Ham would stage Europa League football at their new Olympic Stadium home, kicking off their next European adventure in the third qualifying round at the end of July, the same stage at which they exited in 2015/16.

West Ham may only have secured a place in Europe's second tier tournament due to results elsewhere, but it is worth remembering that it was five years to the day since Avram Grant's disastrous season in charge ended in relegation to the Championship after a miserable defeat at Wigan Athletic.

Slaven Bilić's debut season as a manager in England should not be regarded as anything other than a success, bearing in mind that even his bosses regarded his appointment as a gamble. Rafa Benitez was apparently two hours from becoming West Ham's new manager when Real Madrid came calling. And he ended the 2015/16 season watching Newcastle United being relegated to the Championship.

UEFA Europa League 2016/17
Third qualifying round first leg:
NK Domžale 2 West Ham United 1

West Ham's latest European adventure began on Thursday, 28 July at the Stadion Stožice in the Slovenian capital, Ljubljana.

Their opponents in this third qualifying round tie were NK Domžale, who had earned their place in the Europa League by finishing third in their domestic league. Founded in 1921, they are one of Slovenia's oldest clubs and had won their national title in 2007 and 2008. To reach this stage, they had beaten Lusitanos of Andorra (who West Ham beat in the first qualifying round the previous season) and Belarusian side Shakhtyor Soligorsk. They were also two games into their league campaign, sitting third in the table with four points.

West Ham were to endure a chastening defeat in the rain in Slovenia. Even with Andy Carroll at the spearhead of a strong line-up, Slaven Bilić's side came off second best. Bilić had to watch from the stands as he served the second game of his two-match European touchline ban imposed a year earlier. He saw Mark Noble equalise from the spot either side of Matic Črnic's two goals. West Ham only avoided a 3-1 final scoreline when Adrián made a brilliant late double save.

Any pre-season optimism had quickly evaporated when West Ham fell behind inside 11 minutes. Debutant Håvard Nordtveit handled in the area and Črnic rifled home the penalty. Domžale's lead did not last long as Axel Maraval clattered into Winston Reid from behind and Noble equalised from the penalty spot. Chances fell at both ends, with Črnic missing the best of them. He made amends four minutes into the second half when Antonio was caught out of position, enabling Črnic to charge into the area and slot a low shot past Adrián without a single tackle worth the name being attempted.

Captain Noble admitted the Slovenians were worthy winners and that: 'We have to get on with it. The second leg is something to look forward to, but we have to go there positively. It will be our first game at the Olympic Stadium and the fans will be behind us. We had a good enough team to win here but we did not do that.'

Third qualifying round second leg: West Ham 3 NK Domžale 0 Aggregate 4-2

A week later, West Ham played the second leg at their new home, the London Stadium, perhaps better known as the Olympic Stadium. It was not the glamour tie with which the East London club had planned to cut the ribbon (they played Juventus the following Sunday in the official curtain-raiser) but the Europa League second leg against the side from Slovenia would give supporters a taste of what life after Upton Park might be like.

Slaven Bilić admitted that the game would 'not feel like a home game' and that it would be down to supporters to recreate the noise of Upton Park. Fifty-four thousand of them were expected. I would love to know when a Europa League tie had attracted that sort of attendance for any round up to and including the final!

Pending a safety certificate, West Ham's new stadium was to have a 60,000 capacity – big enough to hold the 12,588 residents of Domžale five times over. Domžale play their home games at Sports Park, a stadium that can hold all of 2,813. It is so small that the first leg was moved to the Stadion Stožice in Ljubljana.

As housewarming parties go, West Ham could not have wished for a better introduction to life at their new Stratford home. The roof did not cave in, the floodlights worked and, most importantly, Slaven Bilić's side shook off the pre-season rust to reach the Europa League play-offs at the expense of NK Domžale. A Cheikhou Kouyaté double and a maiden strike for new signing Sofiane Feghouli crowned an historic night.

The Hammers dominated the first half and the opening goal came as the result of a slick move. Mark Noble released Enner Valencia, who laid the ball back to full-back Sam Byram. He slid the ball across goal for Kouyaté to push it past the goalkeeper and give the hosts a seventh-minute lead. The same player doubled the lead 17 minutes later, prodding home after a move involving Andy Carroll, who knocked back a Michail Antonio cross. There was joy for winger Feghouli late on as he secured the team's progress with a fine right-foot finish. The manager declared himself happy with a 'mature performance' at a stage of the season when there was still the potential to be embarrassed.

The following Sunday, West Ham played Juventus for the Betway Cup (no, me neither) in the official opening of their new home. The match had an exhibition feel to it, but both managers fielded strong sides. It started like one of those parties where the guests turn up early and drink all the booze, with West Ham finding themselves two goals down after 21 minutes. Carroll forced his side back into the match with a goal either side of half-time – both far-post headers – only for Juventus substitute Simone Zaza to hit the winner with five minutes remaining.

Alan Sealey scores West Ham's second goal in their 1965 Cup Winners' Cup victory over TSV Munich

West Ham celebrate their victory

Johnny Byrne scores West Ham's goal in their 3-1 defeat to Borussia Dortmund in the 1966 semi-final second leg of the Cup Winners' Cup.

Dinamo Tbilisi celebrate a goal in their 4-1 thrashing of West Ham at Upton Park in the 1981 Cup Winners' Cup quarter-final.

Paolo Di Canio and Marc-Vivien Foe. Both players would help West Ham win the now forgotten InterToto Cup in 1999

West Ham lose 2-1 to Romanian minnows Astra Giurgin, and are out of the 2015/16 Europa League before the end of August

West Ham line up before their 2-0 defeat of Seville on 12 March 2022, in their Round of 16 second leg tie in the UEFA Cup

Jarrod Bowen scores his team's second goal in a 2-0 win over Anderlecht in the 2022/23 Conference League group stage

Captain Declan Rice cradles the 2023 Conference League trophy. It was his last game for the club before a £105m move to Arsenal, and the club's first major trophy in 43 years.

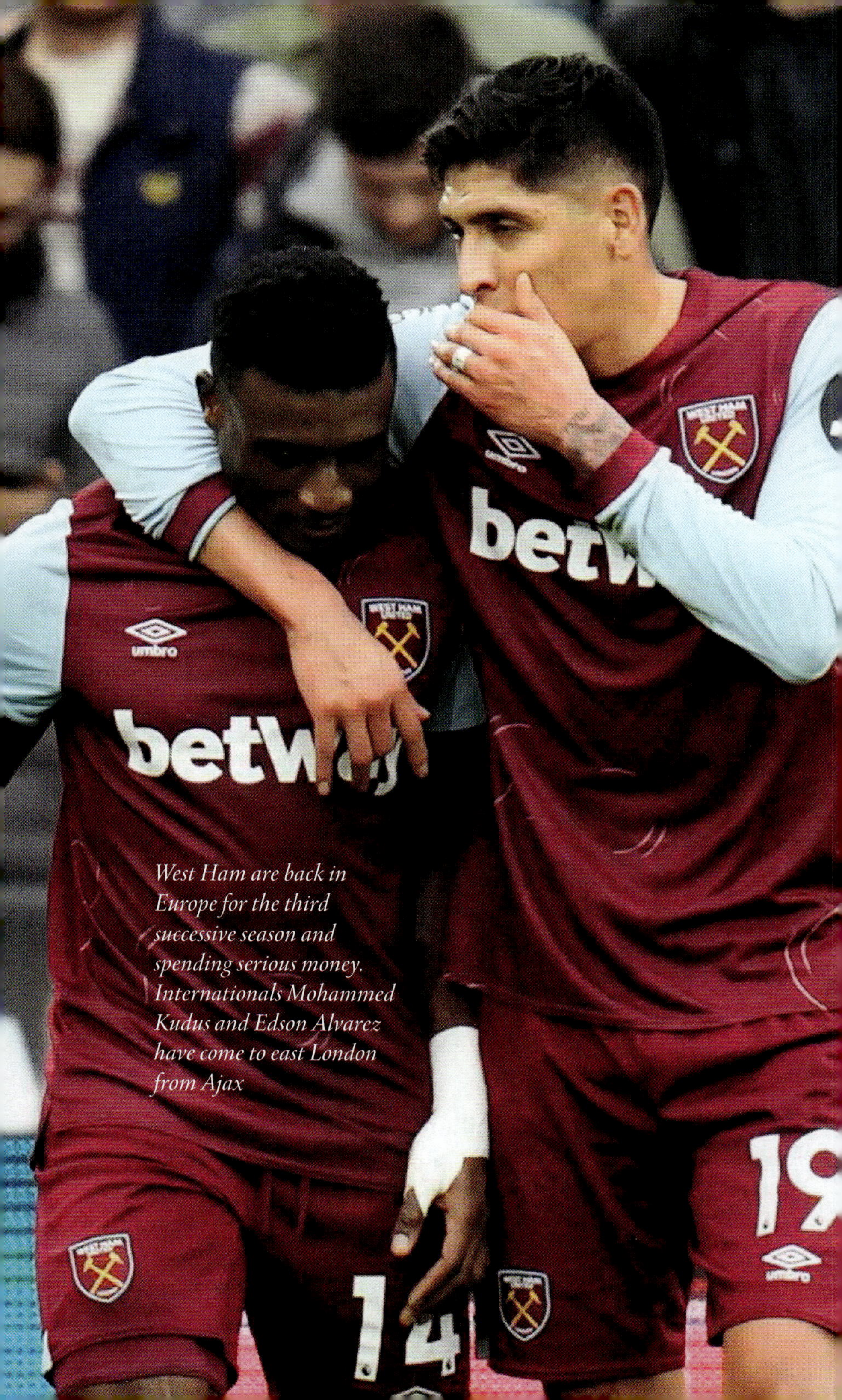

West Ham are back in Europe for the third successive season and spending serious money. Internationals Mohammed Kudus and Edson Alvarez have come to east London from Ajax

Freiburg beat West Ham 1-0 in the Round of 16 match in the 2023/23 UEFA Cup. But the Londoners would win the home leg 5-0 to progress to the quarter-finals

Ron Greenwood and John Lyall – the architects of West Ham's success in the 1960s and 70s

David Moyes would deliver European success and European involvement for three successive seasons

Play-off round first leg: Astra Giurgiu 1 West Ham 1

Ironically, West Ham were drawn against the Romanian side Astra Giurgiu, who had knocked them out in the third qualifying round the previous season by drawing 2-2 at Upton Park and winning 2-1 at home.

Astra had reached the 2016/17 Champions League qualifiers, only to be knocked out at the first stage by Danish side FC Copenhagen, causing them to drop into the Europa League.

Slaven Bilić promised to take the competition seriously this time and apparently warned his players that he would not accept failure. After a 1-1 draw near the banks of the River Danube, a dismayed Bilić concluded that his team needed to be more ruthless in front of goal if they were to avoid another embarrassing elimination from the Europa League.

West Ham dominated the majority of this low-quality game and took a deserved half-time lead through Mark Noble. He converted another penalty (his 23rd from his last 24 attempts) after a handball by Cristian Săpunaru and it seemed the game was West Ham's for the taking. The best chance of the second half fell to Michail Antonio, but he shot wide. The miss came back to haunt Bilić's team when, with seven minutes remaining, substitute Denis Alibec turned in the box and let fly with a fierce shot into the roof of Darren

Randolph's goal. Bilić summed it up afterwards. 'It is very simple – if we can't beat them at home, then we shouldn't be in the Europa League.'

Play-off round second leg:
West Ham 0 Astra Giurgiu 1
Aggregate 1-2

Slaven Bilić's words came back to haunt him as his team lost 1-0 to the Romanian team at the London Stadium to crash out 1-2 on aggregate. Had the Hammers managed to emerge victorious, they would have gone into the following day's draw for the group stage, with European competition until at least Christmas for their desperate fans, almost 57,000 of whom turned up on a warm, humid evening.

West Ham went into the game on the back of a hard-fought 1-0 victory over Bournemouth in the Premier League, with an 85th-minute header from Michail Antonio giving them their first three points at their new home.

Hammers fans can't say they weren't warned about the European disappointment which followed. Bilić had said: 'Billericay Town could rent Wembley and play their home games there, but would it suddenly make them a big club?' And his team, shorn of most of their best players, looked like Billericay on an off day as the Romanians knocked West Ham out of the Europa

League at the qualifying stage for the second time in as many seasons.

Without nine first-team regulars, Bilić had no alternative but to persist with a largely inexperienced line-up akin to that which drew 1-1 in Romania. Even captain Mark Noble was missing with a minor injury. The side had no guile, no imagination and no tempo. As a result, West Ham were functional at best and inferior to Astra in technique and even collective desire.

The home side had their moments but were foiled by fine goalkeeping from Silviu Lung and some poor finishing, especially from loanee Jonathan Calleri. The Hammers were punished on the stroke of half-time when Reece Burke lost possession and, with Sam Byram having pushed forward from right-back, former West Brom midfielder Filipe Teixeira exploited the space to sidefoot Astra ahead. It was a sign of how desperate West Ham were in attack that James Collins was brought on after 88 minutes to play up front. All he succeeded in doing was committing a couple of fouls and being booked. This just about summed up West Ham's night.

In August 2016, West Ham paid Swansea City a record £20.5m for forward Andre Ayew. He was injured in the first league game at Chelsea and was out until October. He would go on to make 50 appearances for the Hammers, scoring 12 goals, before being sent back to Swansea in January 2018. After impressing in that pre-season friendly against Juventus, Simone Zaza was signed on loan but, after an under-performing six months, was loaned on to Valencia.

A surprising departure was James Tomkins, transferred to Crystal Palace for £10m after 225 starts for West Ham.

But the biggest headaches came from the Frenchman Dimitri Payet. He had joined West Ham in June 2015 for a £10.7m fee. In February 2016, he signed a new five-and-a-half-year contract worth £125,000 a week. Following an outstanding first season in English football, he was named Premier League Player of the Year at the London Football Awards and was shortlisted by the Premier League for the 2016 Players' Player of the Year awards. Perhaps it all went to his head. In January 2017, manager Bilić announced that Payet no longer wanted to play for the club. Publicly, the club maintained they wanted to keep Payet but then, on 29 January 2017, he was transferred back to Marseille for £25m.

The new season at the London Stadium – which had begun with a 1-0 win over Bournemouth – saw the London side slide into the relegation zone by October. An early home game against Watford summed up West Ham's form. Two-nil ahead and playing brilliantly, they somehow contrived to lose 4-2 to a background of running battles among home supporters. West Ham also lost 4-2 at West Brom after being 4-0 down by half-time.

There were 1-0 wins at Crystal Palace and at home to a Sunderland side managed by David Moyes. Chelsea were despatched 2-1 at home in the League Cup, though a 4-1 loss at Manchester United ended interest in that competition. There was also a humiliating 5-1 defeat at home to Arsenal.

The January signings of Robert Snodgrass and Jose Font did nothing to inspire Hammers fans. Interest in the FA Cup ended at the first hurdle, after a 5-0 humiliation at home to Manchester City.

Nevertheless, six wins from nine games either side of Christmas ensured that even a late run of defeats did not plunge the Irons back into danger. A 3-1 win at Southampton on 4 February had even taken them as high as ninth place but by the beginning of April, they had slipped down to 15th.

For the probable highlight of the season, supporters had to wait until May and a 1-0 win over bitter rivals Tottenham, thanks to a Manuel Lanzini goal. Liverpool would hand out a 4-0 thrashing in Stratford, though a final day 2-1 win at Burnley ensured a tough season ended with an 11th-place finish.

Chapter 11

Bilić, Moyes, Pellegrini … and Moyes Again

2017/18

West Ham were splashing the cash. Forwards Javier Hernández joined for £16m from Bayer Leverkusen and Marko Arnautović from Stoke City for £20m. Right-back Pablo Zabaleta came in from Manchester City on a free transfer, while goalkeeper Joe Hart arrived on loan.

But the first three league fixtures had to be played away from home due to the World Athletics Championships taking place at the London Stadium. Ominously, those three away games ended in defeats – 4-0 at Manchester United, 3-2 at Southampton and 3-0 at Newcastle.

The first league victory came on 11 September, a 2-0 success over promoted Huddersfield Town. Brighton left Stratford with a 3-0 win under their belts – the Seagulls would only score ten away goals all season.

The Hammers would only secure two wins in their opening 11 league games. One of those defeats was a 3-2 loss at home to mortal enemies Spurs, though at least West Ham had the satisfaction of knocking the North London outfit out of the League Cup with a 3-2 victory (after being 2-0 down) at their temporary Wembley home.

But when Liverpool strolled to a 4-1 win at the London Stadium on 4 November, the team were languishing in 17th place and, two days later, Slaven Bilić was sacked.

He was replaced by former Everton boss David Moyes, but only on a contract until the end of the season. His brief was simple: keep West Ham United in the Premier League.

There was no immediate new manager 'bounce'. Moyes's first game was a run-of-the-mill 2-0 loss at Watford, while his first home game was a 1-1 draw with Leicester City. His old club, Everton, dished out a 4-0 thrashing before a first win finally came on 9 December, 1-0 at home to Chelsea.

Interest in the League Cup ended with a 1-0 loss at Arsenal but there were some encouraging results. Stoke City were beaten 3-0 at the Britannia Stadium, while the first weeks of 2018 witnessed a 1-1 draw away to Tottenham and a 4-1 win at Huddersfield.

In the FA Cup, West Ham squeezed past Shrewsbury Town 1-0 in a replay after a 0-0 draw. But an all-too-familiar exit occurred in the fourth round when Wigan beat the Hammers 2-0.

As if to show upheaval at West Ham was not confined to the pitch, director of player recruitment Tony Henry was accused of pursuing a club policy not to sign African players, allegedly with the knowledge of 'club management', who promptly fired him.

Away form would nosedive. A 3-1 loss at Brighton was followed by a 4-1 defeat at Swansea. But the worst was yet to come. On 10 March, not only did West Ham lose limply 3-0 at home to Burnley, but a small number of fans ran on to the pitch, while others harangued the directors, who were ushered away. There was the unwanted sight of 'Mr West Ham', skipper Mark Noble, wrestling with fans.

When Southampton were beaten 3-0 at the end of March, West Ham found themselves five points above the relegation zone with seven games remaining. Two of those witnessed successive 4-1 defeats, at the Emirates and at home to Manchester City. But the team dragged themselves off the floor to record a 2–0 win at Leicester and finished the season with a 3-1 win against Everton – now managed by Sam Allardyce.

Consequently, West Ham finished 13th, with 41 points. But 38 league games had delivered only seven victories and the fanbase were disillusioned by the move from Upton Park. Five supporters were banned for life after the Burnley fiasco and others were banned for throwing coins or objects 'with intent to injure or harm'.

Moyes's reward for saving the club from relegation was not to be offered a new contract and, on 22 May, the club appointed former Manchester City boss Manuel Pellegrini as the new manager on a three-year contract.

Moyes departed with a warning, telling West Ham that 'everybody always thinks the grass is greener. I would say, more often than not, it's proved wrong'. The Scot had read the situation well. West Ham moved on, hiring Pellegrini and spending heavily, but the rewards were minimal.

2018/19

The new manager wasted no time in spending the club's money. Issa Diop was first through the Stratford door for £22m, closely followed by goalkeeper Łukasz Fabiański for £7m.

While Jack Wilshere came on a free, Andriy Yarmolenko cost £17.5m and £34.2m was given to Lazio for Felipe Anderson.

The league campaign opened with a 4-0 thrashing at Anfield and three more defeats followed before the Londoners pulled off a surprise 3-1 win at Goodison Park. The only consistency about West Ham would be the inconsistency, as usual. A 3-1 victory over Manchester United would be followed by 1-0 losses to Brighton and

Spurs. December would be a good month. Four wins would come before Watford won 2-0 in East London. At least the season would end on a positive note with victories at Spurs and Watford, with a comfortable 3-0 home win over Southampton in between.

West Ham's EFL Cup bid was ended in the fourth round at Tottenham. Their FA Cup campaign only lasted until the same stage, when AFC Wimbledon pulled off a shock (well, maybe not, this is West Ham) 4-2 victory live on TV.

Tenth in the Premier League was a fair reflection of their league form. Nevertheless, the club's own review of the 2018/19 season talked of 'undoubted progression and development at all levels'. And how, 'after a disappointing start to the season, Pellegrini's project has begun to bear fruit in the shape of entertaining, attacking football in the West Ham tradition'. The club could claim the third highest average home attendance in English football, in excess of 58,000, with the East Stand being officially named after Billy Bonds in March.

The club would claim confidently that 'the 2019/20 season will see West Ham United benefit from the next stage of the Pellegrini project'.

2019/20

In July 2019, West Ham bought striker Sébastien Haller from Eintracht Frankfurt, where he had scored 20 goals in 41 games, for a club record £45m. But he would contribute only seven goals in his first season and, in January 2021, was transferred to Ajax, where he would be an inevitable success.

Another of Pellegrini's expensive signings was Felipe Anderson, signed from Lazio for £34.2 million in July 2018. After a reasonable 2018/19, he went off the boil (one goal and four assists) and was loaned to Porto before, in July 2021, he was sold back to Lazio. His 63 appearances had contributed ten goals. A more successful import, eventually, would be Pablo Fornals, for a cool £24m from Villarreal.

The league season opened with a 5-0 thrashing at the London Stadium by Manchester City. There were some good results among the dross (2-0 at home to Manchester United and 1-0 at Chelsea) but by the time they played Leicester on 28 December, West Ham were one point above the relegation zone. They lost 2-1 and Pellegrini was dismissed after a run of nine losses in 12 games.

David Moyes was invited back to steady the ship and asked once again to save the team from relegation. Certain sections of the West Ham fanbase no doubt saw this as a regression. Perhaps they judged the appointment as further evidence of broken promises from the two Davids, Gold and Sullivan. His first game in his second coming was a 4-0 win over Bournemouth on New Year's Day but when they lost 1-0 at Arsenal on 7 March, relegation was still a real possibility. Arsenal manager Mikel Arteta was diagnosed with Covid-19 a few days later and on 13 March 2020, the pandemic would cause the suspension of the season.

Football resumed in June, but in empty stadiums. West Ham restarted on 19 June with a 2-0 defeat at home to Wolves. Yet somehow the Hammers put together enough results, including a 3-2 home win over Chelsea and a 4-0 thrashing of Norwich at Carrow Road when Antonio scored all four goals, to finish 16th, only two places and five points above relegated Bournemouth. It was on 22 July 2020, following a 1-1 draw at Manchester United, that the club secured Premier League status.

West Ham's cup form followed its all-too-predictable course. West Bromwich Albion (now managed by Slaven Bilić) dumped them out of the FA Cup in round four, winning 1-0 at the London Stadium, while the Hammers contrived to leave the EFL Cup in the third round when they were humiliated 4-0 at League One Oxford United.

A 16th-place finish was a major disappointment for the Hammers. Eleven points from their opening six league fixtures had left them in fifth position and the early season talk was of them being contenders for European football. Then goalkeeper Łukasz Fabiański tore a hip muscle in the 2-2 draw at Bournemouth and was ruled out for three months. In the period when the Polish shot-stopper was absent, West Ham's season capitulated. The former Arsenal keeper was injured on 28 September and the Irons wouldn't pick up another three points until a shock win at Chelsea on 30 November. Fabianski's stand-in, Roberto, burdened a large portion of the blame for the shocking run.

If there was one shaft of light, it was the form of 21-year-old academy graduate Declan Rice. The holding midfielder put in countless outstanding displays and featured in every minute of West Ham's campaign. And the club arguably oversaw their best transfer window in recent years under the former Manchester United boss, with January signings Jarrod Bowen and Tomáš Souček among the club's best performers in the second half of the season.

2020/21

The predictions for West Ham in 2020/21 were understandably pessimistic after the previous season's mediocre performance. *When Saturday Comes* foresaw a 14th-place finish while the *Daily Telegraph* said that 'pushing for Europe would be an incredible turnaround' and predicted a 18th-place finish. In *The Times,* three writers predicted relegation, although Matt Dickinson felt West Ham could be a surprise package 'if they can get through the campaign without imploding'. The paper predicted the Hammers would finish 16th. Supporter and writer Pete May predicted 15th, as did *The Guardian* for a 'club in crisis mode'. *FourFourTwo* saw West Ham languishing somewhere between 16th and 20th. So, not a lot of optimism there.

In his programme notes for the opening day match against Newcastle, even skipper Mark Noble was cautious: 'We are going to experience highs and lows again this season, as we do every year, so it's important we all stick together and give everything for our club.'

The highly rated youth academy prospect Grady Diangana left the club to join West Bromwich Albion in an £18m deal, leaving both the fans and the players perplexed. Captain Noble went public with his criticism of the transfer.

In one last summer transfer deal, Felipe Anderson joined FC Porto on a season-long loan. January started with the sale of club record signing Sébastien Haller to AFC Ajax for around £22.5m. A sign perhaps that Moyes was rejecting the over-spending of the recent past and wanted to build his own team.

After the concluding match of the season, a 3-0 victory over Southampton at the London Stadium in front of a Covid-restricted 10,000 crowd, Moyes was heard to shout: 'Get the passports out, because we are going to Europe.'

The last time that a crowd numbered in the thousands had walked across the Olympic Park to watch a football match, 449 days earlier, many of them would have marched in protest at the club's ownership as West Ham languished just above the relegation zone. This time, the only similarities were the opponents and the outcome of the match. And they finished the season above Tottenham.

West Ham would lose their opening two games of the 2020/21 season but, such was their improvement in form, they were fifth by the end of November. From then on they never dropped out of the European qualification places and would go on to qualify for the 2021/22 UEFA Europa League group stages with a sixth-place finish – just two points behind fourth-placed Chelsea and the prize of a Champions League spot. The Hammers collected 65 points, their most in the Premier League era, and registered 19 league wins.

The end-of-season reviews adopted a completely different tone to those of pre-season. The *Daily Telegraph* said: 'David Moyes is surely the manager of the year. He has taken a side that fought relegation last season and transformed them into one of the most impressive teams in the league.' Moyes also featured in *The Guardian*'s roll of honour for the season along with Tomáš Souček, as one of the best players, and Vladimír Coufal, who was rated among the most successful signings. The thrilling 3-3 draw at Tottenham was among the newspaper's outstanding games.

After initially joining on loan, Souček had been signed for £15m in the summer of 2000. During the 2020/21 season, he would play 41 games and score ten goals while fellow countryman Coufal proved a bargain buy at £5m.

For once, West Ham used the loan system successfully. Centre-back Craig Dawson came from relegated Watford in October and made 24 appearances, chipping in with four goals. Jesse Lingard did not come to Stratford from Manchester United until the end of January, but his 16 appearances produced a total of 14 goals and assists.

Despite their fine league form, West Ham's EFL Cup campaign was ended in the fourth round with a 4-1 defeat at Everton and their FA Cup hopes were terminated at Manchester United in round five with a 1-0 defeat. But at least they went out to Premier League sides.

Due to a Covid-extended 2019/20 season, the 2020/21 campaign did not start until 12 September. The Hammers put in probably their worst performance of the season in a 2-0 home loss to Newcastle United ('One game in and already the club are in crisis,' commented *The Observer*). A 2-1 defeat at Arsenal followed and West Ham fans had that 'here we go again' feeling. However, Wolves were tonked 4-0 at the London Stadium and Leicester 3-0 at the King Power. Then, in an extraordinary game at Tottenham, the home side were

3-0 up inside 16 minutes only for goals in the 82nd, 85th and 95th minutes to salvage a point.

The improved form continued throughout the season as the Hammers rapidly climbed up the table into the top six. 'I think breaking the points total was something that we really hoped to do,' Moyes said in an end-of-season interview with whufc.com. 'It was a challenge when we heard what it was and we had a little bit of a dip just after the last international break, so it was great that we picked it up again and we've finished with a couple of wins which shows that the players kept it going right to the end.'

In June 2021, Moyes signed a new three-year contract, despite interest from his old club Everton who, once again, were hunting a new manager.

Moyes sculpted a brilliant season that only ran out of legs when injuries and fatigue hit hardest in the final weeks. He did it by creating a team in his own image; out went the expensive signings whom he believed were not pulling their weight, notably Felipe Anderson.

And it worked. Moyes oversaw a team he could believe in, a group of players he was confident were expert in playing his style of football. With his plan in place, West Ham first hauled themselves up the league and then threatened to gatecrash the top four party. The Hammers were secure in the league again and, for once, got neck ache from looking up the table rather than down. Crucially, West Ham United was finally a club at peace with itself.

While the wild 3-3 draws away to Spurs and at home to Arsenal were, for contrasting reasons, perhaps West Ham's most memorable games, in the wider context of their season, they weren't all that instructive. The routine 3-0 final-day win over Southampton was more typical of a team that was just consistently very good in a season when, after all, only five other teams came anywhere near being so.

And, strangely, West Ham may have benefitted from the absence of crowds for the majority of the season. The combination of the London Stadium – probably the most sterile and least atmospheric ground in the division – and a fanbase deeply hostile to the running of the club was a potentially toxic one. Covid restrictions meant the team were left to develop away from such hostility.

Chapter 12:

European Semi-Finalists: The Europa League 2021/22

THE FOUNDATIONS for West Ham's 2021/22 season were a club record Premier League points tally, a sixth-place finish and direct qualification for the UEFA Europa League group stage.

Despite this, once again, there was more than a hint of pessimism about the coming season. *The Times* forecast an eighth-place finish, while supporter Pete May made the same prediction in *The Observer.* In *When Saturday Comes,* Mark Segal wrote that 'between eighth and 12th and one or two memorable European nights would be fine'. *FourFourTwo* pointed out how 'in the past ten campaigns, 31 English clubs have qualified for the Europa League via the league and only nine have improved their final position the following year'. One of those was West Ham 'through cunningly getting knocked out before the kids were even back at school'. *The Guardian* foresaw a tenth-place finish, warning that: 'David Moyes must strike against the very rhythms of Hammers history. Part of the enigma that is the West Ham Way is that serious slumps habitually follow success.'

The Hammers were unbeaten in their seven pre-season fixtures, winning five, including a 6-2 victory at Celtic Park and a 2-0 Betway Cup triumph over Atalanta.

There were concerns over the size of the squad, especially with Europe looming. Goalkeeper Alphonse Areola arrived on loan from Paris Saint-Germain, followed by French international defender Kurt Zouma from Chelsea.

For the second successive season, West Ham kicked off their Premier League campaign against Newcastle United, but this time in front of a full house and at St James' Park. The score was different, too, with the visitors twice coming from behind to triumph 4-2.

The Hammers then had the opportunity to play in front of a full home crowd for the first time in 541 days. Leicester City were despatched 4-1, with two goals from Michail Antonio making him the club's all-time Premier League scorer. The result put West Ham on top of the Premier League, albeit after only two games, for only the second time ever and the first time in 15 years.

Two draws would follow. A dogged 2-2 draw at home to Crystal Palace was followed by a 0-0 draw at Southampton in a game more notable for the late and stupid dismissal of Michail Antonio after collecting two yellow cards – the second in the fifth minute of added time. The Hammers' next match – on 16 September 2021 – was their first on the continent in six seasons and their first ever in the UEFA Europa League proper.

Europa League group stage: Dinamo Zagreb 0 West Ham United 2

According to Jacob Steinberg in *The Guardian*: 'It was some way for West Ham to silence the doubts about their inexperience on the European stage. They answered the questions by playing like seasoned travellers. There were no stumbles from David Moyes's players as they took their first steps into the unknown and in the end, with Dinamo Zagreb confounded by West Ham's organisation, it was hard to tell which team were supposed to be the novices at this level. Dinamo were outplayed and had no answers to goals from Michail Antonio and Declan Rice, who killed the game as a contest with a stunning solo effort early in the second half.'

Three days later, the Londoners came back down to earth, with their first defeat of the season coming at the hands of Manchester United, 2-1, at the London Stadium. It was 1-1 when Jesse Lingard put United 2-1 up after 88 minutes 20 seconds. Then, in the fourth minute of injury time, West Ham were awarded a penalty. Mark Noble was brought on to take it. It was his first touch of the ball and it was sufficiently poor to enable David de Gea to save a spot kick for the first time since April 2016, having failed to keep out the previous 40 he had faced.

Ironically, the Hammers' next match was also against Manchester United, a Carabao Cup third round game at Old Trafford. Moyes made ten changes, but an early Manuel Lanzini goal and a stubborn defensive display secured their first victory at Old Trafford in 15 years.

Then, away to Leeds United, an injury-time Antonio winner secured a 2-1 come-from-behind victory. The headline on *The Times* report was: 'Moyes has Everton mojo back.'

Europa League group stage: West Ham United 2 Rapid Vienna 0

On 30 September, the day after the club unveiled a statue paying tribute to the club's 1965 European Cup Winners' Cup team, the Hammers secured a comfortable 2-0 victory over Rapid Vienna in the team's first home Europa League game.

The Times reported that: 'Their victory over Rapid Vienna was not quite as emphatic as the Austrian media had predicted, but West Ham were, mostly, a class apart, even if they did need VAR to intervene after a penalty had been awarded against them. West Ham top Group H and have yet to concede a goal after two games. The anticipation was palpable for the first main draw European night at home for West Ham since 2006, when they faced Palermo. Rapid Vienna were under pressure from the start. Declan Rice's header hit the far upright and then Issa Diop failed to tap in the rebound. A second header, this time from Craig Dawson, struck the woodwork, before Rice, the man of the moment after some fulsome praise from his manager, scored, with Michail Antonio the unselfish provider. Deep into stoppage time Benrahma skipped into the area and casually deceived Gartler with the finish.'

A seventh game in 23 days would end in disappointment. West Ham played newly promoted Brentford in their first meeting since 1993, but lost another home game, 2-1, with Brentford scoring their winner with the last kick of the match. Perhaps the home side were jaded after their European exploits.

Moyes would then take his side back to Merseyside and his old club and a 74th-minute goal from Angelo Ogbonna secured a deserved three points. The breakthrough had arrived from a familiar source – a set piece. Since Moyes's first game back at West Ham in January 2020, his team had scored more goals from set pieces – 29, not including penalties – than any other top flight side.

Europa League group stage: West Ham United 3 Genk 0

David Moyes described the prospect of securing European football after Christmas as a 'major boost'. That boost now looked likely as his side edged closer to qualification for the Europa League knockout stages with victory over Genk on 21 October 2021. If West Ham were newcomers on this European stage, their performances so far had not shown it. Three wins, seven goals scored and none conceded put them six points clear in Group H. With West Ham's attack struggling to break the deadlock, it was fitting that their opener came from a set piece. Central defender Craig Dawson required a stroke of luck as his attempted header ricocheted off his shoulder and into the net in first-half stoppage time. Diop headed West Ham's second following a free kick and, only a few minutes later, Jarrod Bowen added a third.

If there is one team West Ham fans want to see their side beat it is Tottenham Hotspur. The home side hauled themselves above their North London rivals with a hard-fought 1-0 win, Antonio nodding in from a 72nd-minute corner. The icing on the cake was West Ham replacing their rivals in the top four.

Next up were Manchester City in the Carabao Cup fourth round. West Ham had not beaten City in any competition in Pep Guardiola's time and some of the defeats had been horrific. This time, the Mancunians were held to a 0-0 draw and goalkeeper Alphonse Areola starred in a 5-3 penalty shoot-out win. City's defeat came five years and one day after their previous loss in the competition.

The following Sunday, in front of the TV cameras, West Ham travelled to Villa Park and returned to London with three points thanks to a 4-1 win. Goals from Ben Johnson, Rice, Fornals and Bowen meant the team set a new club record of eight away games unbeaten, eclipsing the record set in November 1986. Five consecutive away victories equalled another club record.

Europa League group stage: Genk 2 West Ham United 2

Perhaps it was a fitting celebration of David Moyes'ss 1,000th game in management that West Ham United were embroiled in an intense rollercoaster of a match, with the draw at Genk on 4 November 2021 ensuring their qualification for the Europa League knockout stages. In 95 thrilling minutes in Belgium, a brace from Saïd Benrahma was only enough for a point to keep West Ham top of Group H with two matches left to play after an 88th-minute own goal from Tomáš Souček.

The next visitors to the London Stadium were Liverpool. The Merseysiders travelled to Stratford on a 25-game unbeaten run and amid talk of them matching the Arsenal 'Invincibles'. They went home with that prospect shattered after the Hammers inflicted their first defeat of the season. The 3-2 win came courtesy of an own goal from goalkeeper Alisson and goals from Pablo Fornals and Kurt Zouma. It also meant the Hammers moved third in the table, a point ahead of their opponents. Heady times indeed.

Czech businessman Daniel Křetínský completed his purchase of a 27 per cent stake in West Ham United in a deal worth between £180m and £200m that made him the second largest shareholder. The deal reduced David Sullivan's shareholding from 51.5 per cent to 38.8, David Gold's by ten per cent to 25.1 and 'Tripp' Smith's by two per cent to eight, with the number of shares in the hands of other investors falling from 3.4 per cent to 1.1.

West Ham were sitting, heads held high, in third place during the latest international break but after a 1-0 loss away to Wolverhampton Wanderers, David Moyes ruefully admitted that 'we can't hit heights week in, week out'.

Europa League group stage: Rapid Vienna 0 West Ham United 2

Victory in Vienna on 25 November 2021 secured top spot in Group H with a game to spare, with the team that eased past Rapid Vienna a largely second string one. In a game played behind closed doors due to a Covid lockdown in Austria, a fall in intensity was Moyes's biggest concern, one which dissipated as his team dominated. 'When we started in the tournament, I was unsure how we would be because it's relatively new to a lot of the players, but we've done so well and it's a great achievement for us to be in European football come March,' Moyes said.

They may have aspired to the Premier League summit, but next West Ham came up against the reality that was Manchester City at the Etihad. City kept the Londoners on a long leash as the snow fell and a 95th-minute goal from Manuel Lanzini was but a consolation. The Hammers did not manage a shot on target between the 28th and 77th minutes.

The next visitors to the London Stadium were Brighton & Hove Albion, a team they had failed to beat in nine Premier League meetings. A late goal from Neal Maupay rescued a point for the Seagulls after Souček's fifth-minute opener. This was the player's sixth headed Premier League goal since his debut in February 2020, a record bettered by only two other players.

Chelsea were the next visitors to the London Stadium. It was 2-2 as the game entered its closing stages when Arthur Masuaku grabbed a fortunate winner, scoring with what was more a cross than a shot. Twice Chelsea had led, twice they were pegged back because of sloppy defending.

A website published a fair play table that had David Moyes's team as the cleanest in the Premier League.

Their worst offender was Michail Antonio. The 'dirtiest' side were, surprise, surprise, Leeds United.

Europa League group stage: West Ham United 0 Dinamo Zagreb 1

In the luxurious and unexpected position of already being in the Europa League's round of 16, David Moyes dipped into West Ham United's youth system and plucked a few more graduates from their famed academy for the final group game on 9 December. It may have ended the Hammers' unbeaten record in this competition thanks to a determined display by Dinamo Zagreb and a deadly strike from Mislav Oršić, but it allowed seven youngsters, all aged 20 or under, to offer an insight into their futures on a night when they were given a reminder of the gulf between youth and senior level.

A disappointing 0-0 draw at relegation-bound Burnley followed. West Ham failed to convert long, promising spells of pressure against a struggling opponent. Not surprising, perhaps, given that forwards Antonio and Benrahma had managed only one goal between them since mid-September.

A 2-0 defeat at Arsenal would follow. West Ham were certainly hindered by Coufal's sending-off after receiving two yellow cards. The loss pushed West Ham down into fifth place, a point behind their conquerors.

West Ham's poor run continued when they lost 2-1 at Tottenham in a Carabao Cup quarter-final decided by three goals scored in the space of five first-half minutes. Steven Bergwijn put the home side ahead in the 29th minute before Bowen pounced on Eric Dier's mistake to level after 32 minutes. Only two minutes later, Lucas Moura scored what proved to be the winner. West Ham had played a full part in a proper cup tie and must have wondered how they let the game get away from them.

Southampton arrived in East London on Boxing Day without a win in six matches. Imbued with Christmas spirit, West Ham gave them three points with 3-2 defeat. The only excuse was that the home side were without three key defenders in Aaron Cresswell, Kurt Zouma and Angelo Ogbonna.

In their final game of the calendar year, West Ham travelled to Watford. The home side were deep in the relegation dogfight while the Hammers needed three points to reignite their top-four hopes after a run of poor results. In the end, it was the visitors who battled back from a fourth-minute concession to run out emphatic winners. Bowen recorded three assists and Nikola Vlašić scored what would prove to be his only league goal for the club.

A 'half-time' report might have noted that there had been a slight slump recently, but there had been progression with league wins over five of the so-called 'Big Six' and a surprisingly comfortable passage through the Europa League group stage. The downside was that a relatively small squad was beginning to look stretched.

The Hammers made it a happy start to the New Year with a 3-2 win at Crystal Palace. Lanzini was again the Eagles' nemesis with a brace – including a strike that would be voted the club's goal of the season – after Antonio had opened the scoring with his second goal in a week after a nine-match barren spell.

A week later, Leeds United were the visitors to Stratford in an FA Cup third round tie. Lanzini was on target again as West Ham advanced with a controlled and largely untroubled 2-0 win over Premier League opposition.

When Bowen bagged a brace in a 2-0 Premier League win over Norwich City it meant that no English player had been involved in more goals than he had so far that season. The goals came as part of a mid-season run of seven goals in seven games for Bowen.

At the end of January, Leeds were again the visitors to the London Stadium, this time in the Premier League. Marcelo Bielsa's men were without nine players through injury, but a Jack Harrison hat-trick ensured they returned to Yorkshire with three points.

Old Trafford was the next destination in the search for league points. A 90th-minute Marcus Rashford goal separated the sides in what had been an even, if uninspiring, contest.

The fourth round of the FA Cup took West Ham to the Aggborough Stadium, home of non-league Kidderminster Harriers, the lowest ranked team left in the competition. The home side went ahead in the 19th minute but somehow West Ham slithered out of this barnstorming tie with a spot in the fifth round. After Declan Rice, who was sent on by David Moyes at half-time to bring some order to an abject performance, struck in second-half stoppage time to take the game to extra time, Bowen prevented penalties by snaffling a winner with 13 seconds left on the clock.

Bowen was on target again with a deflected effort to help the Irons defeat Watford 1-0. If the game itself was largely forgettable, it came amid some unwanted newspaper headlines after defender Kurt Zouma was filmed kicking his cat. The match report headline in *The Times* was typical: 'Animal lover Moyes ignores outcry and picks shamed Zouma.'

Back-to-back draws at Leicester City – 2-2 courtesy of Craig Dawson's last-gasp header – and 1-1 at home to a rejuvenated Newcastle United saw David Moyes's side slip back to fifth. Were they running out of steam?

West Ham kept themselves in the hunt for Champions League qualification with a dominant, albeit only 1-0, win against Wolves. They were comfortably superior and prevailed through a Tomáš Souček goal.

On the first day of March, West Ham travelled to Southampton with realistic hopes of progressing to the next round of the FA Cup. But they would lose 3-1 and David Moyes was left lamenting that 'we are lacking quality at the moment in the final third' after his team had passed up a number of presentable chances.

A visit to Anfield was probably not West Ham's preferred next destination and they would duly lose to Sadio Mané's 27th-minute strike. The Hammers only had 31 per cent possession but matched Liverpool's 13 shots on target. They deserved a draw, but Lanzini missed a clear cut chance to score a late equaliser.

Attention then switched to the continental stage once again. The Irons were paired in the round of 16 with six-time competition winners and competition favourites Sevilla of Spain.

Europa League round of 16 first leg: Sevilla 1 West Ham United 0

West Ham returned to European action on 10 March 2022 and according to Jacob Steinberg in *The Guardian*: 'This was a game of fine margins and in the end, it belonged to the side with greater European expertise. Sevilla were everything we have come to expect in this competition

– clinical when the moment arrived, obdurate enough to hold out once they were ahead.'

Caught cold when a clever set piece routine allowed Munir El Haddadi to give Sevilla the lead with a sweet strike on the hour, the primary emotion for West Ham was frustration. Moyes's side missed several excellent chances in both halves but there was a robustness to this West Ham team and they did not look out of their depth during the first half. Their football was crisp and their boldness unsettled Sevilla at times, particularly with Antonio running the channels and doing everything possible to ruffle a defence that looked vulnerable with Nemanja Gudelj alongside Jules Koundé instead of the injured Diego Carlos.

The game was nicely balanced at the break. West Ham had settled, Rice winning his tackles and oozing confidence. Gaps appeared and the Hammers went close at the start of the second half, Antonio teeing up Souček to draw another fine save from Sevilla goalkeeper Bono.

A goal was coming. Marcos Acuña trotted across from left-back to take a free kick and West Ham momentarily forget themselves, nobody spotting El Haddadi lurking on the left of the area. Nobody, that is, apart from Acuña, whose delivery caught out West Ham and sat up perfectly for El Haddadi to clip a beautiful finish.

Before the return leg, West Ham had to face Aston Villa in the Premier League and not since West Ham moved to the London Stadium in 2016 had a goal been celebrated with such emotion. When the deadlock was broken midway through the second half, both sets of supporters rose to applaud Andriy Yarmolenko's brilliant strike and salute his return from compassionate leave owing to the war in his homeland of Ukraine. Pablo Fornals added a second and Ramsey pulled a late goal back for the visitors, but those goals paled into insignificance.

Europa League round of 16 second leg: West Ham United 2 Sevilla 0 (aet) Aggregate 2-1

This will go down as one of the greatest nights in West Ham's history. The game on 17 March was an occasion to rival the farewell to Upton Park and it could not have been more fitting that the decisive touch came from Yarmolenko, who was the calmest person in the London Stadium when the ball fell to him in front of goal with eight minutes of extra time remaining.

One-nil down at the start of play, West Ham simply would not be denied. 'We were massive,' Moyes said. 'We played with great passion. It's not just Yarmolenko. It was the team. His message and his name will be heard all round Europe. But the story is not just about Yarmolenko. The story was about West Ham.'

There were heroes everywhere in claret and blue. Rice was imperious in midfield, winning his tackles and spreading the play. Zouma and Dawson headed everything away at the back and Johnson pinned down Sevilla forward Anthony Martial, who offered little before being taken off.

Then there was Antonio, tirelessly running the channels, holding the ball up front and giving Sevilla's defenders a torrid time. It was his cross that allowed Souček to set West Ham on their way just before half-time, the Czech's headed goal arriving just when it seemed Julen Lopetegui's side were beginning to take control.

After 39 minutes, Benrahma linked with Antonio, who drove down the left and crossed to the far post. Souček, who had pulled on to Ludwig Augustinsson's shoulder, rose above the left-back and guided a fine header beyond Bono. The noise was extraordinary when the ball went in.

West Ham threatened during the second half. Souček tested Bono and the Sevilla goalkeeper also denied Lanzini. The tension rose, Sevilla pushing towards the end of normal time, but West Ham somehow found a second wind during extra time. Souček went close again but it seemed penalties were on the way until Yarmolenko, on for Benrahma, popped up.

It was a night of very raw emotion at the London Stadium as West Ham United overcame Sevilla in extra time to claim a place in the quarter-finals of the Europa League. For the second time in five days, Yarmolenko scored a goal of an emotional significance which carried far beyond mere football. By the end, it felt as though the whole evening might have a similar feeling; this stretched further than simply reaching the last eight of a European competition. The Sevilla match might just end up being remembered as the night that West Ham finally came home.

The club has made changes around the ground but, with the benefit of hindsight, it feels as though West Ham reacted more positively than most to matches being played behind closed doors. It was as if a firebreak between the club and its fans was almost necessary. By the time crowds were allowed back in again at the start of the 2021/22 season, the team's fortunes on the pitch had been transformed from battling against relegation to pushing for European football. The sense of a club coming back together again was noticeable from a distance as the season progressed.

As such, the five days which covered the Aston Villa and Sevilla games were a barometer for this change. The quiet, sullen London Stadium of a couple of years ago might now be considered a memory that could fade over time. If West Ham supporters could replicate the wall of sound that accompanied those two wins, they could safely be said to have come home again, even if it had taken almost six years to get there. Because, to be sure, there were no questions being asked at the London

Stadium against Sevilla about the club's identity. From the spectacular light show before the match to the post-match celebrations of both fans and players, it was an evening defined by the whole club pulling together as one.

In the modern age, it is increasingly untenable to describe a football club as 'belonging' to the fans in anything like a literal sense. The gap between the owners and those who pay to support the team has never been wider. But belonging isn't only about possession. A sense of belonging is also important to supporters and when West Ham left Upton Park for Stratford, they lost a part of their identity that mattered to them. Football clubs are rooted in their geographical location and although West Ham only moved four miles, such short distances matter in London. It took six years and it wasn't without its growing pains, but it felt as though West Ham came home against Sevilla and that the positive effect on the club could long outlive the Europa League run.

March ended with a 3-1 loss away to Tottenham and the Irons just did not play well. Apart from the fact it was enemy-in-chief Tottenham, it was a loss to a side also pushing for a top-four place. After 30 games, West Ham were now seventh, six points behind Arsenal in fourth place.

There followed a 2-1 home win over Everton, with Cresswell netting direct from a free kick and Bowen scoring on his first game back from injury.

Europa League quarter-final first leg: West Ham United 1 Olympique Lyonnais 1

When it was all done, after the controversy and the fury and the lunacy of this game on 7 April, there were cuddles and giggles between the managers. David Moyes had calmed down and tried his best not to talk himself into more trouble when reflecting on the moment that reduced West Ham to ten men, sparking his rage and earning him a yellow card.

Not only did West Ham believe that Moussa Dembélé was running wide of goal when his arm was pulled by Aaron Cresswell – an offence for which the left-back was dismissed – they also felt there was a foul on Jarrod Bowen at the start of the Lyon move on the stroke of half-time which led to the red card.

The Hammers, returning after the interval nursing a sense of injustice, survived what Lyon threw at them and then took the lead through Bowen. Tetê came on and wriggled clear to create the equaliser for Tanguy Ndombele after Areola had pushed the cross back into play. Moyes had spoken previously of the need not to be duped by the dark arts and his team were well goaded. Lyon took every opportunity to go down easily, trying to disrupt the game and suck out the intensity. West Ham allowed themselves to become infuriated and exasperated and Moyes's temperature rose, earning himself a booking when he gave referee Felix Zwayer a piece of his mind at half-time.

In the aftermath of the first leg, a weary West Ham lost 2-0 to Brentford in West London, realistically ending their hopes of sneaking into the top four. The Hammers lacked intensity and looked spent. They created nothing and offered up too many chances to the home team. Moyes had increasingly banked on the same players from a small squad and here they seemed to run out of ideas and energy.

Europa League quarter-final second leg: Olympique Lyonnais 0 West Ham United 3 Aggregate 1-4

David Moyes's plan worked to perfection in the return leg on 14 April. Clinical goals from Dawson, Rice and Bowen were no more than West Ham deserved. Their blend of physical power and counter-attacking prowess was too much for Lyon.

West Ham had stood firm. They had survived a torrid opening spell in which Lyon's Karl Toko Ekambi had struck the woodwork, Coufal had survived a penalty appeal for handball and Diop had picked up a booking for a clumsy foul on Moussa Dembélé.

After a while, though, West Ham began to impose themselves, Lanzini knitting things together in the middle, and their threat grew whenever they were able to work Antonio into dangerous positions. Lyon were terrified of the striker's pace. Antonio was involved when the tireless Fornals had a shot from 20 yards and he almost created an opening goal with a cross for Bowen, who was unlucky not to turn the ball home at the far post.

West Ham were growing in confidence at that stage. Rice and Souček were outplaying Ndombele and Thiago Mendes in midfield and Lyon were looking vulnerable under the high ball. Set pieces were an obvious path to goal for West Ham and so it proved when Fornals sent in a corner after 38 minutes. Dawson simply wanted it more than Lyon's defenders and his header meant West Ham were ahead on aggregate.

Lyon cracked again before half-time. Johnson, filling in for Cresswell, crossed from the left and Emerson Palmieri's poor clearance was collected by Rice on the edge of the area. He took a touch and sent a low shot beyond Julian Pollersbeck. West Ham were in their element. Three minutes into the second half, they stopped a Lyon attack and countered when Rice, Fornals and Lanzini played their way out of trouble and got the ball up to Antonio. He found Fornals and when the Spaniard sent Bowen clear, all that was left was for the winger to score with a calm finish from 20 yards. The tie was over.

Lyon never really looked likely to stage a resurrection. It was a textbook Hammers performance against ideal opponents for Moyes's style of play. Lyon, content to keep possession but without much thrust, were easily suffocated and picked off. West Ham were in their first European semi-final in 46 years.

The Hammers returned to the London Stadium and could only manage a tepid 1-1 draw against relegation candidates Burnley. It took a 74th-minute equaliser from Souček to salvage a point.

Then it was off to Stamford Bridge. The Hammers fell to a 90th-minute goal from Christian Pulisic. By then, they were down to ten men after Dawson was sent off, although at least Fabiański saved the resultant penalty.

Europa League semi-final first leg: West Ham United 1 Eintracht Frankfurt 2

West Ham were paired with Eintracht Frankfurt, the Bundesliga club the Irons had defeated at the same stage of the journey to their last European final in 1976. And after the first leg on 28 April, the current Hammers team knew that, just as in 1976, they would have to come from behind to get through. In 1976, the Hammers also lost the first leg 2-1, but on that occasion the defeat was in Frankfurt, not on home soil.

This meeting at the London Stadium was a quick, open game, won deservedly by Eintracht Frankfurt, who were slicker and more clinical in attack. Moyes's side gave a fine account of themselves, responding tigerishly to the blow of a first-minute goal and they might even have travelled to Germany on level terms had Bowen's late overhead kick crept underneath the crossbar – one of three occasions West Ham struck the woodwork.

The game started disastrously. Frankfurt worked a clever rotation on the left, Rafael Borré whipped in a beauty of a cross and Fornals failed to spot Ansgar Knauff ghosting in behind him. His cushioned header left Areola rooted to the spot.

Frankfurt continued to look dangerous on the break, but the hosts were not to be denied. After 21 minutes, Lanzini clipped in a free kick from a central position, Zouma rose to nod the ball across the goalmouth and Antonio hooked it in at the far post.

Yet Frankfurt carried the greater threat throughout the match and they duly regained the lead after half-time with a goal of exquisite construction. Djibril Sow played a quick one-two with Jesper Lindstrøm whose return pass sent Sow swooping down on Areola. His shot was parried but only to the feet of Daichi Kamada, who tapped the ball into an empty net.

In the end, the only consolation for West Ham was that they were still alive. Nobody should mistake this for a hard-luck story, even if Bowen was desperately unfortunate when he hit the bar with his acrobatic effort in added time. The reality was that Eintracht Frankfurt were dominant for long spells and when Moyes picked through his side's messy performance, his overriding emotion would have been relief that West

Ham's hopes of reaching the Europa League Final had not been consigned to dust.

Falling in between the two legs of the semi-final, Arsenal visited the London Stadium looking to secure a European berth of their own. The Hammers enjoyed the majority of possession, territory and play against Mikel Arteta's side, only for defensive lapses and a failure to make the most of promising positions in attack to cost them a result. Headers from defenders Rob Holding and Gabriel meant Bowen's smartly taken reply on the stroke of half-time counted for little. West Ham's back four was stitched together due to injuries and suspensions; they were paying the price of European success and the increased number of games it brought.

Europa League semi-final second leg: Eintracht Frankfurt 1 West Ham United 0 Aggregate 3-1

The odds and history were stacked against West Ham going into the second leg on 5 May. No away team had ever won a Europa League semi-final after losing the first leg at home. Eintracht had won all nine previous UEFA ties in which they recorded an away victory in the first leg. And in the semi-final of the 1965/66 European Cup Winners' Cup, when West Ham lost the semi-final first leg at home to another German club, Borussia Dortmund, they had lost the away leg 3-1.

The disappointment was too much for West Ham to bear. Moyes had lost control by the time a demoralising night deep in the German forests drew to a close. Any thoughts of an heroic comeback had long since passed and, for all that Moyes's side fought after going down to ten men, nothing summed up their lack of composure more than the sight of their manager making a lonely trudge down the tunnel after seeing red for losing his cool with a ball boy during the dying stages.

The harsh reality is that West Ham had not done enough to win this Europa League semi-final. For Moyes, who later apologised for booting the ball at a time-wasting local ball boy as Frankfurt closed in on victory, this stung. More than anything, it was the sense that West Ham could have done more to reach the final. The frustration was immense and, in the cold light of day, it was hard not to feel that Moyes's flash of temper owed much to his team's inability to seize the moment against Frankfurt, who simply managed the details better throughout the tie.

All the same, West Ham created their own problems. They had let themselves down with a disjointed performance at the London Stadium and their hopes of turning it round were all but over after Cresswell was sent off for a foolish offence with only 19 minutes played.

It was galling for Moyes to see one of his most experienced players gift Frankfurt the initiative. West

Ham could not afford any false moves and Cresswell had nobody but himself to blame when he failed to deal with a hopeful punt, the slightest hint of hesitation from the left-back enough to give Jens Petter Hauge a chance to steal possession and burst through on goal. Cresswell was too slow to respond. Hauge was far more assertive and the only surprise was that Jesús Gil Manzano, the Spanish referee, initially reached for a yellow card when Cresswell dragged the Frankfurt forward down just outside the area.

It was a clear denial of a goalscoring opportunity from Cresswell, who had learned nothing from being sent off for the same offence against Lyon in the previous round. Frankfurt appealed for a red and the outcome was inevitable when Manzano checked the pitchside VAR monitor.

The numerical advantage soon told. West Ham adjusted after going down to ten men, shoring up their defence by replacing Lanzini with Johnson, but it was not enough. Frankfurt simply had too much space. They kept the ball moving and were ahead after carving West Ham apart in the 26th minute, Knauff surging past Johnson on the right and pulling the ball back for Borré to beat Areola with a low finish.

At least West Ham continued to fight. Antonio threatened, almost running through before Evan Ndicka stepped in with a fine challenge. Hope flared and the equaliser almost arrived when a free kick from Bowen reached Zouma, who was unable to turn the ball over the line.

So, the Irons' focus returned to the Premier League and their bid to secure back-to-back qualification for Europe through their league position for the first time in the club's history.

On a balmy afternoon in East Anglia, the Hammers found the perfect balm for their Europa League wounds by putting four goals past Norwich City. They established a three-goal advantage by half-time through a Benrahma brace and an Antonio finish. A second-half Lanzini penalty completed the scoring.

West Ham's final home game of the season was against Manchester City, themselves needing the points to clinch another Premier League title. For his last match before retirement, Mark Noble was among the substitutes and he received an incredible reception as he came out of the tunnel. Noble would be introduced on 77 minutes, receiving the biggest ovation of the afternoon as he took the captain's armband.

The game itself did not disappoint. It was Bowen who stole the first half as his two clinical strikes gave the home side a 2-0 lead. City inevitably hit back in the second half. Jack Grealish halved the deficit before Coufal's headed own goal levelled the match. There was time for even more drama when the away side were awarded a penalty late on. Riyad Mahrez stepped up but Fabiański made a superb save, his third stop from five penalties on target in 2021/22.

That 2-2 draw meant that when the Hammers travelled to the Amex Stadium to meet Brighton & Hove Albion on the final day, they were still in the hunt for a Europa League place. They were battling Manchester United for the final spot in Europe's second tier competition and the Old Trafford club did their bit by losing to Crystal Palace at Selhurst Park. At the Amex, Antonio gave the visitors a half-time lead, but Brighton turned it around in the second half and ran out 3-1 winners. 'It was a huge opportunity,' lamented Moyes. 'We didn't play well enough. You could have driven a bus through us.'

It meant West Ham finished seventh with 56 points and would be going on another European tour in 2022/23, albeit in the UEFA Europa Conference League. Another first.

Captain Noble had made his 550th and final appearance in claret and blue. He said: 'We can look back with a lot of pride on the last nine months. To qualify for Europe twice in a row, with what we've done already this year, is a great achievement. Overall, it's a fantastic ending for me, because these past 12 months have been incredible.'

The Guardian, who had predicted a tenth-place finish, summed up 2021/22: 'West Ham had a great season. They maintained their league form while giving their fans the joy of a cup run in Europe. Their wins in Zagreb, Vienna and Lyon will live long in the memory, and victory over Seville gave the London Stadium its best night since the Olympics in 2012.'

In their end-of-season 'awards', the same paper nominated Bowen as player of the season (and he would go on to win his first England caps that summer), Yarmolenko for goal of the season (against Aston Villa) and West Ham 3 Chelsea 2 as one of the games of the season.

Overall, not a bad season for West Ham United. Some decent cup runs and a league campaign spent looking up rather than down.

Chapter 13

After 58 Years, European Winners Again: The Europa Conference League 2022/23

MANY MEDIA outlets were predicting an eighth-place finish in the Premier League and a decent run in the Europa Conference League.

There was considerable activity by West Ham on the transfer front. Goalkeeper Alphonse Areola's loan became a permanent transfer, while £30m was spent on Moroccan defender Nayef Aguerd from Rennes. Crucially, Declan Rice (now captain, after Mark Noble's retirement) and Jarrod Bowen were staying … at least until January.

Forward Gianluca Scamacca's £30.5m arrival from Sassuolo provided another attacking option and hopefully lifted some of the goalscoring pressure from Michail Antonio. The Italian international had scored 16 goals for Sassuolo in Serie A the previous season.

Ivorian winger Maxwel Cornet signed from relegated Burnley, German international defender Thilo Kehrer arrived from Paris Saint-Germain and full-back Emerson Palmieri crossed London from Chelsea. The icing on the cake was the signing of Brazilian international midfielder Lucas Paquetá from Lyon.

Pre-season results were a mixed bag, with the Hammers winning two and drawing four, while losing one. Prior to facing Swiss club Servette, David Moyes had put his squad through an intense training camp in St Andrews – 'brutal' was how captain Rice described it – and Tomáš Souček said it could be one reason for their 'leggy' performances in pre-season.

The 2022/23 Season

Three months after playing in the semi-final of one European competition and coming agonisingly close to securing a place in the Champions League, West Ham were about to start the campaign in another. So, instead of taking their place in Europe's number one competition for the first time, the Hammers found themselves in the third tier competition, the Europa Conference League.

West Ham had to come through two games against Danish outfit Viborg, who were only promoted two seasons ago, to enter the competition proper in September.

Europa Conference League qualifying round first leg:
West Ham United 3 Viborg 1

The road to European glory kicked off on 18 August at the London Stadium, with Gianluca Scamacca climbing high to open his West Ham account while, up in the stand, David Moyes fumed as his side made heavy weather of seeing off Viborg. Goals from the Italy forward and Jarrod Bowen gave the Hammers a two-goal advantage that they nearly squandered when Jakob Bonde reduced the deficit for a side who had finished seventh in Denmark the previous season.

Michail Antonio tapped home to restore the Irons' two-goal advantage for the second leg, but it did not make for comfortable viewing for Moyes, who was serving a ban for kicking the ball towards a ball boy during the Europa League semi-final defeat by Eintracht Frankfurt in May.

But there were also Premier League games to play.

West Ham opened their league season at home to Manchester City. The previous season's 2-2 draw was an aberration against these opponents. The norm was for the Mancunians to leave East London with three points. And they had signed Erling Haaland. He would be the difference, his two goals giving City a 2-0 win. Then the Hammers faced newly promoted Nottingham Forest, who scraped a 1-0 victory, with Rice missing a penalty.

A home loss against bogey side Brighton & Hove Albion meant the Hammers would be bottom of the Premiership without a point, having lost their first three top flight games without scoring for the first time since 1971.

Europa Conference League qualifying round second leg:
Viborg 0 West Ham United 3
Aggregate 6-1

The Hammers held a 3-1 first leg advantage going into the return leg on 25 August and Scamacca settled any nerves by converting at the near post to extend the lead before Saïd Benrahma and Tomáš Souček scored after the break for a comfortable 3-0 win.

However, league form continued to be inconsistent. A first victory would come at Villa Park, but the Hammers could only manage a 1-1 draw at home to Spurs, followed by a 2-1 defeat at Chelsea.

Thankfully West Ham's European form was the opposite of that in the league.

Europa Conference League group stage:
West Ham United 3 FCSB 1

David Moyes admitted that team selections would be a balancing act as his team sought to combine Thursday night European football with the need to climb the

Premier League table. However, he was forced to call upon a trio of rested stars at half-time to secure victory in their opening game in Group B against the Romanian side FCSB on 8 September. What was it with West Ham and Romanian sides?

Andrei Cordea gave the visitors the lead before the break and West Ham were fortunate to be awarded a penalty from which one of the substitutes, Bowen, equalised midway through the second half. Another substitute, Antonio, added a third after Emerson had given the Hammers the lead in a much-improved second-half showing.

Because of the cancellation of the weekend's league programme due to the Queen's death, West Ham's next match was their second in the Conference League on Thursday, 15 September.

Europa Conference League group stage: Silkeborg 2 West Ham United 3

For eight surreal minutes, Silkeborg were in dreamland. Kasper Kusk had coolly side-footed past Areola from the edge of the area after a neat cutback from the left and the Danish side were displaying their aesthetically pleasing possession style, but it was not to last. After Silkeborg's opener, West Ham's superior European nous came to the fore. Tobias Salquist's push in the back offered Cornet the chance to take a tumble on the artificial turf and Manuel Lanzini coolly converted from the penalty spot. The neat passing interchanges of the home side highlighted their comfort on the fast surface, but the bright Cornet nicked the ball and fed Scamacca, who turned before unleashing a ferocious strike into the roof of the net. West Ham grew into the match, with Craig Dawson adding their third with a trademark header from a corner before half-time. The introduction of Bowen as part of a raft of changes gave Silkeborg late hope, as the forward's error resulted in a breakaway that Søren Tengstedt converted after an Areola parry.

West Ham had put together a decent record against Everton in recent seasons, but they would show their inconsistent league form this time, going down to a 1-0 defeat at Goodison Park. After seven league outings, they were in the relegation zone with four points. Only in 1973/74 had the club had fewer points at this stage of a top flight campaign (in 1973/74 it was two points for a win). On the first day of October, West Ham finally secured a home league win, with a 2-0 victory over fellow strugglers Wolverhampton Wanderers. Something had had to give, with two managers under pressure.

In late September, it was announced that Mark Noble would be returning to West Ham as sporting director just months after his retirement as a player. The former captain was to start work in January in a newly created post at his boyhood club, where he played for 18 years. With coaching currently not a priority for Noble, it was announced that the 35-year-old would 'provide input, advice and assistance across West Ham's football operation, with responsibilities including a focus on player recruitment, developing the academy and player and staff well-being'.

Europa Conference League group stage: Anderlecht 0 West Ham United 1

With 20 minutes to play in Belgium on 6 October, the game goalless and West Ham United in need of a moment of inspiration to break the deadlock, David Moyes turned and looked at his bench. His side had been guilty of missing a host of chances. Then, on came Rice, Paquetá and Scamacca – 'three star acts', as Moyes described them. Nine minutes later, the trio combined to give West Ham the lead. Rice switched the play from left to right. Coufal's cushioned header found Paquetá, before the Brazilian picked out Scamacca in a pocket of space in the penalty area. The Italian, buoyed by his first Premier League goal of the season the previous Saturday, glanced over his left shoulder at the goal and struck a clinical right-footed shot into the far left corner from 12 yards.

Europa Conference League group stage: West Ham United 2 Anderlecht 1

Anderlecht issued an apology after their fans lit flares and threw seats at West Ham United supporters during the return fixture at the London Stadium on 13 October. Police had to intervene to separate the two sets of supporters and the Belgian side said their fans' behaviour was unacceptable. One Anderlecht fan was apprehended by security after running on to the pitch.

In the match itself, Bowen underlined again that he could make a late sprint for Gareth Southgate's World Cup squad. By the time the 25-year-old had struck West Ham's second goal in the 30th minute, the former Hereford United and Hull City forward had already bewildered Anderlecht's defenders with his power and pace, and a series of slaloming runs down the right wing. Benrahma had given the Londoners the lead after winning and converting a 14th-minute free kick. And while Anderlecht pulled a goal back late on from the penalty spot through Sebastiano Esposito, the points were rarely in doubt.

League form continued to be a mixed bag. A 3-1 home win over Fulham was followed by a 1-1 draw at Southampton and while the Hammers did play well at Anfield, a record of one victory since the distant 60s produced the predictable outcome. A Monday night fixture against Bournemouth, though, yielded a 2-0 victory, a fifth home win on the bounce in all competitions for the first time since the move from Upton Park.

Europa Conference League group stage: West Ham United 1 Silkeborg 0

The Hammers sailed serenely into the round of 16 as group winners with a game to spare thanks to a one-goal win against Danish club Silkeborg on 27 October. Lanzini's first-half penalty was enough to maintain a 100 per cent record for West Ham, who had already secured qualification but needed a point to finish top of Group B and avoid a play-off round in February. Goalkeeper Nicolai Larsen presented West Ham with a rather fortuitous penalty midway through the first half. Antonio chased Benrahma's pass down the left side of Silkeborg's box. Larsen charged out to confront Antonio but belatedly withdrew from the challenge. Antonio reached the ball first and needed no invitation to go to ground. There was negligible contact but the referee, Jouni Hyytiä, pointed to the spot and Lanzini scored.

Europa Conference League group stage: FCSB 0 West Ham United 3

West Ham finished off their group campaign with a comfortable win against FCSB on 3 November thanks to two strikes from Fornals either side of an own goal. With a place in the last 16 already secured, manager Moyes was able to leave out a host of key players and hand first-team bows to academy graduates Divin Mubama and Oliver Scarles.

The previous season, West Ham lost 1-0 at Old Trafford in the Premier League thanks to a last-minute Marcus Rashford goal. This time around, the result and the scorer were the same. West Ham then had three home matches before the Premier League paused for the World Cup. First up were Crystal Palace who took away three points thanks to a 90th-minute winner. West Ham did not play their first Carabao Cup tie of this peculiar season until 9 November. Championship side Blackburn Rovers were the visitors to the London Stadium. It went to penalties, Angelo Ogbanna the only player to miss, hitting the crossbar as the Hammers were eliminated. West Ham would finish the first part of the season at home to Leicester City. It would be another defeat, 0-2, in front of an impatient crowd. After 15 games, the Hammers would sit in 16th place, one point above the bottom three, as the season took a World Cup-enforced break.

As domestic football paused for the World Cup, the knives were out for David Moyes. West Ham were one point above the relegation zone even though only Arsenal, Chelsea and Manchester United had a higher net spend than West Ham in the past five years. But at least Hammers supporters still had Europe to look forward to in the spring.

After the World Cup hiatus (in which Declan Rice starred in England's passage to the quarter-finals) West

Ham played three friendlies, all away from home, before the league season re-commenced. Cambridge United were beaten 4-2 and Udinese 3-1 before a 1-1 draw at Fulham.

The Hammers restarted their Premier League campaign on Boxing Day evening with a short trip to the Emirates Stadium. Arsenal were the league leaders, while the Hammers were looking down rather than up. Somehow, they managed to lead 1-0 at half-time via a Benrahma penalty, but Arsenal delivered a superb second-half performance and scored three unanswered goals.

West Ham closed out the year at home to another London outfit, Brentford. A 0-2 loss was the Irons' fifth successive defeat and the players left the pitch to boos from those among the 62,467 crowd who bothered to stay to the end. West Ham closed out 2022 with 14 points from 17 games and remained just outside the relegation places. Inevitably, there was more speculation about Moyes's job.

A few days into the New Year, joint chairman David Gold died aged 86 following several months of poor health.

West Ham started 2023 at Elland Road. At least they stopped the run of defeats with a 2-2 draw that Henry Winter described in *The Times* as 'one of the Premier League games of the season, a rollercoaster ride threatening to derail at any moment with both sides giving everything'.

The Premier League paused in January for the third round of the FA Cup. Benrahma came off the bench to knock his old club Brentford out of the competition. It was a vindication for Moyes, who went with a strong line-up, making only four changes from the midweek draw at Leeds. In the fourth round, West Ham were drawn away again, to League One Derby County, and the TV cameras were there to record the hoped for upset. They were disappointed as the Hammers got to the fifth round with goals from Bowen and Antonio. However, West Ham's FA Cup campaign ended once again at Old Trafford. Benrahma gave them a 54th-minute lead but a series of defensive errors meant that Manchester United won through to the next round, 3-1 this time.

West Ham made only one signing in the January transfer window with 30-year-old striker Danny Ings brought in from Aston Villa with the aim of fixing the Hammers' goalscoring problems.

Alas, it was business as usual in the Premier League. Wolverhampton Wanderers leapfrogged the Hammers and pulled out of the relegation zone for the first time since mid-October with a 1-0 win. Two Bowen goals gave West Ham an invaluable three points against fellow strugglers Everton at the London Stadium. It was rumoured Moyes would have lost his job if his team had lost (the 'sack race', one newspaper called it) but in the event it was the man in the away dugout who would be fired. That his name was Frank Lampard probably didn't elicit much sympathy among the West Ham faithful.

West Ham travelled to the North-East to face high-flying Newcastle United. Callum Wilson scored his inevitable goal against the Hammers after only three minutes, but a Paquetá strike after 32 minutes enabled the London side to travel home with a hard-earned point. A week later saw was another 1-1 draw, at home to Chelsea.

West Ham then made the short trip to North London to meet arch rivals Tottenham Hotspur. The latter were experiencing their own problems, but their visitors caused them few problems and their 2-0 victory was too easy. It was so typical of West Ham that against Forest, they oozed attacking intent from the outset and, by the end, had a four-goal win. That said, all the goals arrived in the last 20 minutes. They included a three-minute brace for Ings. Moyes could finally enjoy a celebratory glass of wine. Inevitably perhaps, it was followed by a 4-0 thrashing at Brighton, a game one scribe described as 'as one-sided as it gets in the Premier League'. The manager was predictably jeered by the away fans, who were unsparing in their criticism.

With such awful league form, West Ham's saving grace had been their European campaign. It might only have been the third tier European competition, but it represented the Hammers' only chance of salvaging something from a season that was nosediving into mediocrity or worse.

European Conference League round of 16 first leg: AEK Larnaca 0 West Ham United 2

West Ham United put one foot into the quarter-finals thanks to two first-half goals from Antonio as they resumed their European campaign in Cyprus on 9 March 2023.

Manager Moyes had spoken of his belief that a strong showing in Europe could boost his team's fragile confidence and domestic form, having travelled to Cyprus severely bruised by that 4-0 defeat by Brighton & Hove Albion, which left them only a point above the relegation zone.

Antonio's first goal, in the 36th minute, came from West Ham's first real moment of quality. The excellent Benrahma found space on the left wing, cut inside on to his right foot and whipped in a magnificent cross towards the West Ham striker. Antonio barely had to move and, with a flick of his head, the ball nestled in the bottom corner. His second, just before half-time, was the kind of moment of inspiration Antonio was capable of but had produced far too infrequently during the season. Rice broke forward from midfield and found Antonio, who was given time and space to control and turn on the edge of the penalty area. Antonio set himself and curled a fine shot round the AEK defender.

European Conference League round of 16 second leg: West Ham United 4 AEK Larnaca 0 Aggregate 6-0

Jarrod Bowen was the inspiration for West Ham as they cruised into the last eight of the Europa Conference League with an emphatic win on 16 March. Bowen struck twice at the beginning of the second half to take his overall tally to eight across two European campaigns, making him the Hammers' leading European goalscorer. The victory equalled West Ham's biggest in Europe and meant that, for a second season running, they had reached the quarter-finals of a European competition.

Already two goals down from the first leg, Larnaca were outclassed at the London Stadium as the Hammers strolled to victory. The Cypriots gifted the opening goal to Scamacca and then had Gustavo Ledes sent off just before the break for a poor challenge on Fornals that was upgraded from a yellow card to red following a VAR intervention. Bowen took the home side further clear. His second in particular was impressive as he looped a header from Creswell's cross over the Larnaca keeper and into the corner for his tenth goal of the season, only four of which had come in the Premier League. West

Ham's victory was rounded off by 18-year-old local boy Mubama, who had been with the club since the age of eight and scored his first senior goal on only his third first-team appearance.

Back on Premier League duty, the Hammers were held to another 1-1 draw, this time at home to rapidly improving Aston Villa. West Ham then hosted Southampton in one of those 'six-pointers' so beloved by journalists. It was a dreadful game, high on tension and low on quality, but did yield a 1-0 win. West Ham then came up against Champions League-chasing Newcastle United. This was always going to be a tough game for the home side, but a 5-1 defeat was largely self-inflicted. There were rumours that Moyes would be sacked if his team lost at Fulham, but they gained only their second away win of the campaign courtesy of a Harrison Reed own goal. It was an attritional, pragmatic 90 minutes during which West Ham had only 23 per cent possession.

Amid the discontent, attention turned back to Europe and another visit to Belgium for a quarter-final tie with Gent on 13 April.

Europa Conference League quarter-final first leg:
Gent 1 West Ham United 1

David Moyes admitted the result was better than the performance after West Ham escaped with a 1-1 draw.

Ings put the Hammers ahead against the run of play just before half-time with what was the first European goal of his career. But Gent, who were fourth in the Belgian top flight, deservedly levelled in the second half through Hugo Cuypers. Moyes insisted the Hammers had not taken their unfancied opponents lightly, despite him making six changes to his starting line-up with one eye on the Premier League relegation battle and a visit from leaders Arsenal on the Sunday.

Aguerd had a goal ruled out for handball before Ings, making his first European start since an appearance for Liverpool in October 2015, struck. Moyes had fallen foul of ball boys in Europe before; he was sent off for kicking a ball at one in the semi-final defeat at Eintracht Frankfurt the previous season. But this time, he was grateful to the Gent youngster who lobbed the ball straight to Coufal, allowing the right-back to immediately find Bowen, who crossed for Ings to tap home at the far post.

Europa Conference League quarter-final second leg:
West Ham United 4 Gent 1
Aggregate 5-2

There had not been many times all season when David Moyes had been able to stand back and admire his team's play from a position of comfort. The complaints over West Ham's football had been relentless and, given how much criticism had been thrown in his direction, it was easy to understand why Moyes was celebrating so passionately on 20 April when captain Rice put this quarter-final out of Gent's reach once and for all.

A spirit of defiance had helped West Ham draw with Arsenal, but this performance was stylish. Antonio was in bulldozing form up front, scoring twice, and Paquetá oozed class. But Rice stole the show. The 24-year-old capped off a towering performance by running from his own half to score the best goal of his career to date.

Gent played the slicker football during the first half and West Ham soon trailed. Paquetá squandered possession in the 26th minute, Gift Orban drove down the left and Emerson failed to read the danger, showing a lack of basic defensive instincts. He was nowhere to be seen when Orban's cross exposed West Ham's loss of shape and Matisse Samoise had time to tee up Cuypers, who bundled the ball in from close range. Gent were not ahead for long, though. West Ham levelled with a simple goal. Eight minutes before half-time, Bowen whipped in a free kick from the right and Antonio, who was too strong for his markers, headed in at the near post.

Joseph Okumu's inexplicable handball from a Coufal cross summed up Gent's loss of composure. Paquetá, with a nonchalant run-up, duly punished the Gent defender's blunder with a cool penalty.

Now it was over to Rice. Freed from his defensive responsibilities, the midfielder silenced those who claimed he lacked quality in the final third by powering away, deceiving Okumu and slipping a lovely low finish past Davy Roef.

Gent had collapsed. Paquetá soon stirred again, dropping deep to find Antonio, who cut inside and finished powerfully. West Ham had well and truly lifted the handbrake.

When league leaders Arsenal visited the London Stadium, the Hammers trailed 2-0 after ten minutes but emerged with a surprising 2-2 draw. In thumping Bournemouth 4-0 at the Vitality Stadium, Moyes's side finally looked like their old selves. Crystal Palace v West Ham featured the two oldest managers in the division, though Roy Hodgson still had 15 years on David Moyes. Palace would come from behind to lead 3-1 and win 4-2.

West Ham were as wretched as they were when Moyes's position was in serious doubt in the preceding months. The Irons then travelled to the Etihad Stadium and, to no one's surprise, lost 3-0 to a side pushing for yet another Premier League title. So, it would be an understatement to say West Ham needed three points at the London Stadium against Manchester United. Thanks to goalkeeper David de Gea having one of those moments, when he allowed a soft Benrahma shot to go through his hands, the home side had a rare victory against the visitors. It was the perfect tonic ahead of the Europa Conference League semi-final first leg four days later on Thursday, 11 May.

Europa Conference League semi-final first leg: West Ham United 2 AZ Alkmaar 1

It may have been scrappy, it may have been messy, but West Ham could see only the beauty. They celebrated wildly when Antonio bundled the ball over the line with 15 minutes left, completing a turnaround few people had anticipated, and in those moments, it was possible to forget that the evening had been such a slog. It would only be when the dust settled that West Ham remembered that they were going nowhere until the AZ Alkmaar goalkeeper Mat Ryan misjudged the flight of the ball and almost took Bowen's head off midway through the second half.

Moyes's side toiled for long spells against a limited AZ side, creating little and treating the ball with insufficient care. Their football was unimaginative, too reliant on physical power and counter-attacks and, for a while, it seemed that the first leg of this semi-final would be defined by Alphonse Areola handing AZ the lead when he allowed a soft shot from Tijjani Reijnders to squirm past him.

The mood turned when Ryan fouled Bowen and Benrahma equalised from the spot. Soon it was 2-1, Antonio scoring after a scramble and West Ham finally had their young opponents where they wanted them.

West Ham had failed to handle the occasion when they faced Eintracht Frankfurt in the previous year's Europa League semi-final. They lacked nous and were always chasing the game after conceding in the first minute of the first leg, but it was different against AZ. This time, West Ham responded to adversity. They were resilient enough to keep plugging away, yet Moyes was not entirely happy with West Ham's performance against the fourth best team in the Eredivisie. The Scot saw a lack of quality in the final third and he wondered if his forwards were over excited. Everything felt too frantic.

Three days after the AZ game, the Hammers suffered a dismal 2-0 defeat away to bogey side Brentford.

It was hardly ideal preparation for the European second leg in the Netherlands four days later on Thursday, 18 May. Then, on the eve of the game, it was reported that West Ham were set to appoint a director of football in an attempt to address misgivings over their recent transfer strategy. Where that left manager Moyes was an unanswered question.

Europa Conference League semi-final second leg: AZ Alkmaar 0 West Ham United 1 Aggregate 1-3

All the drama came at the end, with substitute Fornals settling the tie deep into added time and the moronic reaction of some thuggish AZ Alkmaar fans briefly threatening to ruin West Ham's evening. The mood had turned acrid at the AFAS Stadion, with hooligans shaming the beaten hosts when they found the pain of defeat too much to bear and responded to the final whistle by charging at the pitchside section housing West Ham's sponsors, club officials and the team's families.

Ultimately, it never seemed likely that AZ would find a way through the wall of black shirts protecting Areola's goal. The statistics suggested an evening of Dutch dominance. AZ had more shots, more of the ball and more corners. Yet Pascal Jansen's young side would pay for their lack of incision and, in the end, it was not a surprise when Fornals's clinical goal gave West Ham the chance to dream of beating Fiorentina in the final in Prague on 7 June.

There were, of course, some hairy moments during the second half. With 20 minutes left, captain Rice could be seen urging his leggy team-mates to give it one last push. West Ham had to dig deep and, from AZ's perspective, there were questions over whether the game would have turned out differently if they had been awarded a penalty for Aguerd's risky challenge on Vangelis Pavlidis just before the hour.

It was, however, a professional display from West Ham. Moyes, who had never won a trophy in a career spanning a thousand matches, made no apologies for focusing on keeping a clean sheet. The Scot had endured a difficult season; now he stood one win away from cementing his place as a West Ham legend.

Sent on to provide more energy during the dying stages, Fornals did more than that. Deep into added time, a loose ball broke to the Spaniard and when he drove a low shot past Ryan from 20 yards, the Hammers' celebrations could begin. Moyes had become the first British manager since Sir Alex Ferguson in 2011 to reach a European final.

West Ham's final home Premier League game was against a Leeds United side desperate for points and managed for their final four league games by one Sam Allardyce. Leeds got themselves in front, then simply capitulated against a West Ham team with nothing but pride to play for. The Hammers would finish their league campaign at the King Power Stadium against Leicester City. The home side needed a win to stand any chance of staying in the Premier League. They managed a 2-1 win, but it was not enough for the Foxes. It meant West Ham finished the campaign in 14th place with 40 points.

Europa Conference League Final (Prague): West Ham United 2 Fiorentina 1

The Lead-Up

West Ham were in their first European final for 47 years. Back in 1976, they lost the Cup Winners' Cup Final 4-2 to Anderlecht in Brussels. They had won the FA Cup at Wembley in 1975 and would do so again in 1980. The Hammers reached the League Cup Final in 1981. Surely finals – and the occasional trophy – would come along every few years? But then came those 43 years of hurt since West Ham United last won a trophy. And let's not talk about the 2006 FA Cup Final.

For Hammers fans who had suffered from 1976 to 2023, it had been a long journey. Was it possible that Declan Rice could become only the third Hammers captain, since Bobby Moore and Billy Bonds, to lift a major trophy?

The story of West Ham's successful European run went back to Andriy Yarmolenko cutting in from the right flank to give West Ham a last-minute win over Chelsea at the start of July 2020. David Moyes remembered it as a turning point; the moment everything started to come together. The Ukraine winger's goal acted as a catalyst, pulling West Ham away from danger during Project Restart, giving them the belief to beat relegation and shed the discord that had threatened to swallow them whole.

Before long, they were fighting back from 3-0 down against Tottenham, rescuing a point thanks to a stoppage-time thunderbolt from Manuel Lanzini. Once so flaky, West Ham discovered resilience. They were punchy during the 2020/21 campaign, defying expectations by finishing sixth and qualifying for Europe. They upset big teams and made the London Stadium feel like home.

It had been emotional. Who could have seen that coming when Moyes returned to the club for a second spell in December 2019? Of course, it had not been all plain sailing. This was, after all, West Ham. Full of confidence after knocking out Sevilla and Lyon in the Europa League, the Hammers were crushed when they lost their semi-final to Eintracht Frankfurt. They qualified for the Europa Conference League after finishing seventh, but their league form nosedived.

The 2022/23 season had been tough. Moyes spent almost £160m in the summer of 2022 and tried to refine the team's style, but it backfired. The league campaign became a slog. West Ham only secured their Premier League status with two games left and Moyes, who had reverted to a more physical tactical approach, had had to fight for his job. Rumours had it that former boss Slaven Bilić would have come in as interim manager if West Ham had lost to Fulham in April.

Yet Moyes had always found ways to survive. The Europa Conference League Final against Italian outfit Fiorentina on Wednesday, 7 June 2023 would be his 1,097th as a manager and with it came the chance to win his first major trophy. West Ham had not tasted success since winning the FA Cup in 1980 and it was 58 years since they won their only European trophy. 'There's a chance to create a legacy where everyone involved will be remembered forever,' said captain Rice.

The Game

The final started in a deafening atmosphere – what a shame that UEFA had underestimated its own competition, deeming a ground with a capacity of 19,370 a worthy venue for a final.

Having won 13 of their previous 14 matches in this competition to reach the final, there had been a growing feeling of optimism among the estimated 20,000 West Ham supporters who descended on Prague's main square during the day. Most of those clad in claret and blue sang 'One more year, one more year, Declan Rice' in hope rather than expectation as they made their way to the stadium and fanzone. But, regardless of their captain's future, for the 4,890 Hammers lucky enough to have secured an official ticket in the 19,370-capacity home of Slavia Prague and a few thousand more who had also somehow found a way in, this was an occasion to savour.

Those fans would be rewarded as the Hammers ended their wait for a major trophy when Jarrod Bowen scored a last-minute goal to beat Fiorentina and win the Europa Conference League. It was the moment when fortune stopped hiding as Lucas Paquetá slid Bowen through and he kept his footing and his composure, took a touch with his right, two with his left and ended 43 years of hurt for West Ham United.

Perfectly summing up a rollercoaster campaign, West Ham's 14th-place finish in the Premier League that season meant their league position was the lowest of any club ever to win a major European trophy.

The final seemed to be heading for extra time after Saïd Benrahma's second-half penalty was cancelled out just seven minutes later by a well-taken effort from Giacomo Bonaventura. It was a testy and sometimes bad-tempered game. At one point, it got downright ugly as Fiorentina captain Cristiano Biraghi was struck by a plastic cup thrown from the West Ham section, leaving him with blood pouring from a head wound.

The match was settled in the most dramatic manner. Bowen timed his run to perfection as Paquetá slid a superb pass through the Fiorentina defence. The England man ran free, steadied himself, then beat Pietro Terracciano with a calm finish to thrill the Hammers fans and send manager Moyes running down the touchline to celebrate the first major silverware of his career.

After 1,097 games of management, absolutely nothing was going to stop him from enjoying his crowning moment. Fortune wasn't hiding any more. Off Moyes went, charging down the touchline, only stopping when he was in front of the fans celebrating behind the Fiorentina goal. He stood there with his arms aloft and drank in the adulation. Here was the Scot's reward for recovering from the tough times and trusting that one day it would be him standing on a podium after leading a team to glory.

The victory also sealed a place in the following season's Europa League, securing European football for a third year running for the first time in the club's history. The manner of victory could not have been any sweeter for West Ham. The reaction on the pitch and in the stands at the final whistle gave a lie to anyone who felt this tournament was beneath them. At the centre of it all was Rice. There was no thought of his future as he lapped up the adulation of the fans who had followed his journey from rising academy star to full England honours. While he was expected to join Arsenal in the summer, having racked up almost 250 appearances since his debut in 2017 as an 18-year-old, Rice showed for one final time that he remained the heartbeat of Moyes's side.

This was a voyage that began back on 18 August and took the Hammers to Denmark, Romania, Denmark again, Belgium, Cyprus, Belgium again, the Netherlands and finally the Czech Republic to take on Italian opposition.

Several images in particular will remain burned into the memories of Hammers fans. Of Paquetá playing the pass. Of time standing still as Bowen ran through and the winger's shot rolled into the Fiorentina net. Of manager Moyes running down the touchline like Pep Guardiola at Stamford Bridge in 2009 (and deciding against copying José Mourinho's 2004 knee slide at Old Trafford). Of captain Rice sitting on the pitch two hours after the final whistle, posing for photos with the trophy and hugging jubilant club staff.

Leaving aside the 1999 Intertoto Cup and a couple of nervy Championship play-off final victories, West Ham had not won anything since beating Arsenal in the 1980 FA Cup Final. Winning the Europa Conference League mattered. Anyone dismissing it as a tinpot competition was missing the point.

It was just over two years since a group of entitled clubs tried to destroy football by creating a European Super League. The game had changed since West Ham, who were in the old Second Division, beat Arsenal at Wembley in 1980, finances making it fiendishly hard for mid-table top flight clubs to challenge for domestic honours. In the Premier League era, shocks became rare. Since 1992, five clubs outside the elite had won the FA Cup: Everton in 1995, pre-Abramovich Chelsea in 1997,

Portsmouth in 2008, Wigan in 2013 and Leicester in 2021. Even Tottenham, who had Harry Kane, a rich pedigree and a huge stadium, had not won a trophy since the League Cup in 2008.

Ultimately, despite having ended their trophy drought, there was little reason to think a club of West Ham's stature would be emulating Leicester's 5,000-1 Premier League title win of 2016 any time soon. And, to emphasise the challenges facing clubs like West Ham, captain Rice would leave for Arsenal within weeks of lifting the Europa Conference League trophy.

All this made West Ham's triumph over Fiorentina special. Not once did West Ham treat European football as an inconvenience. They embraced the Europa League in the 2021/22 season and the London Stadium, once so unloved, rocked when West Ham beat Sevilla in the last 16 and the 3-0 win at Lyon in the quarter-final will never be forgotten. Losing in the last four to Eintracht stung.

It made West Ham even more determined to win the Europa Conference League.

Admittedly, the standard in UEFA's third competition was mixed. West Ham cruised past forgettable opposition during the group stage and were mostly untroubled during the knockout phase. Fiorentina provided by far their toughest test. West Ham did not play particularly well. Victory summed up their season:

they did just about enough by sitting deep and waiting for moments to strike on the break.

That approach was unlikely to take them forward in the league. West Ham had had a disappointing domestic campaign and there were grumbles about the quality of the football under Moyes. There were flaws on show against Fiorentina, yet nobody cared when Rice went up to lift the trophy. West Ham had secured qualification into the Europa League and provided an example for other English teams to follow. They proved the competition was a chance to make some beautiful memories.

The success was a reward for the way manager Moyes had put in the hard yards and fought back from dispiriting spells at Manchester United and Sunderland. He had silenced the critics who wrote him off as a dinosaur and had done a wonderful job since returning to West Ham in December 2019.

By the side of the pitch at the Fortuna Arena, with West Ham's celebrations in full swing, Moyes saw his 87-year-old dad, David Snr. He went straight over, gave him the firmest of hugs and placed round his neck the winner's medal he had been presented with by UEFA president Aleksander Čeferin. Father and son both grinned from ear to ear. The joy on their faces was something to behold. A dad with his lad, someone who has proved himself to be successful in the most unforgiving of professions, had finally, after 25 years, won something. 'He was the first one I thought should get it [the medal] round his neck,' said Moyes. 'I hope he is enjoying it.'

No one from West Ham will ever forget 7 June 2023. The club's first trophy in 43 years. Their first European trophy since 1965. Scorer Bowen, speaking at the post-match press conference, said: 'The party tonight will be crazy. Days like this don't come around often. You have to enjoy them.'

Forty-three years is, indeed, a long time.

Chapter 14

Back in the Europa League 2023/24

Summer News

A matter of days after the Europa Conference League victory, it was announced that, after talks with chairman David Sullivan, David Moyes would continue as West Ham United manager.

The announcement was construed as reassurance from Sullivan for Moyes after the club's poor league form and amid the club's plans to bring in a new head of recruitment. In late June, it was confirmed that Tim Steidten, who had left Bundesliga club Bayer Leverkusen in March, would be joining the club as technical director.

Coincidentally, Moyes lost two of his assistants. Paul Nevin left to join Patrick Vieira's staff at Strasbourg, while Mark Warburton had left his assistant coach role earlier in the summer. Two other trusted members of his backroom staff, Stuart Pearce and Alan Irvine, had left in the summer of 2022.

In mid-July came the long-anticipated news that Declan Rice was to sign for Arsenal for £105m after two earlier bids had been rejected. The 24-year-old had signed his first professional contract with the Hammers in December 2015 and made his first senior appearance on the last day of the 2016/17 Premier League season as a substitute against Burnley, going on to make his first start that August against Southampton. Rice became the club's captain following Mark Noble's retirement in 2022 and, in what proved to be his final season at the London Stadium, was named the Europa Conference League player of the season.

Rice was not the only player to leave Stratford. After only a season, and eight goals in 27 appearances, Gianluca Scamacca joined Atalanta in his native Italy for a reported £21.5m. Also making a permanent move to Italy was Nikola Vlašić, who joined Torino for a reported £11m after a season there on loan. His record in London was one goal in 31 appearances. Other departures were Arthur Masuaku to Beşiktaş for £1.7m and long-serving favourite Manuel Lanzini to River Plate in his native Argentina on a free.

However, with the new season fast approaching, there were no new arrivals as the Declan Rice millions sat in the bank. Already there was speculation about behind-the-scenes conflict between Moyes – who preferred seasoned Premier League players – and the new technical director, who was looking at foreign imports. There were even reports that Moyes was ready to quit the club due to the shambles of a transfer window.

West Ham must have then found the keys to the piggy bank, though, as Mexican international midfielder Edson Álvarez was signed from Ajax in a deal thought to be worth £35m. And despite all the speculation and gossip, there were still pre-season friendlies to be played.

The Hammers kicked off their pre-season with a 4-1 win at Boreham Wood on 10 July. Their next game was on the other side of the world when, only five days later, they lined up against Perth Glory and emerged with a 6-2 victory. It was West Ham's first visit Down Under in 28 years. Their next opponents were more familiar. Tottenham Hotspur were beaten 3-2 in the same Perth stadium.

Then it was back to the UK and the short trip to the Chigwell Construction Stadium for a 2-2 draw with Dagenham and Redbridge.

On 29 July, West Ham travelled to French Ligue 1 outfit Rennes, with the hosts inflicting the Londoners' first defeat in pre-season, 3-1. Worse would follow as Bundesliga side Bayer Leverkusen scored four goals without reply at the BayArena. Not the ideal way to go into a new season.

Predictions

FourFourTwo foresaw a tenth-place finish: 'The plan. Work out a way to move on in the post-Rice era while clinging grimly to the coat tails of the elite cabal at the top of the Premier League. Navigate another European campaign while integrating a host of new players. Do all of this while steering well clear of relegation trouble in a division filled with smarter, better-run clubs. Easy.'

World Soccer predicted: 'The glory of capturing a European trophy should calm the nerves of last campaign and bring mid-table solidity, despite the major loss of midfield lynchpin Declan Rice. His replacement faces a huge task.'

Hammers fan Pete May told *The Observer*: 'Got to be optimistic after our first trophy in 43 years and a Europa League place. But there are still questions for Moyes to answer. Can he get a talented set to perform more consistently and play on the front foot? Thursday-Sunday football will again be a challenge for a small squad.'

In *When Saturday Comes*, supporter Mark Segal tipped West Ham for an 11th-place finish, saying: 'If the money from Declan Rice is invested well, we should be aiming for the top seven. Another joyous European campaign would be a bonus.'

The BBC Sport website, *The Times* and *The Guardian* all predicted the Hammers would finish 11th.

Curiously, no one saw the Hammers challenging for the title!

The 2023/24 Season

West Ham kicked off the new Premier League season with a visit to the seaside for that rarity for them – a 3pm start on a Saturday. Just as it seemed West Ham and Jarrod Bowen would carry on where they left off in last season's Europa Conference League Final, Bournemouth equalised through Dominic Solanke to earn Andoni Iraola a point in his first match in charge in a 1-1 draw.

It emerged that Manchester City had made a £70m offer for Lucas Paquetá. That bid had been rejected but there was a real possibility that Moyes faced losing his two prized assets within weeks of each other.

There was some good news on the incoming transfer front when James Ward-Prowse made his long-rumoured move from relegated Southampton. The fee was reportedly £30m. Useless fact: Ward-Prowse had covered 433.4km in his 38 Premier League matches the previous season, the highest total in the top flight, while averaging 11.4km a game. More to the point, he had missed only two matches in the past four seasons.

Thankfully, Paquetá's potential move to Manchester City was put on ice when news broke that he was being investigated by the FA for alleged breaches of its betting rules. The nature of the allegations was not revealed and it was reported that sources 'close to the player' were shocked by the investigation, insisting that Paquetá had not been accused of making bets. It was understood that City had been close to reaching an agreement with West Ham for the transfer to go ahead before the allegations surfaced.

The new Premier League season continued with the visit of the men from Stamford Bridge and the Hammers secured their first win with a 3-1 triumph. Despite all the attention over the gambling investigation, Paquetá nervelessly stepped up to score a penalty for the third goal in second-half injury time. Nayef Aguerd managed to both score the first goal and get himself sent off after 67 minutes. Alphonse Areola saved a penalty and Ward-Prowse made his debut. 'A ruthless and resilient West Ham once again proved that life under David Moyes is by no means dull,' commented *The Guardian*.

West Ham finished the following weekend on top of the table after a 3-1 victory on the south coast against Brighton, a team they had never beaten in the Premier League in the previous 12 attempts. The performance was a throwback to the West Ham of two seasons previously, having only 21 per cent possession but scoring three times from ruthless counter-attacks. Ward-Prowse, Bowen and Antonio scored, with a late Pascal Gross goal proving no more than a consolation.

Further good news came with Mohammed Kudus, the Ghana international attacking midfielder, signing from Ajax for £38m. Another addition to the squad was Greek international defender Konstantinos Mavropanos from Stuttgart.

In a rare Friday night outing, West Ham played their fourth league game of the season, and the third on the road. They visited newly promoted Luton Town and went home with another three points. Because of building work, this was Luton's first home game of their first ever Premier League season, but the Hammers coped with the attendant extra pressure, with Bowen improving his season's record to three goals, all scored away from home, and one assist. It was not a surprise that Ward-Prowse had slotted in so easily. He provided two assists on his debut against Chelsea, scored against Brighton and swung in a corner for Kurt Zouma to head in West Ham's second goal at Luton.

In the programme for the Chelsea game, Trevor Brooking was asked about the club's chances for the coming season. His comment was that: 'Overall, it would be good to have five or six points from those first half a dozen games which, on paper, look tough.' With ten points after four games, three of which were away from home, it was nice to see Sir Trevor proved wrong!

A true test of West Ham's form came immediately after the international break when champions Manchester

City came to the London Stadium. But for a timely revelation about the FA looking into a breach of betting regulations, Paquetá could have been lining up for the away side.

While West Ham had impressed during their unbeaten start to the season, particularly during the victories over Brighton and Chelsea, the smart money was still on the side which boasted Erling Haaland up front. For 45 minutes on a clammy day in East London, a compact and enterprising West Ham seemed to be giving City their toughest test of the Premier League season so far, going a goal up with a quick-breaking attack. By the last knockings of the second half, however, the scene was more familiar. City were romping towards their fifth straight league win of the season, 3-1 up and heading back to the top of the table.

Europa League group stage: West Ham United 3 FK TSC 1

West Ham's third successive European adventure kicked off on Thursday, 21 September and for much of this contest, the glory days of Prague felt a long way away. By the end, however, West Ham managed to turn a potentially embarrassing evening into a surprisingly spirited victory against the unfancied visitors from Bačka Topola in Serbia. Moyes made nine changes from the team that lost to Manchester City, with only

Ward-Prowse and Paquetá retained, and Kudus and Mavropanos making their full debuts.

TSC punished a lack of urgency when, right at the start of the second half, Petar Stanić dispossessed Angelo Ogbonna near the halfway line and the Italian, the last defender, could do nothing to stop Stanić running through to beat Łukasz Fabiański with a firm finish.

Now West Ham had to stay calm. The entrance of Antonio made a difference, stretching TSC and making space on the flanks. After 66 minutes, Benrahma perked up, twisting and turning before crossing from the left and, as Kudus attacked the ball, Nemanja Petrović turned it into his own net. It was not long before West Ham led. The home team's aerial barrage wore down TSC and Kudus took advantage of poor marking by heading in a Ward-Prowse corner. Tomáš Souček, on as a substitute, made the scoreline look more emphatic by scoring from another Ward-Prowse set piece.

West Ham's record at Liverpool is beyond awful, so a 3-1 defeat on their return to Premier League action should have come as no surprise. Nevertheless, the Hammers were drawing 1-1 at half time after another Bowen goal. Yet they were comfortably eclipsed as Liverpool registered a sixth successive win in all competitions with plenty to spare.

Moyes's visitors started brightly and deserved to head into the interval all square. Once Liverpool's quality on the ball improved in the second half, however, West Ham were subdued and unable to contain the movement around them. Moyes's long wait for a first win at Anfield went on (20 attempts, seven draws, 13 losses). Antonio's confident boast that West Ham would finish above Liverpool looked seriously misplaced.

West Ham made their third-round entrance into the Carabao Cup at League One Lincoln City. It took until the 70th minute to break the deadlock when Souček made a late run into the box to get on the end of Benrahma's corner. Souček was the only player to retain his place from the Liverpool defeat.

Souček played a key role in West Ham finishing sixth in 2020/21. The Czech Republic international offered steel and athleticism in midfield, with his well-timed bursts forward helping him finish as the club's joint top scorer with ten league goals. Yet the next two campaigns were tougher. The 28-year-old looked fatigued at times and there was a slight alteration to his role when Declan Rice began to attack more. Asked to sit back, Souček's goal threat decreased and his passing from deep was scattergun when he was pressed. With Rice sold to Arsenal, Souček was able to push forward again. Moyes had found a nice balance in midfield after signing Ward-Prowse and Álvarez. With Paquetá shifting to an inside-left role, Souček was able to move higher and his goal in West Ham's 2-0 win over Sheffield United was his third in four appearances.

The strange thing was that none of Sheffield United's players even tried to rattle West Ham. Paul Heckingbottom's side were insipid beyond belief on an afternoon devoid of drama and intensity, their defensive foundations crumbling under the slightest pressure, and it said little for their hopes of staying up that they were so easily swatted aside by opponents who scored twice in the opening 37 minutes through Bowen and Souček before spending the second half saving their legs for the upcoming visit to Freiburg in the Europa League. It was manager Moyes's 900th league game and his 666th in the Premier League.

Europa League group stage: SC Freiburg 1 West Ham United 2

West Ham continued their successful start to life in the Europa League with a record-breaking victory on 5 October at Bundesliga outfit Freiburg, who were expected to be their closest rivals in the group stage. Early on, Paquetá leapt highest to head in a well-aimed cross from Bowen to set the Irons on their way. Following their first-half dominance, West Ham were rocked when Roland Sallai struck a close-range equaliser shortly after the restart. However, defender Aguerd nodded a Ward-Prowse corner past Noah Atubolu after 66 minutes to secure the win.

The London club clinched an impressive record by becoming the first English side to go 17 consecutive games in European competition without defeat, winning 16 of them. Pep Guardiola's Manchester City, Don Revie's Leeds and Bill Nicholson's Tottenham had all managed 16 games unbeaten.

Mexican midfielder Álvarez's impressive performances since joining West Ham had helped to soften the blow of losing Rice. Convincing Ajax to sell him for £35m looked like smart business. Álvarez had quickly adjusted to the pace of English football, providing defensive steel and calmness in possession. Tactically aware, he displayed his intelligence by occasionally dropping back to become a third centre-back.

Next up for West Ham were a team who had won their five previous league games and had thumped Paris Saint-Germain 4-1 in the Champions League in midweek. And Newcastle had thrashed Moyes's team 5-1 on their last visit to the London Stadium. Alexander Isak struck twice inside five second-half minutes to cancel out Souček's opening goal. Moyes sent on summer signing Kudus and in the final minute of normal time, he fired in an equaliser from the edge of the penalty area.

In-form Bowen had scored in all four of West Ham's away league games. The only players previously to score in each of their first five away appearances at the start of a Premier League season had been Thierry Henry for Arsenal in 2001/02 and Mohamed Salah for Liverpool in 2021/22. With his goal at Villa Park, Bowen would join that select group. Yet that was the only consolation from a visit to a ground where the Hammers had had some success in recent seasons.

Villa's 4-1 romp against the Hammers was their 11th successive home win, so the Londoners would have been in little doubt about what they were up against in 'El Claretico'. Manager Moyes was predictably upset at his side conceding four goals, blaming individual errors. West Ham entered the game just two points behind Villa but, despite briefly pulling it back to 2-1, never threatened to escape with a point. They would return to European duty sitting ninth in the Premier League.

Europa League group stage: Olympiacos 2 West Ham United 1

David Moyes defended his team selection after West Ham's unbeaten European record was reduced to ruins in Athens on 26 October, their first loss in continental competition in 18 matches.

Moyes made seven changes for their Europa League clash in the Greek capital, but his tinkering backfired as a soft goal from Olympiacos captain Kostas Fortounis after 33 minutes and a deflection from stand-in Hammers skipper Angelo Ogbonna in first-half injury time brought their undefeated run to a halt despite Lucas Paquetá's late volley.

A hostile reception for West Ham was guaranteed at the Georgios Karaiskakis Stadium, with Olympiacos even issuing a warning to their own supporters not to throw missiles or target players with laser pens. That plea came after their match against fierce rivals Panathinaikos the previous Sunday had to be abandoned when a visiting player was hit by a firework hurled from the crowd.

Paquetá halved the deficit with a stunning volley from the edge of the box with four minutes left but, despite a late flurry, the Hammers could not find an equaliser. A victory would have all but secured West Ham's passage into the knockout stages but now they found themselves with work to do, lying level with Freiburg at the top of the group, with Olympiacos two points behind.

West Ham's next opponents, Everton, had made an awful start to the season, but now had three wins from their past five league matches. The latest came against a passive West Ham at the London Stadium, with the Irons seeming to suffer from yet another post-European hangover.

After the first four games of the season, West Ham were already nine points ahead of Everton; six games later, the gap was only four. Moyes's team were, frankly, dreadful in the first half and though they were much improved in the second, they threatened mostly through off-the-cuff individual skills from Paquetá and Kudus rather than slick attacking moves. Dominic

Calvert-Lewin's 51st-minute goal secured the victory for the Toffees.

On Halloween came news that a stake of up to ten per cent in West Ham United had been put up for sale by Vanessa Gold, the daughter of the club's late joint chairman David Gold, and this had reportedly drawn interest from international investors. Gold's family had a 25 per cent shareholding in West Ham and it was understood that if the offer was right, she would be willing to sell the entire shareholding. Czech billionaire Daniel Kretinsky, who bought a 27 per cent share in 2021, was not expected to buy the Gold shares. David Sullivan still retained the biggest stake in West Ham, at just under 39 per cent, while financier Tripp Smith held eight per cent.

Paradoxically, a surprise 3-1 defeat of Arsenal in a Carabao Cup fourth round tie underlined Declan Rice's importance to his new team. Mikel Arteta decided to look at some of his squad players and ended up accusing them of forgetting about the simple things against highly motivated opponents. It must have been jarring for them to hear Arteta talking about Arsenal failing to compete as West Ham, who swept into the quarter-finals thanks to some thrilling attacking from Bowen and Kudus, capitalised on Rice spending the majority of his first return to the London Stadium on the bench.

Moyes, who claimed his first win over Arsenal as West Ham manager, could reflect on a job well done. Álvarez, one of the players brought in to replace Rice, dominated midfield. Bowen starred up front and Kudus scored another magnificent goal. Mavropanos caught the eye against his old side, showing strength and authority next to Aguerd in central defence.

On the following Saturday, West Ham would cross the capital to meet another bogey team and seeking to improve on a dire record in London derbies. Brentford love playing West Ham, having won all four of their meetings since they returned to the top flight.

Fans were beginning to wonder what exactly Moyes says to his players at half-time? That season, West Ham had conceded seven goals during the first 20 minutes of the second half of matches. Moyes put it down to a lack of concentration and focus after his side's 3-2 defeat by Brentford, but there was more to it than that. It felt structural. It felt like a mindset. West Ham had talented attackers, but in the second half against Brentford it was as if they forgot how to play. They dropped back, offered nothing as an attacking force and duly conceded a messy equaliser. Brentford were rewarded for being more assertive. West Ham were in a bind. Their caution was holding them back.

If Moyes found himself struggling to understand how a performance featuring a stunning goal from Kudus had not yielded a reward, he only had to look at his team ceding the initiative during yet another flat second half. It was not enough to point at Antonio failing to convert an open goal when West Ham led 2-1. One miss could not excuse this collective failure. It was the latest example of West Ham floundering after sitting on a lead. They were unambitious, their threat on the counter-attack non-existent. It was a misguided plan. It could not work with Zouma absent in defence and the suspended Álvarez unable to provide defensive security in midfield. The Hammers would end the day in the bottom half of the Premiership (12th) for the first time all season.

Europa League group stage: West Ham United 1 Olympiacos 0

There was something special about West Ham when they played at home on Thursday nights. An English record ninth successive home victory in European competition – surpassing Manchester City's mark – courtesy of a superb goal from Paquetá gave Moyes's side the revenge they craved since losing to the Greek side last time out. The victory on 9 November virtually sealed progression from the Europa League group stage with two games to spare.

This was far from a vintage performance as West Ham laboured for much of this match. But it was mission accomplished for Moyes, who has endured a testing few weeks after the highs of the Europa Conference

League triumph the previous season. Moyes had been sufficiently scarred by the defeat in Greece a fortnight earlier that he made only three changes from the team that made it four losses from their last five matches in all competitions against Brentford at the weekend.

Olympiacos had won against Arsenal on their two last visits to the capital, in 2020 and 2021 in the knockout stages of the Europa League, and despite the best efforts of the graceful Paquetá, the Greek side managed to frustrate West Ham for large periods by slowing the game down. Ward-Prowse set up Paquetá for his winning goal after 73 minutes. The Brazil international timed his run to perfection to connect sweetly with the chipped ball over the Olympiacos defence and an enormous cheer greeted confirmation that the goal would stand after it had initially been ruled out for offside.

Back at the London Stadium three days later, yet another Europa League hangover loomed for West Ham when they trailed 2-1 to Nottingham Forest after 63 minutes. Then Ward-Prowse intervened, whipping two beauties into the box, one headed home by Bowen for the equaliser and the second nodded in by Souček in the 88th minute to provide an unlikely win.

Even though they must have known precisely what was coming, Forest's failure to deal with Ward-Prowse's expert delivery from corners and Souček's aerial prowess cost them the point to which they had been clinging after

Bowen's headed equaliser. It was a welcome first league win in five matches for the Hammers.

Burnley's appalling form continued with defeat at home to West Ham despite leading until the 86th minute. A Dara O'Shea own goal and a Souček volley settled the match late on. Jay Rodriguez had scored from the spot to put the hosts ahead after Luca Koleosho was brought down in the box. Kudus, the man who gave away the penalty, more than made amends for that indiscretion with a second assist for Souček as his cross found the midfielder in space at the back post to strike into an empty net for his fourth in four matches for club and country, silencing Turf Moor in the process.

Europa League group stage: FK TSC 0 West Ham United 1

Tomáš Souček scored yet another late winner as West Ham secured their place in the Europa League knockout stage with victory at the TSC Arena in Bačka Topola, Serbia on 30 November. It had been a turgid display from Moyes's side, with only one shot on target until Souček met Maxwel Cornet's cross after 89 minutes for his fifth goal in his past five games for club and country.

The Czech had scored in three successive West Ham games for the first time, with each of them being a winning goal and coming later than the 88th minute. His goal meant West Ham had scored in 20 successive

European games, winning 18 and losing only once. Their performance was often slow and ponderous, which was likely down to the seven changes Moyes made from their Premier League win at Burnley the previous Saturday.

Losing Rice in the summer was always going to be difficult for West Ham, but one silver lining was clear. Souček had returned to goalscoring form, netting seven goals in all competitions for the Hammers since Rice left. 'He is back at it and that is good for us,' said his manager. 'We need someone to step up. He's playing with more confidence. We tried to get Declan to get a little bit further forward at times and it might have had a slight effect on Tomáš.'

One reason Moyes signed Ward-Prowse was to provide accurate deliveries for his tall centre-backs and the 6ft 4in Souček. Moyes felt his side could do better from set pieces after 11 of their 42 league goals (26 per cent) came from them the previous season and 14 from 60 goals (23 per cent) two seasons previously.

There are some games in which, you suspect, the two managers could have shaken hands on a draw before kick-off and nobody would much have minded. From the moment Odsonne Édouard levelled eight minutes after half-time when the Hammers hosted Crystal Palace, the game felt certain to finish level and all that was left was for the two sides to go through the motions, fulfilling the contract to provide 90 minutes for the Sky cameras. The growing number of empty seats on a dank, raw afternoon in East London suggested few who had paid for tickets felt a similar obligation.

West Ham had taken a 13th minute lead with a goal of misleading quality, Ward-Prowse sweeping a crossfield pass to Coufal, whose first-time cross found Kudus. His shot took a nick off Marc Guéhi on its way past Sam Johnstone. When Crystal Palace did score, the sixth goal West Ham had conceded in the first 15 minutes of the second half since the beginning of October, it was gifted them by Mavropanos's poor backpass. Édouard took the opportunity almost apologetically, squeezing it just inside the far post at a pace in keeping with the general torpor. The West Ham manager had overseen some stirring performances in East London, but after 97 soporific minutes of 'action' against Palace, it was safe to say this would not be remembered among them.

West Ham had now surrendered 12 points from winning positions in the Premier League during the season. Only Burnley had lost more and it was a statistic not helped by a worrying habit of conceding between minutes 45 and 60 (16 times in 2023).

When West Ham visited the Tottenham Hotspur Stadium, their possession count never got above 25 per cent but Moyes's players could afford to be patient. They came, they saw, they counter-attacked. Bowen and Ward-

Prowse scored second-half goals that spun the game out of Tottenham's orbit in their own backyard. From a dominant first-half siege to a desperate chasing of a game and a looming defeat, Spurs could never quite come to terms with themselves.

An embattled West Ham found their feet in the second half and sensed that Spurs would cough up chances. The two goals the Hammers eventually scored were chiselled out of nothing by Moyes's forwards. Fleeting opportunities were turned into something much greater by the hard running of Bowen and Kudus, who were prepared to chase the ball up the pitch and count on getting the returns.

From the sublime to the really ridiculous. A 5-0 defeat to Fulham at Craven Cottage represented West Ham's worst defeat in any competition since 2011. 'We used up too much energy in midweek,' was Moyes's excuse. 'Another Thursday fixture while Fulham had a Wednesday fixture. No excuse for the result but it played a part in it.'

His players looked off the pace and fatigued. The contest was over before half-time as Fulham put three goals past Fabiański. Despite damage-limiting substitutions and a shift to a back five, Fulham scored two more in the second half. It was abundantly clear that many of the visiting players had lost their appetite for a fight and wanted the experience to end.

Captain Zouma issued a scathing assessment of his team's abysmal show, admitting they were 'nowhere near the levels' required and calling it one of the worst displays during his time at the club. 'They were better everywhere on the pitch,' Zouma told the West Ham website. 'They ran more than us, they wanted to win more than us, physically they were sharper than us. We couldn't deal with them today. Physically, we were nowhere near the levels. Even mentally, I would say we were nowhere near the levels – me first. It's a day to forget and we have to take responsibility.'

Zouma refused to follow his manager's lead in using the difference in recovery time as an excuse. 'I don't know … maybe,' the Frenchman said, when asked whether it had affected the result. 'But we're professionals and we're used to playing Thursday and Sunday.'

The Fulham fiasco revived the speculation about Moyes's future. Jacob Steinberg in *The Guardian* wrote that he 'remains secure in his job'. According to Steinberg: 'The club are not in a rush to make a managerial change and are confident Moyes can inspire an improvement as the team head into a key period of the season. There is less confidence that Moyes will still be in his post at the start of next season. The Scot's deal expires next summer and only a strong end to this campaign will convince West Ham to offer him a new deal.

'Equally, there have been misgivings over Moyes's managerial style for a while. He came close to the sack on several occasions last season and there have been complaints over his pragmatic tactics. Doubts have been expressed from within the dressing room and some supporters have grumbled about the football. The stability provided by Moyes means that West Ham are under no pressure to make a change.'

Gary Jacob in *The Times* reported: 'Discontent had been brewing at West Ham United long before their latest poor performance at Fulham.' West Ham had signed some high-quality players in the summer, but Moyes had not adapted his playing style to get the best from them.

Europa League group stage: West Ham United 2 Freiburg 0

West Ham United booked their place in the last 16 of the Europa League with a commanding 2-0 win against Freiburg on 14 December. West Ham spent the best part of £75m on two Ajax players in the summer and their influence on this display was perhaps the best evidence yet that it was money well spent.

Álvarez climbed out of his sickbed to create the first for the excellent Kudus, before the Mexico midfielder added the second shortly before half-time to put West Ham firmly in control. Despite the doubts about Moyes's future at the club beyond the end of the season, the result meant West Ham had now won their group in European competition for the third consecutive season.

Some of West Ham's play during the first half was magnificent. In the 14th minute, Álvarez clipped a simple ball over Freiburg's static back four and Kudus, darting inside from right to left, was through. The Ghana winger had all the time in the world to control with his chest and slip the ball beyond Noah Atubolu with his left foot. Three minutes before half-time, the advantage was doubled. Álvarez found Bowen on the edge of the penalty area and continued his run. Bowen's return pass was both smart and perfectly executed, leaving the midfielder with the simplest of finishes from 12 yards to score his first goal for the club.

By topping their group, West Ham again avoided the round of 32 and would not return to European action until late March 2024. The focus now was on the Premier League and the two domestic cup competitions. It would be a long and testing three months.

Winter of Discontent

Lucas Paquetá may have made David Moyes feel like pulling out his hair at times, but the Brazilian showed his class with three brilliant assists when the Hammers returned to Premier League action against Wolves. The 26-year-old dazzled in tandem with Kudus in a 3-0 win and the West Ham manager admitted his star player, Paquetá, had been given some extra 'leeway' to accommodate his talent. 'He's a special player. I've not had a huge amount of special players with that amount of talent,' said Moyes. 'There's a bit of leeway we have to give him. As I've got a bit older, I've realised when they have that talent you have to let them flourish. But his workrate as well for the team has been excellent.'

Two goals in the space of ten first-half minutes from Kudus inspired West Ham to a fourth successive home victory that left Moyes's side clutching the coat tails of the Premier League's top six.

On to the Carabao Cup and it became 21 visits to Anfield as a manager for Moyes and still no victory to toast. More dispiriting was the fact that at no point did West Ham even threaten to make the evening uncomfortable, with a first shot on target coming with Jarrod Bowen's 77th-minute consolation strike. Otherwise, they were as lamentable and powder-puff as Liverpool were clinical and motivated. The paucity of West Ham's play would have dismayed Moyes and the manner of the loss could not be blamed just on his team selection. Ward-Prowse had started 16 of the past 17 matches and Paquetá 11 of the past 12, but both began on the bench. That might have prompted eyebrows to be raised, given what was at stake, although it perhaps should not have been a surprise given the only game Ward-Prowse did not start of those 17 was the victory over Arsenal in the previous round. Simply put, too many players were too timid and, by the end, were not even bothering to do the basics of tracking runners. That would have infuriated Moyes, who had endured some beatings at Anfield in the past but never anything like this surrender.

Manchester United were the visitors to Stratford on the brink of Christmas. West Ham did not even have to play particularly well and once the home side scored there was only ever going to be one winner. Goalkeeper André Onana allowed Bowen a second bite at the cherry for his goal, while teenager Kobbie Mainoo's mistake was taken advantage of by Kudus.

It was from a Paquetá ball over the top of the United defence that Bowen opened the scoring in the 72nd minute. Onana was given one opportunity to stop the forward but gave him a second chance from close range to net his third goal in three games. One goal would no doubt have been enough for West Ham to beat this toothless United, but the home team put the result beyond doubt six minutes later. Mainoo failed to control a pass out of defence from Jonny Evans and Kudus took the ball before rifling a shot past Onana.

A post-Christmas visit to the Emirates would normally see the East Londoners leave without any late Christmas presents. This was the kind of game which felt hard for Arsenal to lose by one goal, let alone two, against a Moyes team that could be brittle or stubborn in equal measure. With 77 touches in the West Ham penalty area – a Premier League record for an attacking side according to data going back to 2009 – Arsenal had 30 attempts on goal. West Ham had 26 per cent possession and 100 per cent of the benefit of the doubt for the first goal, which was marginal to say the least. When substitute Benrahma had his penalty, given for a foul by Declan Rice, saved by David Raya in the sixth minute of time added on at the end of the game, it was just West Ham's third attempt on target all evening. The two others had resulted in goals.

Moyes's team were capable of pulling off this kind of heist. Thrashed at Craven Cottage and Anfield, winners away at Tottenham and then at home against Manchester United, this was another milestone in the tumultuous West Ham season of 2023/24. From West Ham's first meaningful attack, Emerson whipped in a devilish cross from the left, curving around Rice and causing Gabriel and Oleksandr Zinchenko to get in a horrible tangle. The ball ricocheted off the latter and only just flew past the post, before Bowen poked it back into the six-yard box, where an unmarked Souček sidefooted into the net. The goal stood after VAR could find no conclusive evidence to show the ball had gone out of play before Bowen's cross. When Ben White then had to turn behind a dangerous Emerson cross, it proved a critical moment. From the corner, whipped in with his usual quality by Ward-Prowse, Arsenal old boy Mavropanos got the run on Gabriel and planted an unstoppable header into the net off the crossbar.

West Ham's final Christmas and New Year fixture saw them at home to Brighton on 2 January, which perhaps played a role in a game of low tempo and few opportunities. This was a game that made it hard not to wonder if there is such a thing as too much football. These were two tired, injury-hit teams trying their best and giving their all without ever really suggesting they had the wit or energy to score a goal. Brighton kept their first Premier League clean sheet of the season, the first time in 24 league matches they had not conceded, ending an unwanted club record run. Brighton had more possession and better chances at the London Stadium in what was a largely dour game to open 2024 for both clubs, but were unable to break through a West Ham defence which, in contrast, had now kept four consecutive clean sheets.

It says an awful lot about West Ham fans that more than 62,000 would turn up at the London Stadium on a January Sunday afternoon for an FA Cup tie against a Championship side. Bristol City earned a deserved draw against their Premier League opponents to force an FA Cup third-round replay.

The Hammers wasted little time in moving through the gears, opening the scoring with just four minutes on the clock. Bowen continued his red hot form by scoring his 14th goal of the campaign after rounding goalkeeper Max O'Leary and squeezing the ball under the body of defender Cameron Pring on the line.

The Robins returned for the second period with intent, playing the majority of their football in West Ham's half of the field, and their willingness to commit to the attack paid dividends when academy graduate Tommy Conway found space behind the Hammers' backline before drilling beyond Fabiański to give his side a 1-1 draw.

Moyes had put out a strong side, but he was left counting the cost of three injuries. Paquetá and Mavropanos were both substituted in the first half with issues, while goalscorer Bowen finished the game but required treatment after the final whistle before subsequently limping down the tunnel.

West Ham's next game was the replay at Ashton Gate. Misery, again, for the Londoners, who were needlessly reduced to ten men on a febrile night and looked woefully short in attack without the likes of Bowen. Moyes, who played for Bristol City in the 1980s, conceded they had been 'very good' over the two matches. In only the third minute, Conway, who had struck the equaliser at the London Stadium, intercepted Mavropanos' dreadful pass and rounded Fabiański to slot home from a narrow angle.

It took a solid 20 minutes for a rattled West Ham, deprived of key attacking talent, to impose anything approaching the sparkling displays they had sometimes shown in the Premier League. They came within inches of equalising as Danny Ings received the ball with his back to goal and fired narrowly wide. Any hopes of a fightback were torpedoed by a petulant Benrahma, however, as he kicked out at Joe Williams following the City midfielder's badly-timed challenge. After a melee, calm was restored and referee Darren England sent Benrahma packing. With him went West Ham's FA Cup hopes for the season.

West Ham's next Premier League outing took them to Sheffield United, who were clearly on a one-way trip back to the Championship. This game ended as an advert for the frantic and unpredictable nature of the Premier League, with added time featuring red cards for Rhian Brewster and Coufal, plus a controversial penalty awarded for goalkeeper Areola's challenge on Oli McBurnie. The latter's penalty kick in the 103rd minute of a game that had flared up from the moment, 24 minutes earlier, when Ward-Prowse caused delirium among the away fans directly behind Wes Foderingham's goal by blazing in the penalty to put the visitors ahead for a second time. Cornet's opener – like Ben Brereton Díaz's first equaliser for Sheffield United – was his maiden strike for West Ham since signing two summers earlier.

At the end of January, West Ham announced the signing of England midfielder Kalvin Phillips on loan until the end of the season. It appeared that so much would depend on if, and how quickly, Phillips could rediscover the buzz that made him such a wonderful watch under Marcelo Bielsa at Leeds United. Since signing for Manchester City in August 2022, he had made only two Premier League starts.

If Phillips thought the journey back from the fringes would be an easy one, here was a reminder of the relentless nature of the Premier League. Phillips was only three minutes into his West Ham United debut when a rusty, underhit backpass was snaffled by Bournemouth's Dominic Solanke and slammed in. Ward-Prowse's second-half penalty ensured his mistake did not lead to defeat at the London Stadium but even a draw felt like an opportunity missed in the race for a fourth successive season of European football.

In other transfer news, Pablo Fornals joined Spanish outfit Real Betis on a permanent transfer for an undisclosed fee. The 27-year-old returned to Spain after four and a half seasons with the Hammers, during which he made 203 appearances and scored 23 goals. Benrahma joined French Ligue 1 club Olympique Lyonnais on loan until the end of the 2023/24 season, including an option of making the transfer permanent in the summer. Algeria winger Benrahma signed for West Ham from Brentford in October 2020 and had gone on to play 155 times in claret and blue. German defender Thilo Kehrer joined Ligue 1 club Monaco on loan. The arrival of Phillips apart, there was no sign of any incomings despite the obvious need for a forward to provide support and competition for the injury-prone 34-year-old Antonio.

At the beginning of February, Moyes took his team to Old Trafford. Despite the 0-3 scoreline, it was a tight game. West Ham were determined to ensure United would not have it all their own way. They mustered 22 shots all told but only three were on target – a wastefulness epitomised by Emerson's miss. Even at two goals down, West Ham had a chance to pull one back, only for Diogo Dalot to make a stupendous block after Bowen had delayed his shot a fraction too long after being released by Álvarez.

Alejandro Garnacho scored his second when he shot low into the corner from Scott McTominay's pass after Phillips had lost possession. Phillips's reaction to being hounded off the ball by a combination of McTominay and Højlund left much to be desired. The England midfielder did not even attempt to give chase. Manager Moyes reflected: 'We played better than when we beat them [2-0 at home] in December. I enjoyed my team's performance but not the result.'

West Ham had already beaten title-chasing Arsenal twice during the season, but when the Gunners travelled to the London Stadium on 11 February, Moyes was forced to watch his side turn in one of the worst performances during his time in charge. He admitted his team 'fell apart' and were 'weak' as they suffered their joint-biggest home defeat, with thousands of fans streaming out of the stadium in disgust after conceding four goals before half-time. If losing 5-0 at Fulham was bad, how do you describe a 6-0 loss at home?

Kalvin Phillips came on with the score already 4-0. By the final half hour, with Arsenal taking turns in attempting to tee up Mohamed Elneny for a final banter goal, the notion there was anyone in the West Ham team with a compelling claim to match Rice's levels at the Euros seemed a little distant. Perhaps there was also a clue as to why Rice had sharpened his all-round game under Arteta, for whom midfield is an obsession, as opposed to a coach in Moyes who seems at times to want to play without one.

When the sixth and final goal of this humiliation came, it had to be Rice. The former West Ham hero had already set up goals with whipped dead ball deliveries for William Saliba and Gabriel – goals number one and three – when Ben White cut back, and Leandro Trossard and Martin Ødegaard left it for each other. Enter Rice. The midfielder's shot from outside the area curled away from Areola to find the far corner and the sound you heard was of seats clicking back and thousands more making for the exits. Rice did not celebrate and when he was substituted immediately afterwards, there was generous applause from those West Ham fans who had stayed.

West Ham had beaten Arsenal 2-0 at the Emirates Stadium on 28 December, a result that now seemed to have been lifted from another lifetime. The Hammers had not won since and if the final scoreline was then worse was the complete absence of fight, especially in defensive situations.

There was no secret about what Moyes wanted to do – remain compact and punch hard and fast on the counter. Yet his team could get nothing going. Their first-half performance was an abdication; it was no exaggeration to say that Arsenal could have been 7-0 up by the end of it.

The records that tumbled:

- West Ham suffered the joint-heaviest home defeat in their league history, while the only other time they had lost by six goals in the top flight came back in December 1963 against Blackburn Rovers (8-2).
- For only the second time in the Premier League, a side managed by Moyes conceded six or more goals in a home game – both instances came in matches against Arsenal (Everton 1 Arsenal 6 in August 2009).
- This was Moyes's 683rd game in the Premier League and the first time he had seen his side go in at half-time trailing by four goals. Indeed, it was also the first time a Moyes team had conceded four goals in the first half of a Premier League match.

Former West Ham striker Tony Cottee blamed the club's board for the continuing uncertainty over Moyes's contract, as well as a quiet transfer window that only saw Phillips come into the club on loan from Manchester City. 'Absolute shambles. Club will never change with this board,' Cottee wrote on X. 'No investment in the window and a manager with five months left on his contract. Players, tactics and the result were poor today. Where do we go from here? I don't know.'

Inevitably, there were reports that the 'mood has changed' at West Ham and that the club were 'looking at potential replacements' for Moyes. One report claimed: 'West Ham owner David Sullivan is yet to be convinced whether to hand a new contract to Moyes as he is frustrated with numerous issues at the club.'

Since that win at the Emirates, Bowen had not scored or assisted in any of the five games he had played in, culminating in the no-show against Arsenal. The correlation between his output and the team's struggles was clear and was only exacerbated by the lack of a creative influence in the absence of the injured Paquetá and the dip in form from Kudus, who had struggled to get up to speed since his return from the Africa Cup of Nations.

There was frustration over reports that half a dozen transfer deals had been set up during January but had not materialised due to disagreements between Moyes and technical director Tim Steidten.

It was become a running joke at West Ham; Moyes always seemed one defeat away from the sack. Even in the seasons when he delivered sixth- and seventh-place finishes, a section of the Hammers support remained unhappy with the Scot. And although the Europa Conference League triumph may have cast his Hammers legacy in iron, it was now a distant memory as familiar rumbles of discontent reappeared. So, next up was a trip to relegation strugglers Nottingham Forest at the City Ground.

Towards the end of another chastening afternoon for West Ham, a 'Moyes out' banner was unfurled in the away end from which the majority of travelling supporters had already long departed. The 2-0 defeat was another excruciating experience, with loan signing Phillips sent off after two cautions within two minutes and 56 seconds of each other as West Ham became the first team since 5 November to fail to score against Forest in the Premier League.

Where was the expected response after the 6-0 battering at the hands of Arsenal? Nowhere to be seen. West Ham had their moments, Antonio letting one chance pass him by as he over-elaborated against his former club, but, barring a brief rally before Phillips's 71st-minute red card, the rare Hammers' opportunities came courtesy of Forest's carelessness rather than any great invention on their part.

After Moyes equalled his worst run in charge of the club with eight winless games – an unwanted feat last chalked up when he started his second stint at the helm in early 2020 – the West Ham players went over to applaud the travelling supporters, some of whom held up banners saying 'Moyes out' and 'GSB out' – the latter a reference to Vanessa Gold, David Sullivan and Karren Brady.

Social media was naturally awash with yet more talk about Moyes's future, but the club were doing their best to dampen down speculation. The latest rumour was that the club was under pressure to convince Tim Steidten not to leave his technical director role at the end of the season. There was growing concern that Steidten was not happy in East London and could walk away in the summer. 'Sources' claimed he was frustrated with the way West Ham operated and that he felt he had not been given enough power. There had been uneasiness between Steidten and Moyes the previous summer and internal tensions had grown during the January transfer window, when Moyes was not aligned with the recruitment team on attacking targets.

The trend had long been set. Every time Moyes was on the verge of being sacked, his team put in a performance that pulled him back from the brink. Enter Brentford, who had beaten West Ham home and away in every meeting since they were promoted to the Premier League. All season, it seemed that Moyes's fate depended largely on Jarrod Bowen, whose Europa Conference League Final heroics were fading by the day as the season threatened to descend into darkness. One hat-trick later, taking him to a career-best 14 Premier League goals for the season, and everything seemed rosy again.

It had been a trying start to the year for the striker and his team. Bowen had not scored a Premier League goal since December 2023 and West Ham had not won a league game in 2024, but Bowen's three goals against Brentford demonstrated his clinical edge. The first was a gorgeous outside-of-the-boot finish after five minutes. Two minutes later, he had a simpler chance from a Coufal pass, but there was the briefest delay to Bowen's run, ensuring he could sweep it home without breaking stride. The third, a header, was admittedly made easier by Brentford's Kristoffer Ajer temporarily forgetting about the concept of marking.

'Bowen was unplayable,' lamented Brentford manager Thomas Frank. But look beyond Bowen's hat-trick – and Emerson upstaging all three goals with a faultless long-range fourth – and the key to West Ham's success was the returning Lucas Paquetá. The winless run had coincided with his injury and he was a subtly important presence against Brentford, linking play with a vision and accuracy which his team had badly lacked.

The *Daily Telegraph* suggested that: 'West Ham fans may reflect on the nightmarish vision of what a post-

David Moyes world looks like. Evertonians used to be like them once, back in the days when their team hovered frustratingly in the Europa League places, craving that elusive next step towards the promised land of Champions League qualification and the major trophies they see their legends lifting on the murals around the stadium. All the debates currently aired in London's East End were first broadcast in Merseyside's pubs after the most frustrating defeats between 2002 and 2013; that more "style" was needed, others were moving forward more progressively, and when it came to the killer instinct separating competitors from winners, Moyes was more suited to laying foundations than building upon them.'

On his latest return to Goodison Park, Moyes landed another blow on his old club with a 3-1 victory. Here, the breaker was provided by the right boot of Souček, who flashed a shot beyond Jordan Pickford in stoppage time to set up a victory that for long periods had looked beyond them. It was a strike good enough to be included in *Match of the Day*'s best goals of the month. A breakaway goal in the 95th minute from Álvarez compounded Everton's pain. Everton were even awarded their first penalty of the season, but Areola dived to his left to repel a rather tame effort from Beto. West Ham's first goal had come from a Ward-Prowse corner. His usual pinpoint delivery was met by captain Zouma, who looped a header into the far corner.

Back-to-back wins eased the pressure, temporarily at least, on under-fire Moyes and provided the perfect build-up for the resumption of West Ham's bid for a second European trophy in as many seasons as they returned to Freiburg for the first leg of their Europa League round of 16 tie on 7 March.

Europa League round of 16 first leg: Freiburg 1 West Ham United 0

West Ham's team hotel was targeted by loud pyrotechnics on the night before this clash. Then, on the pitch, there were VAR fireworks that left David Moyes fuming with referee Alejandro Hernández.

Moyes insisted that UEFA referees would normally give a spot-kick when Noah Weißhaupt handled in the area as he challenged Tomáš Souček, but Hernández ruled no penalty after taking several minutes to decide. It meant Michael Gregoritsch's late goal put West Ham's European adventure under severe threat.

A century earlier, West Ham were the first English team to visit Germany after the First World War. The tour included a loss to Freiburg, but at least on that occasion West Ham had the excuse of a six-hour train journey. Now, in 2024, it was hard to tell that West Ham were favourites following their wins over Freiburg during the group stage. The Hammers struggled to put moves together in the first half and wasted their best chances after the interval.

Moyes raged at his team's poor passing for much of a forgettable first half. They created little after Bowen volleyed wide from a Kudus cross. Paquetá repeatedly losing possession was not a good sign. There was no control in midfield. Kudus toiled on the right and Ward-Prowse did nothing in open play. Yet Freiburg, who were ninth in the Bundesliga after a patchy run, also lacked conviction.

In the end, the decisive move came from Freiburg coach Christian Streich, who brought on Gregoritsch as a substitute and saw the Austrian striker tap home from Roland Sallai's cross. This was only Freiburg's second win in 90 minutes in any competition in 2024.

When the Hammers returned to domestic action three days later, Moyes was again left furious after his side were denied a vital late penalty for the second time in a week.

Goals from Paquetá and substitute Danny Ings saw the Hammers come from 2-0 down to draw with struggling Burnley. West Ham were lifeless in a poor first half where they did not manage a shot on target. However, the Hammers reappeared after the break looking like a different side and pulled a goal back within 30 seconds of the restart. Paquetá showed the desire which had previously been missing to press Burnley high, winning back possession to go clean through and calmly stroke the ball past Clarets' keeper James Trafford. Moyes's side continued to press for a leveller but Burnley looked set to hang on for victory until Ings's dramatic late intervention.

The relationship between a section of the West Ham fanbase and their manager had always felt fractious and a home defeat by Burnley would have been further fuel for Moyes's detractors. While the Scot did not escape criticism after a draw against one of the worst sides in the league, the fightback at least meant he did not feel the full brunt of the home support's frustrations at the final whistle. However, the loud boos after Burnley's second goal and at half-time illustrated how quickly Hammers fans could voice their displeasure.

Europa League round of 16 second leg: West Ham United 5 Freiburg 0 Aggregate 5-1

It is not just West Ham's season that hinged on the outcome of this game on 14 March. Domestic rivals Tottenham and Aston Villa were paying close attention, as were Brighton, Wolves, Newcastle and Chelsea. This was because the result could turn out to be crucial in deciding which country got one of UEFA's coveted new European performance spots and an extra place in Europe. The outcome depended on the overall progress of English clubs in Europe and with several already falling by the wayside, success for West Ham could prove vital.

Although this win cannot be considered on a par with the Hammers' big knockout successes against Lyon and Sevilla in the Europa League two years earlier, given Freiburg's limited quality, the way the Hammers despatched the German side was impressively clinical and businesslike.

Paquetá's goal after nine minutes settled the nerves and levelled the scores on aggregate, and the tie was effectively over by the 52nd minute when Aaron Cresswell made it 3-0 with a superb finish. In between, Bowen had scored after 32 minutes to mark his England call-up with a first European goal of the season. Kudus capped off the performance with two brilliant goals after 77 and 85 minutes, illustrating the quality in this Hammers team which the Germans simply could not live with.

While this was a thoroughly professional team display, Kudus utterly stole the show with his two superb goals, particularly his first and West Ham's fourth. Picking up the ball deep inside his own, the Ghanaian dribbled through several Freiburg players before coolly slotting the ball into the bottom corner. It was a magnificent piece of individual quality, even if Freiburg had already thrown in the towel. Kudus's second goal was also eye-catching, an unerring strike from more than 20 yards which flew past the goalkeeper. It proved to be his last contribution before being substituted to a well-deserved standing ovation.

Thursday night in Stratford may not sound like the most glamorous occasion to outsiders but, for those of a West Ham persuasion, these were becoming the occasions to savour above all the rest.

This latest victory at the London Stadium on a European night, over a Freiburg side that was overpowered from the first minute, was West Ham's 11th consecutive home win in European competition.

It had been an impressive and thrilling run, featuring 30 goals, and one which had delighted a fanbase who always came out in full force under the midweek lights. Not even a 5.45pm kick-off, at the height of London's rush hour, deterred the West Ham faithful.

For Moyes, victory secured a third consecutive European quarter-final. 'From where we have come from, to be in another quarter-final is a brilliant achievement,' he said. 'The club has moved on so much.'

Three days after the demolition of Freiburg, the Hammers had two goals ruled out at the London Stadium, with Moyes again left cursing his team's luck after the longest VAR check in Premier League history (five minutes and 37 seconds) saw his side denied a dramatic late winner against Aston Villa. The Hammers were forced to settle for a 1-1 draw after Souček's close-range effort was ruled out deep into stoppage time for handball. Nicolò Zaniolo rescued a point for Champions League-chasers Villa, scoring in the 79th minute.

Antonio had put the Hammers in front after scoring his first Premier League goal since August 2023. The Jamaica international executed a superb diving header, getting on the end of Coufal's pinpoint delivery in the 29th minute. Antonio had a second ruled out for handball shortly after the break when he was adjudged to have used his arm to convert a Bowen cross.

On 20 March, *The Times* ran a piece entitled 'Academies creating golden age of talented youngsters', in which it highlighted the fact that, in 2023/24, 'the number of minutes accrued by players aged 21 and under has climbed by about 25 per cent'. *The Times* printed a table of Premier League minutes played by players who were aged 21 or under. Top came Burnley with 7,553 minutes while Fulham were bottom with 74. Tellingly, West Ham were next to bottom with 76. Surprising perhaps from a club who won the FA Youth Cup the previous season and whose under-21 side were sitting second in Premier League 2. The article provided further evidence for those Hammers fans who were frustrated with Moyes's reluctance to blood youngsters.

On the pitch, Moyes faced more criticism. If it wasn't bad enough that West Ham should lose to Newcastle United at St James' Park after being 3-1 up – conceding goals in the 90th and 94th minutes – there was yet more woe for Kalvin Phillips as he conceded a penalty at 3-1 and then generated headlines by confronting a West Ham fan after the match.

Moyes seemed to forget that he was a 60-year-old, such were the myriad emotions that informed his body language throughout a true rollercoaster of an afternoon. Despite their poor start to 2024, West Ham remained very much in the European race, but their optimism was shaken by a game that soured their manager's Easter. West Ham's defensive frailties were not new, just simply more exposed.

The collapse at Newcastle emphasised the importance of Edson Álvarez, who was missing at St James' Park. In signing the Mexican, Moyes had secured about as good a Rice replacement as could have been expected. Since his full debut, Álvarez had started all but five league games. In those, West Ham shipped three goals at Brentford, five at Fulham, two at Sheffield United, four at Newcastle and two in 45 minutes at home to Burnley before the Mexican's half-time introduction.

After just five minutes of Tottenham's trip across town to the London Stadium, they were strolling and passing as if these were their glory days of September all over again. Pass, pass, pass and then Brennan Johnson converted at the back post. It was pretty football, leading to a pretty goal. Just as they took a grip of this game, though, it slipped away from them in the London rain. West Ham fought back from a set piece, scoring through captain Zouma, and the Hammers had many of the better opportunities over the course of the night.

In the end, both sides had reason to feel that two points had been lost. For Spurs, because this draw left them two points behind Villa. For Moyes and West Ham, now three points behind Manchester United, because they failed to capitalise on the vulnerability in the visiting defence.

Moyes would have been pleased by the defensive performance of his team. Such solidity had not always been found, even at the London Stadium, during the course of the season. Johnson's early goal for Spurs was the 55th West Ham had conceded in the Premier League during the 2023/24 season. To give that number some meaning, consider this: they conceded 55 in the whole of the previous season when they finished 14th. In other words, West Ham were a much better side than they were a year ago, despite being considerably worse defensively. Indeed, not since 2010/11 had a West Ham defence shipped goals as regularly as this one.

When West Ham followed up with a 2-1 win at Wolves on 6 April, former Hammer Gary O'Neil claimed his players felt they were not respected by referees and described the decision to disallow what would have been a 99th-minute equaliser from Max Kilman as one of the worst decisions he had seen. Sadly, instead of this match at Molineux being remembered for the spectacle, it was subsumed by the discourse over refereeing that was continuing to suck the life out of the game.

There had been few matches all season that better embodied the game of two halves cliché. In the first half, Wolves were sublime. In the second period, though, Moyes's tactical changes transformed West Ham into the ascendant side. A double change – Antonio and Ben Johnson for Souček and Coufal – transformed the visiting team, who equalised through Paquetá's penalty, then took the lead when Ward-Prowse scored direct from a corner.

Referee Tony Harrington had been at the centre of most of the big moments in the match. He awarded a penalty to each side, converted by Pablo Sarabia and Paquetá, and disallowed a goal from Emerson. The referee also gave West Ham the corner that Ward-Prowse swung directly into the far corner, although the wind and José Sá were far more influential than the officials on that one.

The win kept alive the Hammers' hopes of qualifying for Europe again via their Premier League position. They could still make it into the Champions League by winning the Europa League – but they were about to face their stiffest test yet as they prepared to face Bayer Leverkusen in their quarter-final first leg on 11 April.

Europa League quarter-final first leg: Bayer Leverkusen 2 West Ham United 0

West Ham knew they had their work cut out against Bayer Leverkusen if they were to reach a third European semi-final in as many seasons. It wasn't just that Leverkusen were nearly home and hosed in their pursuit of a first Bundesliga title. And it wasn't just that they were also in the German Cup Final and were strong favourites against second-tier Kaiserslautern. There was also this: 41 games into the season, with the spring blossom on the trees, the club with a reputation for never winning anything had not yet lost a match and were within touching distance – only 12 games – of an historic unbeaten treble.

Leverkusen had broken Bayern Munich's stranglehold on the Bundesliga and boasted many ways of hurting their opponents. As a further boost ahead of the West Ham tie, highly-rated Spanish manager Xabi Alonso had committed his future to the club.

West Ham were now seasoned European competitors under Moyes and had made a habit of turning up in the big games. However, their chances were not helped by the absence of Bowen and Álvarez for the first leg at the BayArena. Bowen was ruled out by a knee injury sustained in the win at Wolves while Álvarez was suspended. Goalkeeper Areola was also absent through injury, as was the on-loan Phillips, who might have hoped to redeem himself in the absence of Álvarez.

It would be a frustrating night and one which divided opinion among Hammers fans over Moyes's tactical approach. Moyes insisted West Ham were 'still in the tie' despite two late goals condemning his side to defeat after coming within seven minutes of securing a priceless goalless draw. First, after 83 minutes, Jonas Hofmann fired through a crowd of bodies after the visitors struggled to clear a corner. Then, in the first minute of injury time, Victor Boniface doubled the lead with a well-directed header from a Hofmann cross.

The hosts dominated possession but were frustrated by a superbly organised Hammers defence until Hofmann's late intervention. The visitors showed great discipline to limit Leverkusen's chances while also offering an occasional threat on the counter through the pace and power of Antonio. Indeed, he created arguably the best opportunity of the first half as he broke down the left and squared for Kudus, but the Ghana winger's shot was straight at Leverkusen goalkeeper Matěj Kovář.

The statistics pointed to Leverkusen dominance, with the Germans managing a shot count of 33 compared to West Ham's one, and the Hammers needed a couple of smart saves from Fabiański to keep Leverkusen at bay for as long as they did. Moyes's strategy was evident from the off. West Ham were content to sit deep, frustrate their hosts and look to break when the opportunity arose.

They so nearly executed it to perfection, with Leverkusen failing to create any clear chances in the first hour or more. Ultimately, though, the pressure told and the Hammers would now have to end the German side's unbeaten run – and do it in some style – to progress. Their chances were not helped by the fact they would now be without Emerson and, crucially, Paquetá after both received yellow cards in the first leg to trigger one-match suspensions.

The defeat in Germany felt cruel on Moyes and his side when they were within seven minutes of halfway house parity. However, they were visibly always clinging on and a more scrutinous eye would see this as the day when the failings of the January transfer window bit hard. Benrahma and Fornals had both been allowed to leave the club without a replacement being signed. By the time they departed, neither was a first choice nor anything like the former versions of themselves, but the pair had still made 45 appearances between them across the first half of the season, minutes and miles that then had to be redistributed to already overburdened legs in the second half of the campaign. So it was that, while Alonso had Boniface and Hofmann – the men whose goals decided the game – to bring off his bench, Moyes had, well, not much at all.

At the same time West Ham were losing to Leverkusen, Liverpool were surprisingly being beaten

3-0 at home by Atalanta of Italy in their Europa League quarter-final first leg. Ironically, the scorer of two of Atalanta's goals was Gianluca Scamacca, the striker whose brief spell at West Ham had been so disappointing.

Three days after the heartbreak in Germany, Moyes faced another daunting task in trying to raise his shattered side for the visit of Fulham. The road to Dublin and the Europa League Final might just have been closed but, entering the final run-in in the Premier League, the race for European places was still well and truly on.

Fulham had not departed the East End with three points on any of their last dozen Premier League visits and had won just once on the road anywhere (at Old Trafford) since beating Everton on the opening day of the campaign.

Here, though, Andreas Pereira's double earned a 2-0 victory and, in the process, capped an abysmal 72 hours for Moyes's side, who had seen their European aspirations for both the current season and the next suffer twin blows.

In desperation, Moyes turned to teenage midfielder George Earthy as the game entered its final throes, a rare instance of the Scot putting trust in one of a crop of highly rated young Hammers. Just two minutes into the 19-year-old's Premier League debut, though, he was involved in a sickening collision, being accidentally flattened by team-mate Álvarez and seemingly being knocked out cold when his head hit the floor. The incident took any late sting out of an affair that, by then, looked settled.

Moyes might ideally have liked to rotate his side more heavily but neither his squad depth nor the precarious state of the Premier League's race for Europe offered him such a luxury. With Bowen still missing, Ings was brought in as one of three changes, the striker starting in the same team as Antonio for only the second time in his West Ham career. At least Fabiański, the veteran Pole, again showed that for all their depth problems elsewhere, West Ham were still blessed with perhaps the division's most reliable back-up goalkeeper.

West Ham United's two roads back into Europe suddenly looked equally perilous. After being schooled by Bayer Leverkusen, defeat by Fulham meant their chances of finishing in the Premier League's top seven appeared slim at best. Moyes'ss future beyond the end of the season remained uncertain, with his contract expiring in the summer and his team's performance against Fulham doing him few favours. Despite their successes in Europe and a position in the top half of the Premier League table, there remained a sense that many West Ham fans have never truly bought into his pragmatic style. The team's lack of swagger and his attacking conservatism had failed to win over supporters and the lacklustre defeat by Fulham highlighted his side's limitations.

Europa League quarter-final second leg: West Ham United 1 Bayer Leverkusen 1 Aggregate 1-3

West Ham needed a two-goal win just to take Bayer Leverkusen to extra time in the return leg at the London Stadium on 18 April but David Moyes refused to promise his team would adopt a more attacking approach, despite claims from his own players that his first-leg tactics had been too negative.

James Ward-Prowse, quoted on the club's own website, admitted the Hammers had been guilty of showing Leverkusen 'a bit too much respect' in the first leg and Łukasz Fabiański claimed they also made a number of tactical mistakes. 'We have spoken about it,' the goalkeeper said. 'There were certain moments when we were defending too deep and sometimes, we were not brave enough when we regained possession of the ball. In the first game, I don't think we used it well.'

Moyes, though, clearly felt he did not get the appreciation he believed he deserved for guiding West Ham to three successive European qualifications and winning the Europa Conference League. As a result, he was in no mood to concede any ground to his detractors, no matter what his players might have said. 'I still believe that we are playing against one of the best teams in Europe at this moment in time. We should give them respect,' he said. 'We will try not to give them too much but, ultimately, they deserve the respect in terms of their results. It would be hard not to respect any team who are 16 points clear in the Bundesliga.'

Xabi Alonso was confident his team would not suffer from a hangover when looking to maintain their treble charge. Leverkusen, who were now unbeaten in 43 matches in all competitions in the 2023/24 season, had celebrated wildly after winning the first Bundesliga title in the club's history on the Sunday before the second leg.

For West Ham, the stakes were huge. Fail – and that seems a harsh word given the task – to pull off a miracle and, after a period in which the club's perpetual rocky road had been infused with a continental twist, this might just prove an ending of sorts. West Ham were flagging in their domestic push for Europe just when English football's sliding coefficient meant the bar for qualification would be higher. 'It's a club that has been relegated, it has been up and down,' Moyes added. 'But it's never been in Europe three times in a row, I know that. Our plan is to try and make it four.'

It wasn't to be, despite a brave effort from the Hammers who threatened, for 45 minutes at least, to upset the odds but were frustrated by some unsympathetic officiating from Spanish referee José María Sánchez Martínez and, in the end, were cruelly denied even the consolation of being the first team all season to beat Bayer Leverkusen.

'I felt like I didn't get a decision all game,' Michail Antonio complained afterwards. 'It doesn't feel like you're playing against 11 men, it feels like you're playing against 13, 14 including the two linos. You just have to keep pushing and try and make the decisions go your way. And they just weren't.'

Moyes, although having to be more diplomatic, made it clear he agreed. 'I watch a lot of Spanish football and have worked in Spain, so I have an idea of what it's like,' he said. 'If that's the way it is, you wouldn't watch many Spanish games, I wouldn't have thought.'

West Ham were dynamic from the first whistle but, with injuries and suspensions having hit their squad hard and a majority of inexperienced options on the bench, including two goalkeepers, they were out of energy by the end. 'It was a completely different game in the first half than the second half,' admitted Leverkusen's Granit Xhaka, the former Arsenal midfielder.

Alonso's men did indeed begin shakily as West Ham, backed vociferously from the stands, pressed high and hard – and halved the deficit in the 13th minute. Centre-back Odilon Kossounou gave away possession and then failed to stop Antonio heading home Bowen's cross from six yards. Goalkeeper Matěj Kovář had come to meet it, too, and was also found wanting.

Antonio saw another header saved before Bowen, unmarked at the back post, volleyed against Kovář's legs, with Moyes toppling to the turf in frustration. Alonso hooked the hapless Kossounou before half an hour was on the clock and made two more changes at the break, sending on Jeremie Frimpong plus first-leg scorer Victor Boniface, but another big chance came and went for the home side. Bowen dispossessed Piero Hincapié just before the hour mark but his ball across the box could not locate a team-mate.

Home energy levels began to dip and Frimpong, sent sprinting clear with a pass from his own half in the 83rd minute, somehow failed to score. However, the substitute extinguished the Hammers' hopes in the 89th minute with a shot that foxed goalkeeper Fabiański via a hefty deflection off team-mate Aaron Cresswell. The goal not only ensured they would go on to face Roma in the semi-final, but that they would leave London with their 44-match unbeaten run, for now at least, still intact.

West Ham dominated for an hour until a lack of options off the bench again proved to be Moyes's Achilles' heel. Without Paquetá and Emerson through suspension, an already lightweight squad was at its wafer-thin worst. Alonso had had the luxury of making six changes coming into this game and at half-time sent on Frimpong and Boniface. Midway through the second half, the sparky Amine Adli was thrown into the fray, too. All the while, Danny Ings, Ben Johnson and Maxwel Cornet jogged up and down the touchline and Moyes looked the other way.

Moyes was involved in a frosty exchange with a reporter as he was asked about his future at the club following their Europa League exit. After the match, Moyes and the media officer who accompanied him took exception to a question asked at a news conference. Reporter: 'If this is the end of your tenure at the end of the season, how do you reflect on …' Moyes: 'Sorry, I didn't get that question.' Moyes had been in the game too long not to realise questions would keep being asked about his future until a decision was made.

For his part, Xabi Alonso admitted that Leverkusen rode their luck. 'We can say this has been a good lesson and we are delighted to be in the semi-final,' he said.

Three days after bowing out of Europe in defiant style, West Ham folded meekly at Crystal Palace to leave their hopes for another season of Thursday night fun in the mire. So abject was their display that neither Moyes, nor his players, attempted to use the tight turnaround as an excuse, despite it being freely offered up. 'The players got praised for their performance on Thursday night, but today was so bad I cannot put it into words,' Moyes said. 'In truth, I am embarrassed to sit here and be speaking on behalf of the team and the way they have performed.'

Palace were outstanding and fully deserving of their win, racing into a 4-0 lead inside 31 minutes and eventually going on to a 5-2 triumph. West Ham were falling apart. There had been no clean sheet in 15 league matches and only three wins since the turn of the year. It seemed this might make the decision over Moyes's future more straightforward, for the board and the man himself, should the season trundle towards a flat end. Much of the debate which followed boiled down to the question of whether the stability and success of the Moyes era was worth sacrificing in pursuit of something more.

Two seasons earlier, Oliver Glasner's Eintracht Frankfurt team denied Moyes's Hammers in the Europa League semi-final and had Palace not moved for the Austrian, he might have been in contention for the vacancy possibly opening up at the London Stadium. A tactical coup at Anfield for a 1-0 win pointed towards Glasner's progressiveness – a quality which Moyes, for all he had delivered copper-bottomed security and a European trophy, was accused of lacking. If a Moyes team could not supply solidity and shape, then – with entertainment off the menu – it had little to offer a fanbase craving thrills paired with devotion to the cause.

The humiliation at Palace made Moyes's departure all the more inevitable. There was an acceptance within West Ham that a change was needed, although the unpredictable nature of the club meant that nothing could be completely ruled out. Julen Lopetegui was the reported early frontrunner for the job and was understood to have attended at least one game at the London Stadium during the season. However, sources had cautioned that the former Wolves manager was yet to convince David Sullivan, the co-owner, he was the right man to succeed Moyes.

West Ham had looked at Lille's Paulo Fonseca and Fulham's Marco Silva while former Hammer Gary O'Neil was also seen as a potential candidate should he decide to seek a challenge away from Wolves. Former Brighton manager Graham Potter remained available more than a year after his sacking by Chelsea while ex-Nottingham Forest boss Steve Cooper was also touted as a possible target. As the speculation mounted, Rúben Amorim, the highly rated Sporting Lisbon manager, even flew to London for talks with Sullivan, although West Ham knew they would have to pay a hefty £13m buyout clause.

West Ham's penultimate home game was a contest with title-chasing Liverpool. After an entertaining 2-2 draw, the main media focus was on the result dealing a critical blow to the Anfield club's fading title bid and how Jürgen Klopp and Mo Salah had been involved in a touchline spat before the star striker prepared to come on as a substitute.

After an opening period in which Liverpool dominated without taking their chances, West Ham scored an excellent goal from Bowen (his 20th of the season) on one of their clever breaks. After half-time, West Ham again began to look tired (this was their 50th game of the season) and Robertson put the visitors on level terms. Then, from a corner, Liverpool went ahead, with a ball that pinged off Ogbonna, Souček and Areola. West Ham looked finished. They toyed with a complete collapse, only for Areola to thwart Luis Díaz with two outstanding saves. Out of nowhere, an equaliser arrived. Bowen crossed and Antonio punished slack defending by heading past Alisson. Liverpool had found a way not to win. West Ham were lucky.

Moyes was happy after Antonio rescued a creditable point, but he knew that Liverpool were the better team. Confidence was fragile after the thrashing at Crystal Palace. Kudus's dribbling worried Trent Alexander-Arnold on the left, but other moments of flair were sparse. Paquetá simply was not in the game.

The match programme said: 'In the past three seasons West Ham have played and won more matches in European competitions than any other club – a total of 26 victories in 37 matches, compared to Real Madrid's 24 wins in 35 matches and Manchester City's 23 wins in 35 matches.' So what if they were in the Champions League … they had never won the Conference League!

With three games remaining and speculation rife over Moyes's future, it was reported that technical director Steidten had been asked not to enter the team's dressing room for the rest of the season while he continued to speak to potential managers to succeed Moyes.

West Ham's penultimate away fixture of the season took them to Chelsea. Trips to Stamford Bridge had possessed an ominous quality throughout Moyes's managerial career and, after a 5-0 thrashing, he left with a record of 19 visits in the Premier League without a single victory. This now looked likely to be his last visit to Stamford Bridge as West Ham boss and it surely ranked among the worst of a sorry bunch. One newspaper headline after this contest was: 'Ray of hope for Mauricio Pochettino in battle of doomed managers.'

Arriving in West London with their European hopes just about still alive, West Ham turned in the performance of a team playing for nothing at all and were duly dismantled by a Chelsea side whose own late season resurgence had pushed them in the top six mix.

Since the start of March 2023, this was the ninth time Moyes had watched his team lose a Premier League match by three goals or more. The resilience and determination synonymous with the best Moyes teams had disappeared and here it took only Cole Palmer's 15th-minute opener to effectively break any lingering resolve. From the pasting that followed, it was impossible not to sense a team now desperate for the season to end, and a club in need of clarity – even as Moyes continued to insist that no announcement on his future would be made until after the final game, away at Manchester City.

This was yet another defensive performance when West Ham eyes appeared anywhere but on the ball. Only the bottom three had poorer defensive records than the Hammers and it was now 16 consecutive league games without a clean sheet. The forwards, too, were ineffective. Paquetá looked disinterested and only Bowen emerged with any credit, having managed to hit the bar three times.

Afterwards, Moyes would talk about a lack of 'mental toughness' and suggested that the leakiness was down to selling Declan Rice the previous summer. The harsh reality was that the Scot's methods were no longer working. West Ham had become an easy team to play against. Souček and Álvarez, who went off at half-time, were not providing enough protection in midfield. Zouma and Ogbonna toiled in central defence. Emerson, the former Chelsea left-back, was given a torrid time by Noni Madueke.

After the Chelsea debacle the West Ham board finally accepted the inevitable and confirmed that Moyes would leave his post when his contract expired at the end of the season. It was reported that they were closing in on the appointment of Lopetegui as his replacement. Lopetegui, who had been out of work since leaving Wolves the previous summer, had agreed a deal in principle to take over after holding multiple rounds of talks with the London Stadium club. The 57-year-old Spaniard was lined up after West Ham decided to shelve plans to hand a new deal to Moyes, who was to depart after four and a half mostly successful years in East London.

The humiliation at Stamford Bridge convinced the club to provide clarity around the situation. Although Moyes was ending on a disappointing note, the club's decision to confirm his exit ahead of the final home game against Luton Town at least gave supporters a chance to give him a proper send-off.

In a statement issued through the club, Moyes said: 'I have enjoyed four and a half brilliant years at West Ham, and the club is in a stronger position than when I returned back in 2019. When I joined West Ham for a second time, the club was one place above the relegation zone, and it has been a terrific journey to have achieved three consecutive seasons in Europe.

'After leading the club to safety, we guided the team to finishes of sixth and seventh in the Premier League, and I was delighted when we won the Europa Conference League title last June – the club's first major trophy in 43 years. I would like to thank all the players for their support, and all the success they have achieved, over the last four and a half years.'

On 11 May, West Ham rallied to deliver Moyes a fitting home send-off and leave Luton on the brink of relegation. The Moyes farewell gig almost failed to launch, but eventually his team lit up the London Stadium with some back catalogue favourites to win 3-1. A disinterested crowd were left scratching their heads early on at football's equivalent of obscure album tracks, like Albert Sambi Lokonga's opener for Luton. The hosts needed a full 50 minutes to find their rhythm and start banging out the hits.

But once Ward-Prowse had warmed them up with a crisp leveller, the Moyes tribute band were right back in the pocket. Souček volleyed the Hammers in front, then George Earthy turned in a classic of the genre – the local teenager climbing off the bench to score his maiden club goal with his first touch. Midfielder Earthy turned in Kudus's low cross to put the Hammers 3-1 up, just 30 seconds after replacing Antonio. A glimpse into the future, perhaps, as the 19-year-old hugged his elated team-mates, but also a nod to Moyes's summer departure. The Havering native was concussed and hospitalised on his Premier League debut in April. Now the promising midfielder had delivered the knockout blow to Luton's top-flight status.

A top-half finish at least improved upon the previous term's frustrating 14th and Moyes's summer exit seemed well timed for all parties. Moyes was not quite revelling in being the centre of attention in the build-up to kick-off, but the departing Hammers boss was definitely glad-handing with well-wishing home fans. He made good on his pre-match promise not to deliver any animated message to fans on the pitch at full-time. In some gentle ribbing of Liverpool's all-action boss Jürgen Klopp, Moyes had joked he was not the type of manager to fist pump a crowd. And after shaking hands with all and sundry on the bench, he was off down the tunnel. The end-of-season awards were still to take place on the pitch, but Moyes was as keen as ever to avoid the spotlight, even through the pleasantries.

The ex-Everton boss insisted he had transformed the Hammers to the point where the East Londoners could spend their immediate future looking up. Admitting emotions caught up with him at full-time, Moyes said: 'Sometimes all you hear is negative stuff, but the best part of 50,000 people stayed behind after the final whistle. To join a football club and do something is not easy for any manager. Hopefully I'll walk away with people saying I've done something here and that expectations have been raised.'

Ahead of the final game, West Ham confirmed that defender Thilo Kehrer was to join AS Monaco on a permanent contract for an undisclosed fee, having spent the second half of the 2023/24 season on loan at the French Ligue 1 side. The 27-year-old made 12 appearances for the Hammers at the start of the campaign before linking up with Les Rouges et Blancs in early January in a deal that included an option for him to remain at the Stade

Louis II long term. In total, the Germany international played 50 games for the Irons after signing from Paris Saint-Germain in the summer of 2022, including one as a substitute in the Europa Conference League Final victory.

If Manchester City could have chosen any team to play in their final league game to seal an historic fourth successive Premier League title, then West Ham United would have been near the top of any list. Anything other than a City win would have given Arsenal the title, but Phil Foden scored after just 79 seconds and then had another after 18 minutes. Kudus scored to set City nerves tingling until Rodri fired home with half an hour to play. Arsenal had needed a favour from West Ham, who were already confirmed in ninth place and were playing out the final match of Moyes's second spell as manager.

West Ham, without Bowen due to tonsillitis, could do little to repel the hosts. The Hammers stirred before the break as Kudus forced a save from Stefan Ortega and then pulled one back with a stunning overhead strike. City tightened their grip and West Ham had seen little of the ball when Rodri powerfully guided home City's third from the edge of the box just before the hour. There seemed little motivation from West Ham to respond and City calmly stroked the ball around. Some hearts may have been in mouths when Souček put the ball into the net two minutes from time, but it clearly struck his arm and the goal was disallowed by VAR.

Moyes brought an end to his successful spell in charge of West Ham and admitted he has already rejected job overtures as he looked forward to a break from the game. With Pep Guardiola having won the title yet again for City, Moyes joked: 'I'll wait until Pep goes before I come back.'

During the 2023/24 season, West Ham were actually on top of the Premier League … for two days. They finished ninth, outside the European places, with 52 points (P38 W14 D10 L14 F60 A74). The 74 league goals conceded was their worst since shipping 84 in 1966/67 and the Hammers were the first side to finish as high as ninth when conceding that many since 1963/64 when both Spurs (81 goals, fifth place) and Arsenal (82, eighth) did so.

Looking Back, Looking Forward

'Maybe West Ham are a different sort of club,' David Moyes said before the Leverkusen game. 'This place has never been smooth at any time, I don't think. The people who watch West Ham and come here probably know that's part of it. I don't think anyone comes here to have a smooth time. It's always got a tinge of something else about it. It's a club that has been relegated, it has been up and down. But it's never been in Europe three times in a row.'

Maybe that was part of the reason why the Moyes era at large was so difficult to define, littered with historic success and a fair sprinkling of struggle, the two often at times mere weeks apart. Many of its most memorable results were not four- and five-nil strolls, but turnarounds of the type witnessed in the 2021/22 Europa League campaign or the lockdown epic against Tottenham when the Hammers came from 3-0 down with eight minutes to play to draw, courtesy of Manuel Lanzini's stunner.

A social media post in April 2024 commemorated the late John Lyall, the previous Hammers manager to win a trophy, to a universally warm reception. Perhaps, in the future, Moyes will be remembered as fondly even if the hardcore were never fully convinced. Perhaps that was down to Moyes's outward flintiness. Reportedly, behind the scenes he could be warm, but he always refrained from giving much away in public. Equally, his style of football did not fit the template of whatever the 'West Ham Way' is supposed to be. Despite huge talent within his team, he often seemed most satisfied with performances in which the only discernible quality was the keeping of defensive shape. At the time of writing, it feels that it may take some time for Moyes to receive his deserved recognition.

Above all, David Moyes was the man who made West Ham fans fall in love with their club again. It should not be forgotten that the mood was poisonous when he was brought back on a rescue mission in December

2019. Anger over the move to the London Stadium had not gone away, an underperforming, uncommitted side had slid into another relegation battle and supporters were staging angry protests against the club's unpopular ownership before home games.

Four and a half years on, the mood was different, as were the expectations. European football had come to Stratford for three consecutive seasons and West Ham, as the ironic chant went, were 'massive'. Moyes's place in the club's history is not just about that triumph in the Europa Conference League Final. Beating Fiorentina was great and Moyes's charge down the touchline after Jarrod Bowen's last-minute winner was an iconic image, but the whole journey was unforgettable. 'My goodness, for us to go from a team that was fighting at the bottom of the league to sixth was unbelievable,' Moyes said before his final home game against Luton.

There were no complaints about the manner of his departure. He said it was the right decision for both parties. He talked about having spent a long time away from his family, who still lived in the north, and explained that his batteries were drained after three years of European football. 'I'm pretty beaten up,' Moyes said.

But the overriding emotion was pride. Pride at finishing sixth and seventh. Pride at reaching the semi-finals of the Europa League in 2022. Pride at the long-awaited trophy. Pride at wounding all the big teams in the Premier League. Pride, above all, at leading a group that could usually be trusted to give their all. 'You don't run, you don't play,' was the familiar Moyes refrain. Fans may want entertainment; they also want to watch a team playing for the shirt.

When Moyes left, he could undoubtedly claim to be West Ham's best manager of the Premier League era. When it comes to the best moments under him, it is hard to know where to begin. He often cited Andriy Yarmolenko's last-minute winner against Chelsea during Project Restart as a turning point for West Ham, who were fighting relegation. But he also picked out Michail Antonio scoring four against Norwich as a fond memory. He spoke about securing sixth by beating Southampton when crowds returned in 2021.

West Ham embraced Europe under Moyes. The London Stadium was deafening when West Ham beat Lopetegui's Sevilla in the last 16 of the Europa League in 2022. The Hammers kept defying the odds, winning 3-0 in Lyon in the next round. Craig Dawson scored the opener that night. The centre-back was one of many unfashionable players lifted by Moyes. The manager took Bowen out of the Championship and turned him into an England international. He made Declan Rice a £100m-plus player and found value in the Czech Republic internationals Tomáš Souček and Vladimír Coufal. He briefly reignited Jesse Lingard's spark and helped Pablo Fornals settle in England.

There was the emotion of Yarmolenko, who was granted compassionate leave after Russia's invasion of Ukraine, returning to score the winner against Villa. There was the improbability of almost qualifying for the Champions League with a squad that contained one striker and the likes of Fabián Balbuena, Issa Diop, Ryan Fredericks and Arthur Masuaku. Under Moyes, West Ham won games they weren't supposed to win. They fought, scrapped and made the fans feel proud again. It was a blessing for the board, who no longer heard people complaining about the stadium. Moyes brought stability to a previously dysfunctional club, lifting a disillusioned fanbase. 'You have to raise expectations as a manager,' he said. 'That's part of your job: to come in and give supporters something which maybe they haven't achieved before.'

On 23 May 2024, what had long been assumed was formally confirmed, that Julen Lopetegui would be West Ham United's next head coach (not manager). The 57-year-old Spaniard would officially start on 1 July on a two-year deal, with the option for a third.

So, looking ahead to a new era, what can fans expect? The plan when he arrived at Wolves was to bring in a new style focused around pressing and playing out from the back. He wanted players to win the ball higher up the pitch to allow them to get more players in the box. However, they still struggled for goals and were the lowest scorers in the league. He switched between 4-2-3-1 and 4-4-2 formations rather than the 4-3-3 he used during his successful three-year spell at Sevilla, where he won the Europa League and qualified for the Champions League three times.

Off the pitch at Wolves, he was said to have made small but significant changes. There had been an acceptance behind the scenes that standards had slipped since March 2022 and Lopetegui brought those back with the reintroduction of all-staff meal times and rewarded his squad by buying them special meals each time they kept a clean sheet. Players praised his communication skills and his clear messaging enabled Wolves to go on an impressive home run that was key to their safety.

He was aided by a tight inner circle, bringing eight members of staff with him initially and it was expected he would do the same at West Ham. On the touchline, he is a totally different character to David Moyes. He is often erratic and feisty, and Wolves fans often witnessed him screaming, jumping and remonstrating with officials and opposition managers. 'He is an emotional manager,' was the verdict of one Wolves player. Those who know him had spoken of an emotional burnout after he was sacked as Sevilla manager in October 2022. However, after a season out of work, he is likely to have recharged from his nine-month stint at Molineux and will be ready to go again.

Lopetegui's availability made dealing with him easier for the Hammers board. He wants to build a team capable of challenging for the Champions League like his fellow Basque Unai Emery at Aston Villa. But West Ham will need to invest and bolster an ageing, light squad if they are to push on.

Sullivan is believed to have been won over by Lopetegui. The former Spain and Real Madrid manager won the Europa League at Sevilla in 2020 and guided Wolves away from relegation trouble after taking over midway through the 2022/23 season, finishing 13th. He left Wolves because of concerns over their lack of transfer activity. Lopetegui is regarded as a workaholic and a gifted coach.

The question will be whether he can work within West Ham's structure. He was forced to leave the Spain job after agreeing to take over at Madrid on the eve of the 2018 World Cup. He then lasted 128 days at Madrid and his three years at Sevilla ended badly. Arguably, Lopetegui is coming into the most stable situation at West Ham since Harry Redknapp left in 2001. He will be expected to hit the ground running. West Ham must hope so. Otherwise, David Moyes could be getting a third phone call.

Hopefully, someone told him that things rarely run smoothly at West Ham United. The size of his transfer budget could depend on whether Lucas Paquetá, whose contract contains an £85m release clause, is targeted again by Manchester City. On the same day Lopetegui's appointment was announced, Paquetá was finally charged by the FA for allegedly deliberately getting himself booked 'for the improper purpose of affecting the betting market'.

If the charges are proven, Paquetá could be facing a lengthy, even lifetime, ban.

Julen, welcome to the West Ham soap opera.

Line Ups

European Cup Winners Cup 1964/65

First Round: First Leg
Wednesday, September 23, 1964
Jules Otten Stadion, Ghent, Belgium
La Gantoise 0
West Ham 1
Boyce (52)
HT: 0-0
Attendance: 18,000
West Ham United: Jim Standen; John Bond; Martin Peters; Eddie Bovington; Ken Brown.
Bobby Moore (Captain); Alan Sealey; Ron Boyce; Johnny Byrne. Geoff Hurst; Johnny Sissons.

First Round: Second Leg
Wednesday, October 7, 1964
Upton Park, London
West Ham 1
Byrne (43)
La Gantoise 1
Peters (32, og)
HT: 1-1
Attendance: 24,000
West Ham won on aggregate 2-1
West Ham United: Alan Dickie; John Bond; Martin Peters; Eddie Bovington; Ken Brown.
Bobby Moore (Captain); Peter Brabrook; Ron Boyce; Johnny Byrne. Geoff Hurst; Johnny Sissons.

Second Round: First Leg
Wednesday, November 25, 1964
Upton Park, London
West Ham 2
Bond (58), Sealey (82)
Spartak Prague 0
HT: 0-0
Attendance: 27,590
West Ham United: Jim Standen; John Bond; Jack Burkett; Eddie Bovington; Ken Brown (Captain).
Martin Peters; Alan Sealey; Ron Boyce; Johnny Byrne; Geoff Hurst.
Johnny Sissons.

Second Round: Second Leg
Wednesday, December 9, 1964
Letna Stadium, Prague
Spartak Prague 2
Mraz (73, 88)
West Ham 1
Sissons (14)
HT: 0-1
Attendance: 45,000
West Ham won on aggregate 3-2
West Ham United: Jim Standen; John Bond; Jack Burkett; Eddie Bovington; Ken Brown (Captain).
Martin Peters; Alan Sealey; Ron Boyce; Johnny Byrne; Geoff Hurst.
Johnny Sissons.

Quarter Final: First Leg
Wednesday, March 16, 1965
Stade Olympique de la Pontaise, Lausanne, Switzerland.
Lausanne Sports 1
Hosp (80)
West Ham 2
Dear (21) Byrne (53)
HT: 0-1
Attendance: 20,000

West Ham United: Jim Standen; Joe Kirkup; Martin Peters; Ron Boyce; Ken Brown.
Bobby Moore (Captain); Alan Sealey; Geoff Hurst; Johnny Byrne.
Brian Dear; Johnny Sissons.

Quarter Final: Second Leg
Wednesday March 23, 1965
Upton Park, London
West Ham 4
Tachella (42, og), Dear (43, 89) Peters (59)
Lausanne Sports 3
Kerkhoffs (37) Hertig (48) Eschmann (80)
HT: 2-1
Attendance: 31,780
West Ham won on aggregate 6-4
West Ham United: Jim Standen; Joe Kirkup; Martin Peters; Ron Boyce; Ken Brown.
Bobby Moore (Captain); Alan Sealey; Geoff Hurst; Johnny Byrne.
Brian Dear; Johnny Sissons.

Semi –Final: First Leg
Wednesday April 7, 1965
Upton Park, London.
West Ham 2
Dear ((9) Byrne (24)
Real Zaragoza 1
Canario (55)
HT: 2-0
Attendance: 35,000
West Ham United: Jim Standen; Joe Kirkup; Jack Burkett; Martin Peters; Ken Brown.
Bobby Moore (Captain); Ron Boyce; Brian Dear; Johnny Byrne.
Geoff Hurst; Johnny Sissons.

Semi –Final: Second Leg
Wednesday April 28, 1965
Estadio de La Romareda, Zaragoza, Spain
Real Zaragoza 1
Lapetra (24)
West Ham 1
Sissons (54)
HT: 1-0
Attendance: 29,400
West Ham won on aggregate 3-2
West Ham United: Jim Standen; Joe Kirkup; Jack Burkett; Martin Peters; Ken Brown.
Bobby Moore (Captain); Alan Sealey; Ron Boyce; Johnny Byrne.
Geoff Hurst; Johnny Sissons.

European Cup-Winners' Cup Final
Wednesday May 19, 1965
v.TSV Munich 1860 (West Germany)
Wembley Stadium, London
Attendance: 97,974
West Ham 2
Sealey (69, 71)
TSV Munich 0
HT: 0-0
West Ham United: Jim Standen; Joe Kirkup; Jack Burkett; Martin Peters; Ken Brown.
Bobby Moore (Captain); Alan Sealey; Ron Boyce; Geoff Hurst.
Brian Dear; Johnny Sissons.

European Cup Winners Cup 1965/66

Second Round: First Leg
Nov 24, 1965
Upton Park, London
West Ham 4
Hurst 23,43, Byrne 65, Brabrook 82
Olympiakos 0
HT: 2-0
Attendance 27,250
West Ham United: Jim Standen; Joe Kirkup; John Charles; Eddie Bovington; Ken Brown.
Bobby Moore (Captain); Peter Brabrook; Martin Peters; Johnny Byrne.
Geoff Hurst; Johnny Sissons.

Second Round: Second Leg
Dec 1, 1965
Kariaskis Stadium,Athens
Olympiakos 2
Bovington 57 og, Polihronlou 81
West Ham 2
Peters 28 ,53.
HT: 0-1
West Ham won on aggregate 6-2
Attendance 40,000
West Ham United: Jim Standen; Joe Kirkup; John Charles; Eddie Bovington; Ken Brown.

Bobby Moore (Captain); Peter Brabrook; Martin Peters; Johnny Byrne.
Geoff Hurst; Johnny Sissons.

Quarter Final: First Leg
March 2, 1966
Upton Park, London
West Ham 1
Byrne 46
Magdeburg 0
HT: 0-0
Attendance 30,620
West Ham United: Jim Standen; Denis Burnett; Jack Burkett; Eddie Bovington; Ken Brown.
Bobby Moore (Captain); Peter Brabrook; Ron Boyce; Johnny Byrne.
Geoff Hurst; Johnny Sissons.

Quarter Final: Second Leg
March 16, 1966
Ernst Grube Stadium, Magdeburg, East Germany
Magdeburg 1
Walter 77
West Ham 1
Sissons 78
HT: 0-0
West Ham won on aggregate 2-1
Attendance 35,000
West Ham United: Jim Standen; Denis Burnett; Jack Burkett; Eddie Bovington; Ken Brown.
Bobby Moore (Captain); Peter Brabrook; Ron Boyce; Geoff Hurst.
Martin Peters; Johnny Sissons.

Semi-Final: First Leg
April 5, 1966
Upton Park, London
West Ham 1
Peters 52
Borussia Dortmund 2
Emmerich 86, 88
HT: 0-0
Attendance 28,130
West Ham United: Jim Standen; Ken Brown; John Charles; Martin Peters; Ron Boyce.
Bobby Moore (Captain); Peter Brabrook; Jimmy Bloomfield.
Johnny Byrne; Geoff Hurst; Brian Dear.

Semi-Final: Second Leg
April 13, 1966
Westfalenstadion,Dortmund
Borussia Dortmund 3
Emmerich1, 28, Cyliax 86
West Ham 1
Byrne 43
Borussia Dortmund won on aggregate 5-2
HT: 1-2
Attendance 35,000
West Ham United: Jim Standen; Eddie Bovington; John Charles; Martin Peters; Ken Brown.
Bobby Moore (Captain); Peter Brabrook; Ron Boyce; Johnny Byrne; Geoff Hurst.
Jimmy Bloomfield.

Season 1975/76

Anglo-Italian Cup Winners Cup

First Leg
Sep 3, 1975
Stadio Communale, Florence
Fiorentina 1
Guernini 20
West Ham 0
HT: 1 - 0
Attendance 35,000
West Ham United: Mervyn Day; John McDowell; Frank Lampard; Billy Bonds (Capt); Tommy Taylor; Kevin Lock; Alan Taylor; Graham Paddon; Pat Holland (Jennings 46).
Trevor Brooking; Keith Robson.

Second Leg
Dec 10, 1975
Upton Park, London
West Ham 0
Fiorentina 1
Speggiorin 20
H. T: 0-1
Attendance 14,699
West Ham United: Mervyn Day; John McDowell (Coleman 46); Frank Lampard (Capt); Pat Holland; Tommy Taylor; Kevin Lock; Alan Taylor; Graham Paddon; Billy Jennings.
Trevor Brooking; Johnny Ayris (Curbishley 70).

European Cup Winners Cup 1975/76

First Round: First Leg
Sep 17, 1975
Olympic Stadium, Helsinki
Lahden Reipas 2
Lindholm 4, Tupasela 53
West Ham 2
Brooking 29 Bonds 76
HT: 1-1
Attendance 6,000
West Ham United: Mervyn Day; John McDowell; Frank Lampard; Billy Bonds (Capt); Tommy Taylor; Kevin Lock; Pat Holland; Graham Paddon; Alan Taylor; Trevor Brooking; Keith Robson (Jennings 71).

First Round: Second Leg
Oct 1, 1975
Upton Park, London
West Ham 3
Robson 60, Holland 86, Taylor A. 89
Lahden Reipas 0
H. T: 0-0
Attendance: 24, 131
West Ham: Mervyn Day; John McDowell; Frank Lampard; Billy Bonds (Capt); Tommy Taylor; Kevin Lock; Alan Taylor (Jennings 72); Graham Paddon; Keith Robson; Trevor Brooking; Pat Holland.
West Ham won on aggregate 5-2

Second Round: First Leg
Oct 22, 1975
Rasdan Stadium, Erevan
Ararat Erevan 1
Petrosian 66
West Ham 1
A. Taylor 56
HT: 0-0
Attendance 66,662
West Ham: Mervyn Day; John McDowell; Frank Lampard; Billy Bonds (Capt).
Tommy Taylor; Keith Coleman; Alan Taylor; Graham Paddon.
Bobby Gould; Pat Holland; Keith Robson.

Second Round: Second Leg
Nov 5, 1975
Upton Park, London
West Ham 3
Paddon 16, Robson 27, Taylor A. 59
Arrarat Erevan 1
Petroslan 48
HT: 2-0
West Ham won on aggregate 4-2
Attendance 30,399
West Ham United: Mervyn Day; John McDowell; Frank Lampard; Billy Bonds (Capt).
Tommy Taylor; Keith Coleman; Alan Taylor; Graham Paddon.
Pat Holland; Trevor Brooking; Keith Robson.

Quarter-Final: First Leg
March 3, 1976
Zuiderparkstadion,The Hague
FC Den Haag 4
Mansveld 12, 16 pen, 40 pen; Schoenmaker 44
West Ham 2
Jennings 51, 59
HT: 0-4
Attendance 26,000
West Ham United: Mervyn Day; Mick McGiven (Keith Coleman 46); Frank Lampard.
Billy Bonds (Capt); Tommy Taylor; Kevin Lock; Alan Taylor.
Graham Paddon; Billy Jennings; Alan Curbishley; Keith Robson.

Quarter-Final: Second Leg
March 17, 1976
Upton Park,London
West Ham 3
A Taylor 29, Lampard 33, Bonds 36 (pen).
FC Den Haag 1
Schoenmaker 59
HT: 3-0
Aggregate 5-5: West Ham won on away goals.
Attendance 29,829
West Ham: Mervyn Day; Keith Coleman; Frank Lampard; Billy Bonds (Capt); Tommy Taylor; Kevin Lock; Alan Taylor; Graham Paddon; Billy Jennings; Trevor Brooking; Keith Robson.

Semi-Final: First Leg
March 31, 1976
Waldstadion , Frankfurt
Eintracht Frankfurt 2

Neuberger 29, Kraus 47
West Ham 1
Paddon 9
HT: 1-1
Attendance 45,000
West Ham United: Mervyn Day; Keith Coleman; Frank Lampard; Billy Bonds (Capt).
Tommy Taylor; John McDowell; Pat Holland; Graham Paddon.
Billy Jennings; Trevor Brooking; Keith Robson.

Semi-Final: Second Leg
April 14, 1976
Upton Park, London
West Ham 3
Brooking 49, 77, Robson 68
Eintracht Frankfurt 1
Beverungen 88
HT: 0-0
West Ham won on aggregate 4-3
Attendance 39,202
West Ham United: Mervyn Day; Keith Coleman; Frank Lampard; Billy Bonds (Capt).
Tommy Taylor; John McDowell; Pat Holland; Graham Paddon.
Billy Jennings; Trevor Brooking; Keith Robson.

European Cup Winners Cup Final
May 5, 1976
Heysel Stadium, Brussels
Attendance 58,000
West Ham 2
Holland 29, Robson 69
Anderlecht 4
Rensenbrink 42, 73 (Pen), Van der Elst 48,88
HT: 1-1
West Ham United: Mervyn Day; Keith Coleman; Frank Lampard; (Alan Taylor 46); Billy Bonds (Capt); Tommy Taylor; John McDowell; Pat Holland; Graham Paddon; Billy Jennings; Trevor Brooking; Keith Robson.

European Cup Winners Cup 1980/81

First Round, First Leg
Sep 17, 1980
Bernabeu Stadium, Madrid
Castilla 3
Paco 64, Balin 71, Cidon 75
West Ham 1
Cross 18
HT: 0-1
Attendance 40,000
West Ham United: Phil Parkes; Ray Stewart; Frank Lampard; Billy Bonds (Capt).
Alvin Martin; Alan Devonshire (Brush 86); Nicky Morgan (Barnes 73).
Paul Goddard; David Cross; Trevor Brooking; Geoff Pike.

First Round, Second Leg
Oct 1, 1980
Upton Park, London
West Ham 5
Pike 19, Cross 30,103,119, Goddard 40
Castilla 1
Bernal 56
West Ham won on aggregate 6-4
HT: 2-0
Attendance 262
West Ham United: Phil Parkes; Ray Stewart; Frank Lampard; Billy Bonds (Capt).
Alvin Martin; Alan Devonshire; Pat Holland (Brush 106); Paul Goddard (Morgan 91); David Cross; Trevor Brooking; Geoff Pike.

Second Round: First Leg
Oct 22, 1980
Upton Park, London
West Ham 4
Bonds 24, Goddard 27, Stewart 30(Pen), Cross 83,
Timisoara 0
HT: 3-0
Attendance 27,257
West Ham United: Phil Parkes; Ray Stewart; Frank Lampard; Billy Bonds (Capt); Alvin Martin; Alan Devonshire; Pat Holland; Paul Goddard (Morgan 88).
David Cross; Jimmy Neighbour; Geoff Pike.

Second Round, Second Leg
Nov 5, 1980
1 Mat, Timisoara
Timisoara 1

Paltinisanu 53
West Ham 0
HT: 0-0
Attendance 25,000
West Ham United: Phil Parkes; Ray Stewart (Brush 38); Frank Lampard; Billy Bonds (Capt).
Alvin Martin; Paul Allen; Pat Holland; Paul Goddard; David Cross.
Jimmy Neighbour (Brooking 60); Geoff Pike.
West Ham won on aggregate :4-1

Quarter Final: First Leg
March 4, 1981
Upton Park, London
West Ham 1
Cross 54
Dynamo Tblisi 4
Chivadze 24; Gutsayev 32; Shengalia 55,67.
HT: 0-2
Attendance 34,957
West Ham United: Phil Parkes; Ray Stewart; Frank Lampard; Billy Bonds (Capt).
Alvin Martin; Alan Devonshire (Allen 46); Jimmy Neighbour.
Paul Goddard; David Cross; Trevor Brooking; Geoff Pike.

Quarter Final: Second Leg
March 18, 1981
Lenin Stadium, Tbilisi
Dynamo Tblisi 0
West Ham 1
Pearson 87
Attendance 80,000
Dynamo Tbilisi won on aggregate 4-2
West Ham United: Phil Parkes; Ray Stewart; Frank Lampard; Billy Bonds (Capt).
Alvin Martin; Paul Brush; Jimmy Neighbour; Paul Goddard (Pearson 65)
David Cross; Trevor Brooking; Geoff Pike.

Anglo-Italian Cup 1992/93

Preliminary Round: Sep 2, 1992
Upton Park,London
West Ham 2
Dicks (2)
Bristol Rovers 2
Stewart (2)
HT: 1-0
Attendance: 4,809
West Ham United: Steven Banks; Steve Potts; Julian Dicks; Tony Gale; Alvin Martin.
Martin Allen; Mark Robson (Rush); Peter Butler; Trevor Morley.
Clive Allen; Kevin Keen.

Preliminary Round: Sep 30, 1992
Roots Hall, Southend
Southend United 0
West Ham 3
Morley, Dicks (pen), Holmes
HT: 0-2
Attendance: 6,482
West Ham United: Ludek Miklosko; Tim Breaker; Julian Dicks; Steve Potts; Alvin Martin.
Martin Allen; Mark Robson; Matty Holmes; Trevor Morley.
Clive Allen; Kevin Keen.

Nov 11, 1992
Stadio Giovanni Zini
Cremonese 2
Florjanic (2)
West Ham 0
HT: 0-0
Attendance: 1,639
West Ham United: Ludek Miklosko; Kenny Brown; Julian Dicks: Steve Potts; Alvin Martin.
Martin Allen; Mark Robson; George Parris (Keen); Trevor Morley.
Clive Allen; Matty Holmes.

Nov 24, 1992
Upton Park, London
West Ham 2
Clive Allen (2)
Reggiana 0
HT: 0-0
Attendance: 6,872
West Ham United: Ludek Miklosko; Tim Breaker; Julian Dicks; Steve Potts; Alvin Martin (Kenny Brown); Martin Allen; Mark Robson (Bishop); Matty Holmes; Trevor Morley; Clive Allen; Kevin Keen.

Dec 8, 1992
Stadio San Vito,Cosenza
Cosenza 0

West Ham 1
C. Allen 44
HT: 0-1
Attendance: 800
West Ham United: Ludek Miklosko; Tim Breaker; Julian Dicks; Steve Potts; Alvin Martin.
Martin Allen; Matthew Rush; George Parris; Steve Jones.
Clive Allen; Kevin Keen (Kenny Brown).

Dec 16, 1992
Upton Park, London
West Ham 0
Pisa 0
HT: 0-0: Attendance: 7,123
West Ham United: Ludek Miklosko; Tim Breaker; Julian Dicks; Steve Potts; Alvin Martin.
Martin Allen; Matthew Rush; Ian Bishop; Alex Bunbury.
Clive Allen (Steve Jones); Kevin Keen (Stewart Robson).

Intertoto Cup 1999/2000

First Round: Bye

Second Round: Bye

Third Round: First Leg
Saturday July 17, 1999
Upton Park, London
West Ham 1
Kitson 18
Jokerit 0
HT: 1-0
Attendance: 11,908
West Ham United: Craig Forrest; Steve Lomas; Scott Minto; Steve Potts (Marc Keller 46)
Rio Ferdinand; Neil Ruddock; Frank Lampard; Joe Cole
Paul Kitson; Paulo Di Canio; Trevor Sinclair (Ian Wright 60).

Third Round: Second Leg
Saturday July 24, 1999
Olympiastadion, Helsinki, Finland
Jokerit 1
Koskela 33
West Ham 1
Lampard 76
HT: 1-0
Attendance: 7,667
West Ham won on aggregate 2-1
West Ham United: Shaka Hislop; Rob Jones (Steve Potts 46); Scott Minto; Steve Lomas
Rio Ferdinand; Neil Ruddock; Frank Lampard; Marc Keller (Michael Carrick 80).
Paul Kitson; Paulo Di Canio (Stan Lazaridis 76); Trevor Sinclair.

Semi-Final: First Leg
Wednesday July 28, 1999
Upton Park, London
West Ham 1
Lampard 7
Heerenveen 0
HT: 1-0
Attendance: 7,485
West Ham United: Shaka Hislop; Steve Potts; Scott Minto; Steve Lomas
Rio Ferdinand; Neil Ruddock (Ian Pearce 52); Frank Lampard; Marc Keller (John Moncur 46); Paulo Wanchope; Paulo Di Canio (Paul Kitson 78); Trevor Sinclair.

Semi-Final: Second Leg
Wednesday August 4, 1999
Abe Lenstra Stadium, Heerenveen
Heerenveen 0
West Ham 1
Wanchope 25
HT: 0-1
Attendance: 13,500
West Ham United: Shaka Hislop; Steve Lomas; Scott Minto; Frank Lampard; Rio Ferdinand.
Ian Pearce; John Moncur (Joe Cole 82); Marc-Vivien-Foe; Paulo Wanchope; Paulo Di Canio (Paul Kitson 69); Trevor Sinclair.

Final: First Leg
Tuesday August 10, 1999
Upton Park, London
West Ham 0
Metz 1
Saha 13
HT: 0-1
Attendance: 25,372
West Ham United: Shaka Hislop; Steve Lomas; Scott Minto; Frank Lampard; Rio Ferdinand.

Steve Potts; John Moncur; Marc-Vivien Foe (Paul Kitson 77); Paulo Wanchope. Paolo Di Canio; Trevor Sinclair.

Final: Second Leg
Tuesday August 24, 1999
Stade Symphorien,Metz
Metz 1
Jestrovic 68
West Ham 3
Sinclair 23, Lampard 43, Wanchope 78
HT: 0-2
Attendance: 19,599
West Ham won aggregate 3-2
West Ham United: Shaka Hislop; Steve Lomas; Marc Keller; Marc-Vivien Foe; Rio Ferdinand.
Steve Potts; John Moncur; Frank Lampard; Paulo Wanchope.
Paolo Di Canio (Joe Cole 81); Trevor Sinclair.

UEFA Cup

First Round: First Leg
Thursday September 16, 1999
Upton Park, London
West Ham 3
Wanchope 39, Di Canio 48, Lampard 58.
NK Osijek 0
HT: 1-0
Attendance: 25,331
West Ham United: Shaka Hislop; Steve Potts; Igor Stimac; Javier Margas; Trevor Sinclair.
Frank Lampard; Steve Lomas; John Moncur (Marc-Vivien Foe 88); Marc Keller.
Paolo Di Canio (Paul Kitson 85); Paulo Wanchope.

First Round: Second Leg
Thursday September 30, 1999
Gradski Vrt
NK Osijek 1
Bubalo 70
West Ham 3
Kitson 27, Ruddock 83, Foe 90
HT: 0-1
Attendance: 15,000
West Ham won on aggregate 6-1
West Ham United: Shaka Hislop; Steve Potts; Rio Ferdinand (Neil Ruddock 83); Steve Lomas.
Igor Stimac; Marc-Vivien Foe; Trevor Sinclair (Adam Newton 46); Paul Kitson.
Paolo Di Canio (Paulo Wanchope 68); Frank Lampard; Marc Keller.

Second Round: First Leg
Thursday October 21, 1999
Stadionul Ghencea, Bucharest
Steaua Bucharest 2
Rosu 40, Illie S 57
West Ham 0
HT: 1-0
Attendance: 12,500
West Ham United: Shaka Hislop; Steve Potts (Javier Margas 61); Neil Ruddock; Steve Lomas; Rio Ferdinand.
Marc-Vivien Foe; Trevor Sinclair; John Moncur; Paolo Di Canio (Joe Cole 55).
Frank Lampard; Paulo Wanchope.

Second Round, Second Leg
Thursday, November 4,1999
Upton Park, London
West Ham 0
Steaua Bucharest 0
HT: 0-0
Steaua win 2-0 on aggregate.
Attendance: 24,514
West Ham United: Shaka Hislop; Rio Ferdinand; Neil Ruddock; Javier Margas; Trevor Sinclair.
Joe Cole; Frank Lampard; Steve Lomas; Marc Keller (Paul Kitson 64); Paolo Di Canio; Paulo Wanchope.

UEFA Cup 2006/07

First Round: First Leg
Thursday September 14, 2006
Upton Park, London
West Ham 0
USC Palermo 1
Caracciolo (45)
HT: 0-1
Attendance: 32,222
West Ham United: Roy Carroll; Tyrone Mears; Paul Konchesky; Danny Gabbidon; Anton Ferdinand; Javier Mascherano; Lee Bowyer (Matthew Etherington 59); Nigel Reo-Coker; Bobby Zamora (Carlton Cole 77); Carlos Tevez (Marlon Harewood 77); Yossi Benayoun.

First Round: Second Leg
Thursday September 28, 2006
Stadio Renzo Barbera, Palermo, Sicily
U.S.C. Palermo 3
Simplico 35, 62, Di Michele 67
West Ham 0
HT: 1-0
Attendance: 19,264
West Ham United: Roy Carroll; Jon Spector; Paul Konchesky; Danny Gabbidon; James Collins; Javier Mascherano (Yossi Benayoun 68); Ian Bowyer; Nigel Reo-Coker; Marlon Harewood (Teddy Sheringham 68); Carlton Cole (Bobby Zamora 60); Carlos Tevez.
Palermo won 4-0 on aggregate.

UEFA Europa League 2015/16

First Qualifying Round: First Leg
Thursday July 2, 2015
Upton Park, London.
West Ham United 3
Sakho 40, 45+2
Tomkins 58
FC Lusitans 0
HT: 2-0
Attendance: 34,966
West Ham United: Darren Randolph; James Tomkins (Captain); Matt Jarvis; Mauro Zarate (Djair Parfitt-Williams 73); Diafra Sakho (Elliott Lee 62); Joey O'Brien (Josh Cullen 60); Morgan Amalfitano; Diego Poyet; Reece Burke; Reece Oxford; Lewis Page.

First Qualifying Round: Second Leg
Thursday July 9, 2015
Estadi Comunal D'Andorra La Vella, Andorra La Vella
FC Lusitans 0
West Ham United 1
Lee 21
HT: 1-0
West Ham win on aggregate 4-0
Attendance: 1,300
West Ham United: Darren Randolph; Joey O'Brien (Reece Burke 60); James Tomkins (Captain); Reece Oxford; Lewis Page; Diego Poyet; Josh Cullen (Amos Nasha 85); Matt Jarvis; Morgan Amalfitano (Djair Parfitt-Williams 76); Diafra Sakho; Elliot Lee.

Second Qualifying Round: First Leg
Thursday July 16, 2015
Upton Park, London.
West Ham United 1
Tomkins 90
Birkirkara 0
HT: 0-0
Attendance: 33,048
West Ham United: Adrian; Joey O'Brien; James Tomkins; Winston Reid; Aaron Cresswell; Kevin Nolan (Captain) (Diego Poyet 79); Mark Noble; Matt Jarvis; Morgan Amalfitano (Martin Samuelsen 59); Mauro Zarate; Modibo Maiga (Elliot Lee 67).

Second Qualifying Round: Second Leg
Thursday July 23, 2015
Ta' Qali National Stadium, Valetta, Malta
Birkirkara 1
Miccoli 14
West Ham United 0
HT: 1-0
1-1 on aggregate
West Ham win 5-3 on penalties
Attendance: 15,257
West Ham United: Adrian; Joey O'Brien; James Tomkins; James Collins; Aaron Cresswell; Cheikhou Kouyate; Mark Noble; Kevin Nolan (Captain) (Diego Poyet 59); Matt Jarvis (Martin Samuelsen 120); Morgan Amalfitano (Modibo Maiga 59); Mauro Zarate.

Third Qualifying Round: First Leg
Thursday July 30, 2015
Upton Park, London.
West Ham United 2
Valencia 23, Zarate 51
Astra Giurgiu 2
Boldrin 71, Ogbonna 82 (og)
HT: 1-0
Attendance: 33,858
West Ham United: Adrian; Aaron Creswell; Cheikhou Kouyate; Mauro Zarate (Matt Jarvis 76); Mark Noble (Captain); Joey O'Brien (Reece Burke 36); James Collins; Angelo Ogbonna; Dimitri Payet; Enner Valencia (Modibo Maiga 37); Reece Oxford.

Third Qualifying Round: Second Leg
Thursday August 6, 2015

Stadionul Marin Anastasovici, Giurgiu,Romania
Astra Giurgiu 2
Budescu 32, 36
West Ham United 1
Lanzini 3
HT: 2-1
Astra Giurgiu win 4-3 on aggregate.
Attendance: 6,300
West Ham United: Darren Randolph; Kevin Nolan (Captain); Carl Jenkinson; Modibo Maiga; Dimitri Poyet; Oneil Henry; Manuel Lanzini; Elliot Lee (Jordan Brown 80); Lewis Page (Alex Pike 89); Josh Cullen; Kyle Knoyle.

UEFA Europa League 2016/17

Third Qualifying Round: First Leg
Thursday July 28, 2016
Stadion Stozice, Slovenia
NK Domzale 2
Crnic 11 (Pen), 49
West Ham United 1
Noble 18 (Pen).
HT: 1-1
Attendance: 8,500
West Ham United: Adrian; Michail Antonio (Domingos Quina 81); Havard Nordtveit; Winstone Reid; Sam Byram; Pedro Obiang; Cheikhou Kouyate; Mark Noble (Captain); Sofiane Feghouli; Enner Valencia; Andy Carroll.

Third Qualifying Round: Second Leg
Thursday August 4, 2016
London Stadium, London
West Ham United 3
Kouyate 8, 25; Feghouli 81
NK Domzale 0
HT: 2-0
Attendance: 53,914
West Ham United: Darren Randolph; Michail Antonio; Winstone Reid; Reece Oxford; Sam Byram; Havard Nordtveit; Cheikhou Kouyate (Pedro Obiang 88); Mark Noble (Captain); Sofiane Feghouli; (Domingos Quina 88); Enner Valencia; Andy Carroll (Ashley Fletcher 90).

Play-Off Round: First Leg
Thursday August 18, 2016
Stadionul Marin Anastasovici,Giurgiu.
Astra Giurgiu 1
Alibec 83
West Ham United 1
Noble 45 (Pen).
HT: 0-1
Attendance: 3,360
West Ham United: Darren Randolph; Sam Byram; Reece Oxford; Angelo Ogbonna; Reece Burke; Pedro Obiang; Mark Noble (Captain); Michail Antonio. Enner Valencia (Andy Carroll 62); Gokhan Tore (Marcus Browne 74); Jonathan Calleri (James Collins 63).

Play-Off Round: Second Leg
Thursday August 25, 2016
The London Stadium, London
West Ham United 0
Astra Giurgiu 1
Teixeira 45
HT: 0-1
Astra win 2-1 on aggregate.
Attendance: 56,932
West Ham United: Darren Randolph; Sam Byram; Winstone Reid (Capt); Angelo Ogbonna; Reece Burke (James Collins 88); Havard Nordtveit (Enner Valencia 46); Pedro Obiang; Cheikhou Kouyate; Gokhan Tore; Jonathan Calleri (Ashley Fletcher 61); Michail Antonio.

UEFA Europa League 2021/22

First Round
Thursday September 16,2021
Stadion Maksimir
Dinamo Zagreb 0
West Ham United 2
Antonio 21, Rice 50
HT: 0-1
Attendance: 12,344
West Ham United: Fabianski; Fredericks; Zouma; Diop; Cresswell; Rice (Cap); (Noble 83); Soucek; Lanzini; (Benrahma 52); Vlasic; (Bowen 69); Fornals; (Masuaku 83); Antonio; (Yarmolenko 83).
Dinamo Zagreb: Livakovic; Sutalo; Theophile-Catherine; (Juric 46); Lauritsen; Ristovski; (Moharrami 63); Ademi; (Cap); Misic; (Tolic 75); Franjic; Ivanusec; (Menalo 83); Orsic; (Gojak 83); Petkovic.
Referee: Ruddy Buquet (France)

Second Round
Thursday September 30,2021
The London Stadium, London
West Ham United 2
Rice 29, Benrahma 90+4
Rapid Vienna 0
HT: 1-0
Attendance: 50,004
West Ham United: Areola; Johnson; Dawson; Diop; Cresswell; Noble (Cap); (Soucek 62); Rice; Vlasic; (Lanzine 62); Yarmolenko; (Fornals 75); Benrahma; Antonio; (Bowen 62).
Rapid Vienna: Gartler; Aiwu; Greimi (Stojkovic 62); Wimmer; Ullmann (Auer 74); Petrovic; (Ljubicic 81); Grahovac; Arase; Knasmullner; Fountas (Kitagawa 62); Kara (Grull 62).
Referee: Tobias Stieler (Germany)

Third Round
Thursday October 21,2021
The London Stadium, London
West Ham United 3
Dawson 45+1, Diop 57,Bowen 58.
KRC Genk 0
HT: 1-0
Attendance: 45,980
West Ham United: Areola; Johnson; Dawson; Diop; Cresswell (Fredericks 67); Rice (Cap)(Noble 67); Soucek 58; Yarmolenko; Lanzini (Chesters 88); Vlasic (Fornals 83); Bowen (Benrahma 83).
KRC Genk: Vandevoordt; Preciado 87; Cuesta (Sadick 46); Lucumi; Arteaga; Thorstvedt (Toma 83); Hrosovsky; Heynen; Bongonda (Tresor 73); Onuachu (Ugbo 73); Ito (Oyen 83).
Referee: Donatas Rumsas (Lithuania)

Fourth Round
Thursday November 4,2021
Cegeka Arena
KRC Genk 2
Paintsil 4, Soucek 87 (og)
West Ham United 2
Benrahma 59,82
HT: 1-0
Attendance: 12,239
West Ham United: Areola; Coufal; Dawson; Diop; Cresswell; Rice (Cap); Noble (Soucek 58); Benrahma; Lanzini (Kral 85); Masuaku (Fornals 58); Antonio (Bowen 58).
KRC Genk: Vandevoordt; Munoz (Preciado 87); Sadick; Lucumi; Arteaga; Thorstvedt (Ugbo 97); Hrosovsky, Ito; Heynen; Paintsil (Oyen 90+4); Onuachu.
Referee: Aleksandar Stavrev (Macedonia)

Fifth Round
Thursday November 25,2021
Rapid Vienna 0
West Ham United 2
Yarmolenko 39; Noble 45+2 (Pen)
HT: 0-2
Attendance: 0
West Ham United: Areola; Coufal; Dawson; Diop; Masuaka (Fredericks 77); Noble (Cap); Soucek (Kral 65); Lanzini (Fornals 65); Vlasic (Perkins 77); Yarmolenko; Bowen (Benrahma 65).
Rapid Vienna: Gartler; Hofmann (Cap); Aiwu; Moorman; Petrovic; Ljubicic (Grahovac 90); Arase (Ballo 75); Knasmullner (Grull 59); Fountad (Dtrunz 90); Kitagawa (Kara 59).
Referee: Sergei Ivanov (Russia)

Sixth Round
Thursday December 9,2021
The London Stadium, London
West Ham United 0
GNK Dinamo Zagreb 1
Orsic 3
HT: 0-1
Attendance: 49,401
West Ham United: Areola; Ashby; Baptiste; Alese; Longelo; Noble (Cap); Kral; Yarmolenko (Potts 87); Fornals (Benrahma 46); Vlasis; Perkins (Forson 87).
GNK Dinamo Zagreb: Livakovic; Sutalo; Theophile-Catherine; Peric; Ristovski; Ademi (Cap) (Bulat 71); Gojak; Stefulji (Dilaver 80); Ivanusec; Andric (Juric 64); Orsic (Misic 64).
Referee: Maurizio Mariani (Italy)

Round of 16, First Leg
Thursday March 10,2022
Ramon Sanchez-Pizjuan Stadium, Seville
Sevilla FC 1
Munir 60
West Ham United 0

HT: 0-0
Attendance: 34,728
West Ham United: Areola; Johnson; Dawson; Zouma; Cresswell; Rice (Cap); Soucek; Lanzini (Noble 83); Fornals (Masuaku 90+3); Vlasic (Benrahma 67); Antonio.
Sevilla FC: Bono; Jesus Navas (Cap); Gudelj; Kounde; Acuna; Jardan; Oliver Torres; Corona (Augustinsson 88); Ocampos; En-Nesyri (Rafa Mir 89); Munir (Martial 75).
Referee: Sandro Scharer (Switzerland)

Round of 16, Second Leg
Thursday March 17,2022
The London Stadium, London
West Ham United 2
Soucek 39, Yarmalenko 112
Sevilla FC 0
West Ham United win 2-1 on aggregate, after extra time.
HT: 1-0
Attendance: 59,981
West Ham United: Areola; Johnson; Dawson; Zouma; Cresswell; Rice (Cap); Soucek; Fornals (Diop 119); Lanzini (Noble 115); Benrahma (Yarmolenko 88); Antonio (Fredericks 120).
Sevilla FC: Boubou; Jesus Navas (Cap) (Montiel 106); Kounde; Gudelj (Carmona 111); Augustinsson; Jordan; Delaney; Rakitic (Torres 56); Corona (Munir 96); En-Nesyri (Rafa Mir 91); Martial (Luismi 101).
Referee: Clement Turpin (France)

Quarter Final, First Leg
Thursday April 7,2022
The London Stadium, London
West Ham United 1
Bowen 52
Olympique Lyonnais 1
Ndombele 66
HT: 0-0
Attendance: 59,978
West Ham United: Areola; Fredericks; Dawson; Zouma; Cresswell; Rice. (Cap); Soucek; Fornals; Benrahma (Johnson 46); Bowen; Antonio.
Olympique Lyonnais: Lopes; Gusto; Boateng (Toko Ekambi 64); Lukeba; Emerson; Aouar; Mendes (Denayer 90); Ndombele; Faivre (Tete 64); Lucas Paqueta; Dembele (Cap).
Referee: Felix Zwayer (Germany)

Quarter Final, Second Leg
Thursday April 14,2022
Parc Olympique Lyonnais
West Ham United 3
Dawson 38; Rice 44; Bowen 48.
Olympique Lyonnais 0
West Ham United win 4-1 on aggregate.
HT: 2-0
Attendance: 50,065
West Ham United: Areola; Coufal; Dawson; Diop; Johnson; Rice (Cap) (Benrahma 90); Soucek; Bowen; Lanzini (Noble 77); Fornals; Antonio (Yarmolenko 84).
Olympique Lyonnais: Pollersback; Gusto; Denayer (Reine-Adelaide 89); Lukeba; Emerson; Mendes; faivre (Lucas Paqueta 46); Toko Ekambi; Aouar(B.Barcola 71); Ndombele (Tete 46); Dembele (Cap).
Referee: Sandro Scharer (Switzerland)

Semi-Final, First Leg
Thursday April 28,2022
The London Stadium, London
West Ham United 1
Antonio 21
Eintracht Frankfurt 2
Knauff 1, Kamada 54
HT: 1-1
Attendance: 59,980
West Ham United: Areola; Johnson; Zouma; Dawson; Cresswell; Soucek; Rice (Cap); Bowen; Lanzini (Benrahma 66); Fornals; Antonio.
Eintracht Frankfurt: Trapp; Tata; Hinteregger; Toure; Knauff; Sow; Rode; Kostic; Lindstrom (Hauge 62); Kamada; Borre (Ache 90+3).
Referee: S Gozubuyuk (Netherlands)

Semi-Final, Second Leg
Thursday, May 5,2022
Deutsche Bank Park, Frankfurt
Eintracht Frankfurt 1
Borre 26
West Ham United 0
Eintracht Frankfurt win 3-1 on aggregate.
HT: : 0-1
Attendance:48,000

West Ham United: Areola; Coufal (Yarmolenko 87); Dawson; Zouma; Cresswell; Rice (Cap); Soucek; Bowen; Lanzini (Johnson 22); Fornals (Benrahma 74); Antonio.
Eintracht Frankfurt: Trapp; Tuta; Hinteregger (Toure 8); N'Dicka; Knauff; Sow; Rode (Jakic 76); Kostic; Hauge(Hrustic 82); Kamada; Borre (Paciencia 83).
Referee: Jesus Gil Manzano (Spain)

UEFA Conference League 2022/23

Play-Off Round: First Leg
Thursday August 18,2022
The London Stadium, London
West Ham United 3
Scamacca 23, Bowen 64, Antonio 78
Viborg FF 1
Bonde 69
HT: 1-0
Attendance: 30,230
West Ham United: Areola; Coufal; Johnson; Ogbonna (Cap) (Kehrer 66); Ashby; Soucek; Coventry (Downes 84); Cornet; Lanzini (Fornals 46); Bowen (Benrahma 66); Scamacca (Antonio 66).
Viborg FF: Lund; Anyembe (Gaaei 34); Zaletel; Burgy; Sorensen; Gronning (Cap); Zamburek (Berger 87); Leemans (Sondergaard 66); Bonde (Thorsen 87); Grot; Lonwijk (Mortimer 66).
Referee: Marco Di Bello (Italy).

Play-Off Round: Second Leg
Thursday August 25,2022
Energi Viborg Arena
West Ham United 3
Scamacca 23, Benrahma 51, Soucek 63
Viborg FF 0
West Ham United win 6-1 on aggregate.
HT: 1-0
Attendance: 8,435
West Ham United: Areola; Johnson; Ogbonna; Kehrer; Cresswell (Cap) (Zouma 81; Fornals; Soucek (Downes 68); Benrahma (Coventry 68); Lanzini (Okoflex 82); Cornet; Scamacca (Antonio 68).
Viborg FF: Lund; Gaaei; Burgy; Sorensen; Leemans (Sondergaard 78); Gronning (Cap); Bonde (Zamburek 60); Lonwijk (Mortimer 60); Grot (Jatta 60); Said (Berger 78).
Referee: Harald Lechner (Austria)

UEFA Europa Conference League Group B, Round 1
Thursday September 8,2022
The London Stadium, London
West Ham United 3
Bowen 69 (Pen), Emerson 74, Antonio 90
FCSB 1
Cordea 34
HT: 0-1
Attendance: 39,536
West Ham United: Areola; Coufal; Kehrer; Ogbonna (Dawson 90); Emerson; Rice (Cap); Downes; Benrahma (Bowen 46); Lanzini (Lucas Paqueta 46); Cornet (Fornals 68); Scamacca (Antonio 46).
FCSB: Tarnovanu; Cretu; Dawa (Harut 87); Tamm; Radunovic; Olaru (Rusu 90); Edjouma; Oaida (Radaslavescu 90); Coman (Cap) (Oct. Popescu 71); Cordea; Compagno (Miculescu 70).
Referee: Benoit Bastien (France)

UEFA Europa Conference League Group B, Round 2
Thursday September 15,2022
Jysk Park
West Ham United 3
Lanzini 13 (Pen), Scamacca 25, Dawson 38
Silkeborg IF 2
Kusk 5, Tengstedt 75.
HT: 3-1
Attendance: 6,702
West Ham United: Areola; Coufal; Dawson; Kehrer; Cresswell; Emerson; Lanzini (Coventry 90+3); Rice (Cap) (Soucek 63); Lucas Paqueta (Benrahma 63); Cornet (Fornals 86); Scamacca (Bowen 63).
Silkeborg IF: Larsen; Sonne; Salquist; Felix; Engel (Klitten 46); Poroarson; Brink; Klynge (Kaalund 62); Tengstedt; Kusk (Jorgensen 62); Helenius (Cap) (Adamsen 62)
Referee: Fabio Verissimo (Portugal)

UEFA Europa Conference League
Group B, Round 3
Thursday October 6,2022
Lotto Park, Brussels
West Ham United 1
Scamacca 79
RSC Anderlecht 0
HT: 0-0
Attendance: 17,033
West Ham United: Areola; Coufal; Johnson; Dawson; Ogbonna (Cap); Emerson; Downes; Lanzini (Rice 70); Bowen (Fornals 86); Benrahma (Lucas Paqueta 70); Antonio (Scamacca 70).
RSC Anderlecht: Van Crombrugge (Cap); Debast; Hoedt; Delcroix (N'Diaye 87); Murillo; Ashimeru (Raman 65); Diaware (Esposito 87); Arnstad; Amuzu (Duranville 46); Verschaeren.
Referee: Novak Simovic (Serbia)

UEFA Europa Conference League
Group B, Round 4
Thursday October 13,2022
The London Stadium, London
West Ham United 2
Benrahma 14, Bowen 30
RSC Anderlecht 1
Esposito (Pen) 89
HT: 2-0
Attendance: 40,767
West Ham United: Areola; Coufal; Johnson; Ogbonna (Dawson 22 (Soucek 74)); Cresswell Cap) (Rice 63); Emerson; Lanzini; Downes; Lucas Paqueta (Fornals 46); Benrahma; Bowen (Scamacca 64).
RSC Anderlecht: Van Crombrugge (Cap); Debast; Delcroix (Hoedt 79); N'Diaye ; Murillo; Arnstad; Diawara (Sadiki 59); Verschaeren (Vertonghen 67); Amuzu (Stoeykens 66); Esposito; Silva (Stassin 79).
Referee: Willy Delajod (France)

UEFA Europa Conference League
Group B, Round 5
Thursday October 27,2022
The London Stadium, London
West Ham United 1
Lanzini 24 (Pen
Silkeborg IF 0
HT: 1-0
Attendance: 35,911
West Ham United: Areola; Coufal; Johnson; Aguerd (Kehrer 76); Ogbonna (Cap); Emerson; Lanzini; Coventry (Rice 84); Fornals (Downes 68); Antonio (Soucek 84); Benrahma (Scamacca 68).
Silkeborg IF: Larsen; Ostrom; Salquist; Felix; Klitten; Poroarson; Gojani (Oggesen 48); Klynge (Kaalund 69); Tengstedt (Lind 84); Jorgensen (Kusk 46); Helenius (Cap) (Adamsen 68).
Referee: Joni Hyytia (Finland)

UEFA Europa Conference League
Group B, Round 6
Thursday November 3, 2022
Arena National
West Ham United 3
Fornals 40,65, Dawa 56 (og)
FCSB 0
HT: 1-0
Attendance: 20,172
West Ham United: Areola; Coufal (Ashby 67); Johnson (Casey 77); Aguerd; Ogbonna (Cap); Scarles; Lanzini; Coventry; Downes (Appiah-Forsen 67); Fornals (Potts 67); Mubama (Swyer 67).
FCSB: Tarnovanu; Pantes; Dawa; Bouhenna; Radunovic; Edjouma; Dulca (Radaslavescu 46); Oaida (Olaru 46); Cordea (Cap)(Stoica 46); Compagno (Rusu 59); Popescu (Coman 60).
Referee: Sascha Stegemann (Germany)

UEFA Europa Conference League
Round of 16, First Leg
Thursday March 9,2023
AEK Arena-Georgios Karapatakis
West Ham United 2
Antonio 36, 45+1
AEK Larnaca 0
HT: 2-0
Attendance: 6,654
West Ham United: Areola; Kehrer; Zouma; Aguerd; Cresswell, Rice (Cap) (Soucek 60); Lanzini (Paqueta 77); Downes; Fornals (Cornet 82); Benrahma (Bowen 60); Antonio (Scamacca 60).
AEK Larnaca: Piric; Casas (Faraj 58); Milicevic; Tomavic; Englezou (Cap); Mamas (Altman 58); Ledes; Sanjurjo; Rosales (Christoforou 87); Jakolis (Trickovski 77); Lopes (Nikolic 58).
Referee: Espen Eskas (Norway)

UEFA Europa Conference League
Round of 16, Second Leg
Thursday March 16,2023
The London Stadium, London
West Ham United 4
Scamacca 20; Bowen 47,49, Mubama 65
AEK Larnaca 0
West Ham United win 6-0 on aggregate.
HT: 1-0
Attendance: 40,482
West Ham United: Areola; Johnson; Zouma (Laing 68); Ogbanna (Cap); Cresswell; Soucek (Potts 68); Paqueta (Cornet 54); Lanzini; Bowen (Mubama 54); Fornals; Scamacca (Ings 54).
AEK Larnaca: Piric; Casas; Tomavic; Gonzalez(Cap)(Christoforou 46); Englezou; Gus; Oier (Pons 66); Mamas; Jalolis (Altman 66); Naoum (Faraj 81); Nikolic (Lopes 66).
Referee: Georgi Kabakov (Bulgaria)

UEFA Europa Conference League
Quarter-Final, First Leg
Thursday April 13,2023
KAA Gent Stadium
West Ham United 1
Ings 45+3
KAA Gent 1
Cuypers , 56
HT: 1-0
Attendance: 19,037
West Ham United: Areola; Coufal; Johnson; Aguerd; Ogbonna; Emerson (Cresswell 87); Rice (Cap); Downes (Paqueta 74); Lanzini (Benrahma 61); Bowen; Ings (Antonio 61)
KAA Gent: Roef; Castro-Mentes; Piatkowski; Okumu; Torunarigha (Fortuna 65); Hong (Odjidja-Offoe 65); Kums (Cap); De Sart; Fofana (Samoise 65); Cuypers; Orban (Tissoudali 83).
Referee: Tasos Sidiropoulos (Greece)

UEFA Europa Conference Quarter-Final, Second Leg
Thursday April 20,2023
The London Stadium, London
West Ham United 4
Antonio 47,63, Paqueta 55 (pen), Rice 58.
KAA Gent 1
Cupyers 26
West Ham won 5-2 on aggregate.
HT: 0-1
Attendance: 53,475
West Ham United: Areola; Coufal; Zouma (Kehrer 70); Aguerd; Emerson; Rice (Cap) (Downes 70); Soucek; Paqueta; Benrahma (Fornals 79); Bowen (Cornet 79).
KAA Gent: Roef; Samoise; Piatkowski; Okumu; Nurio-Fortuna; Kums (Cap); De Sart (Odjidja-Offoe 71); Castro-Montes (Fofana 85); Hong (Depoitre 72); Cuypers (Godeau 84); Orban (Tissoudali 72).
Referee: Orel Grinfield (Israel)

UEFA Europa Conference League
Semi-Final, First Leg
Thursday May 11,2023
The London Stadium, London
West Ham United 2
Benrahma 67 (Pen), Antonio 75
AZ Alkmaar 1
Reijnders 41
HT: 0-1
Attendance: 62,471
West Ham United: Areola; Kehrer; Zouma; Aguerd; Cresswell,Rice (Cap); Soucek; Paqueta; Benrahma (Fornals 90); Antonio (Ings 79); Bowen.
AZ Alkmaar: Ryan; Sugawara; Beukema; Hatzidiakos; M.de Wit; Clasie (Cap); Mijnans; Reijnders; Odgaard (Lahdo 68); van Brederade (Mihaliovic 80); Pavlidis.
Referee: Thalil Umut Meler (Turkey)

UEFA Europa Conference League
Semi-Final, Second Leg
Thursday May 18,2023
AZ Stadion
West Ham United 1
Fornals 90+4
AZ Alkmaar 0
West Ham United win 3-1 on aggregate.
HT: 0-0
Attendance: 19,009
West Ham United: Areola; Kehrer; Zouma; Aguerd; Cresswell; Soucek; Rice (Cap); Paqueta(Downes 90+5); Bowen; Antonio (Ings 84); Benrahma (Fornals 75).
AZ Alkmaar: Ryan; Sugawara; Beukema; Hatzidiakos; Kerkez (M.de Wit 85); Reijnders; Mijnans(D. de Wit 70); Clasie (Cap); van Brederode (Lahdo 78);

Pavlidis; Karlsson (Meerdink 85).
Referee: Ivan Kruzliak (Slovskia).

UEFA Europa Conference League Final
Wednesday June 7,2023
Eden Arena, Prague
West Ham United 2
Benrahma 62 (Pen), Bowen 90
ACF Fiorentina 1
Bonaventura 67
HT: 0-0
Attendance:17,363
West Ham United: Areola; Coufal; Zouma (Kehrer 61); Aguerd; Emerson; Soucek; Rice (Cap); Paqueta; Bowen; Benrahma (Fornals 76); Antonio (Ogbonna 90+3).
ACF Fiorentina: Terracciano; Dodo; Milenkovic; Ranieri (Igor 84); Biraghi (Cap); Bonaventura; Amrabat; Mandragora; Gonzalez; Jovic (Cabral 46); Kouame (Saponara 62).
Referee: Carlos Del Cerro Grande (Spain)

UEFA Europa League 2023/24

Thursday September 21,2023
The London Stadium
UEFA Europa League Group A-Round 1
West Ham United 3
Petrovic 66 og, Kudus 70, Soucek 82
FK TSC 1
Stanic 47
Half-Time: 0-0
Attendance: 41,374
Position in Group: 1st.
West Ham United: Fabianski; Kehrer; Mavropanos; Ogbonna; Cresswell (Emerson 46); Paquetá (Cornet 86); Ward-Prowse; Fornals (Antonio 61); Kudus; Ings (Soucek 76); Benrahma
Backa Topola : Simic; Cvetokovic; Antonic; Dordevic (Krstic 69); Petrovic (Rakonjac 81); Radin; Dakovac (Cirkovic 80); Stojic; Kuveljic (Vulic 80); Stanic; Jovanovic (Mirchevski 90+2).
Referee F Glova.
Thursday October 5 ,2023

UEFA Europa League Group A-Round 2
Europa-Park Stadium
SC Freiburg 1
Sallai 49
West Ham United 2
Paqueta 8, Aguerd 66
Half-Time: 0-1
Attendance: 34,100
Position in Group: 1st.
Freiburg: Atubolu; Sildillia; Ginter; Lienhart; Kübler (Weisshaupt 76); Sallai; Eggestein (Röhl 76); Höfler; Grifo (Breunig 87); Adamu (Doan 45); Höler (Philipp 76).
West Ham United: Fabianski; Coufal; Mavropanos; Aguerd; Kehrer (Emerson 71); Álvarez; Ward-Prowse (Ings 90); Kudus (Benrahma 80); Paquetá (Mubama 90); Fornals (Soucek 71); Bowen.
Referee M Al-Hakim (Swe).

UEFA Europa League, Group A, Round 3
Thursday October 26,2023
Georgios Karaiskakis Stadium
Olympiacos 2
Fortounis 33, de Almeida 45+1
West Ham United 1
Paqueta 87
Half-Time: 2-0
Attendance: 30,623
Position in Group: 1st=
Olympiacos: Paschalis; Rodinei (Quini 74); Retsos; Porozo; Ortega; Alexandropoulos (Masouras 85); Camara; Hezze; Podence (Solbakken 85); El Kaabi(Scarpa 90+5); Fortounis (Jovetic 90+5).
West Ham United: Areola; Kehrer; Mavropanos; Ogbonna; Emerson; Ward-Prowse (Álvarez 72); Soucek; Benrahma (Bowen 58); Fornals (Paquetá 57); Kudus (Cornet 72); Ings (Antonio 58).
Referee: Andris Teimanis

UEFA Europa League, Group A, round 4
Thursday November 9, 2023
London Stadium
West Ham United 1
Paqueta 73
Olympiacos 0
Half-Time:0-0
Attendance: 55,811
Position in Group: 1st.
West Ham United: Fabianski; Coufal; Mavropanos; Aguerd; Emerson; Álvarez (Soucek 80); Ward-Prowse; Kudus (Mubama 89); Paquetá;

Benrahma(Cornet 84); Bowen.
Olympiacos: Paschalakis; Rodinei; Porozo; Restos; Ortega; Hezze (Biel Mas Jaume 90); Alexandropoulos (Scarpa 76); Camara; Podence (Masouras 76); Jovetic (El Kaabi 56); Fortunas.
Referee M Jug (Slovenia)

Europa League, Group A, Round 5
Thursday November 30, 2023
TSC Arena
Backa Topola 0
West Ham United 1
Soucek 89
Half-Time: 0-0
Attendance: 4,256
Position in Group: 1st.
Backa Topola: Ilic; Cvetkovic; Antonic; Stojic; Calusic; Petrovic; Kuveljic (Vulic 77); Radin (Vlalukin 77); Dakovac; Milovanovic (Pantovic 77); Cirkovic(Sos 86).
West Ham United: Fabianski; Johnson (Kehrer 79); K Mavropanos; Aguerd; Cresswell (Emerson 79); Ward-Prowse; Paquetá; Fornals; Soucek; Benrahma (Cornet 67); Mubama (Ings 67).
Referee A Lindhout (Neth).

UEFA Europa League Group A, Round 6
Thursday December 14,2023
London Stadium
West Ham United 2
Kudus 14, Alvarez 42
Freiburg 0
Half-time 2-0
Attendance:48,876
Position in Group: 1st.
West Ham United: Fabianski; Coufal (Kehrer 88min); Mavropanos; Aguerd; Emerson; Álvarez (Fornals 54); Soucek; Kudus (Cornet 88); Ward-Prowse; Paquetá (Mubama 72); Bowen.
Freiburg: Atubolu; Sildialli; Ginter; Gulde; Makengo (Kübler 74); Doan; Eggestein (Höler 56); Höfler; Grifo (Weisshaupt 69); Sallai (Röhl 45); Gregoritsch(Adamu 56).
Referee J Pinheiro (Por).

UEFA Europa League, Round of 16, First Leg
Thursday March 7,2024
Europa-Park Stadium
Freiburg 1
Gregotitsch 81
West Ham United 0
Half Time: 0-0
Attendance: 34,700
Referee: Alejandro Hernandez (Spain)
Freiburg
Atubolu; Sildillia (Kubler 82); Ginter; Gulde; Günter; Hofler; Doan(Muslija 82); Eggestein; Holer(Gregoritsch 71); Grifo (Weishaupt 71; Sallai 6.
West Ham United: Fabianski; Coufal; Mavropanos; Zouma; Emerson (Cresswell 68); Ward-Prowse (Phillips 82); Alvarez; , Soucek; Paqueta; , Bowen; Kudus.
Referee: Alejandro Hernandez (Spain)

UEFA Europa League, Round of 16, Second Leg
Thursday March 14,2024
The London Stadium
West Ham United 5
Paqueta 9, Bowen 32, Cresswell 52, Kudus 77,85
Freiburg 0
West Ham win on aggregate 5-1
Half Time: 2-0
Attendance: 51,014
West Ham United: Fabianski; Coufal; Zouma; Mavropanos ; Cresswell; Alvarez (Phillips 86) ; Soucek; Bowen (Earthy 86); Paqueta (Ward-Prowse 62) ; Kudus(Ings 86 ; Antonio (Johnson 78).
Freiburg: Atubolu; Sildillia (Röhl 68); Ginter ; Gulde (Kübler 62), Günter; Höfler (Muslija 62); Eggestein; Doan; Sallai ; Grifo (Gregoritsch 45); Holer (Philipp 68).
Referee: Marco Guida (Italy)

UEFA Cup, Quarter Finals, First Leg
Thursday April 11, 2024
BayArena
Bayer Leverkusen 2
Hofmann 83, Boniface 90+1
West Ham United 0
Half-Time: 0-0
Attendance:30,210
Bayer Leverkusen: Kovar: Stanisic

(Hincapié 66); Tah; Tapsoba ; Frimpong (Tella 67) ; Palacios; Xhaka; Grimaldo; Wirtz; Adli (Hofmann 76); Schick (Boniface 76).
West Ham United: Fabianski; Mavropanos (Aguerd 86); Zouma; Cresswell; Coufal; Soucek; Ward-Prowse; Emerson; Kudus (Johnson 86); Paquetà; Antonio.
Referee Artur Manuel Soares Dias

UEFA EUROPA League, Quarter Final Second Leg
Thursday April 18, 2924
West Ham United 1
Antonio 13
Bayer Leverkusen 1
Frimpong 89
Half-Tine: 1-0
Bayer Leverkusen win on aggregate: 3-1
Attendance: 62,473
West Ham United: Fabianski; Coufal (Johnson 83); Zouma; Aguerd (Ogbonna 45); Cresswell; Ward-Prowse; Álvarez (Cornet 83); Soucek; Bowen; Antonio; Kudus
Bayer Leverkusen: Kovar; Stanisic; Tah; Kossounou (Tapsoba 29); Hincapie; Xhaka; Palacios; Tella (Frimpong 45); F Wirtz (Andrich 87), Grimaldo (Adli 68); Schick (Boniface 45,).
Referee J Sanchez (Sp).

Bibliography

Banks, Robert: *An Irrational Hatred of Luton*. Independent UK Sports Publications (London) 1995

Banks, Robert: *An Irrational Hatred of Everything*. Biteback Publishing (London) 2018

Belton, Brian: *They Nearly Reached the Sky*. Fonthill, 2017

Blows, Kirk: *Terminator-The Authorised Julian Dicks Story*. Polar Publishing (Leicester) 1996

Blows, Kirk and Hogg, Tony: *The Essential History of West Ham United*. Headline (London) 2000

Blows, Kirk and Sharratt, Ben: *Bring me the Head of Trevor Brooking*. Mainstream (Edinburgh) 2010

Bonds, Billy: *Bonzo – An Autobiography*. Weidenfeld & Nicolson (London) 1988

Brand, Paul: Fortune's Always Hiding: From Stratford to Saville. Pitch Publishing (Chichester) 2023

Brand, Russell: *Irons in the Fire*. Hodder & Stoughton (London) 2007

Brooking, Trevor: *An Autobiography*. Pelham Books (London) 1981

Di Canio, Paolo: *The Autobiography*. Collins Willow (London) 2000

Dickinson, Matt: *Bobby Moore- The Man in Full*. Yellow Jersey Press (London) 2014

Fuller, Stuart: *Passport to Football*. SportsBooks (Cheltenham) 2009

Goldblatt, David: *The Ball is Round-A Global History of Football*. Viking (London) 2006

Greenwood, Ron: *Yours Sincerely*. Willow Books (London) 1984

Hurley, Daniel: *The Games That Made Us*. Pitch (Chichester) 2022

Hurst, Geoff: *The World Game*. Sportsman's Book Club (London) 1968

Johnson, Graham Martin: *Any Old Iron.* Superwize (London) 2011
Korr, Charle: *West Ham United.* Duckworth (London) 1986
Lyall, John: *Just Like My Dreams-My Life with West Ham.* Viking (London) 1989
MacDonald, Roger: *Britain versus Europe.* Pelham Books (London) 1968
Martin, Alvin: *A 21 Year Stretch.* Testimonial Brochure (1995)
May, Pete: *Hammers in the Heart.* Mainstream (Edinburgh) 2005
Moynihan, John: *The West Ham Story.* Arthur Barker (London) 1984
Noble, Mark: *Boleyn Boy-My Autobiography.* Harper Collins (Dublin) 2023
Northcutt, John and Shoesmith, Roy: *West Ham United-A Complete Record.* Breedon Books (Derby) 1993
Northcutt, John & Shoesmith, Roy: *West Ham – an Illustrated History.* Breedon Books (Derby) 1998
Northcutt, John & Marsh, John: *West Ham United– The Complete Record.* deCoubertin Books (Liverpool) 2015
Powell, Jeff: *Bobby Moore-The Life and Times of a Sporting Hero.* Robson Books (London) 1993
Stevens, Dr. Phil: *John Lyall – A Life in Football.* Apex Publishing (Clacton-on-Sea) 2015
Stewart, Ray: *Spot on with Tonka.* Testimonial Brochure
Tomas, Jason: *The Hammers – The West Ham United Dream Team.* Mainstream (Edinburgh) 1997
Weeks, David:*And on the 6th day God created Bobby Moore.* New Breed Publishing (London) 2012
Williams, Brian: *Nearly Reach the Sky – A Farewell to Upton Park.* Biteback Publishing (London) 2015

Sky Sports Football Yearbooks
European Cup Winners' Cup 50 Years On
Club brochure, issued with 2014/15 Membership.
West Ham Programmes

Websites
Wikipedia
West Ham United F.C.in European Football
UEFA.com
bb.co.uk/sport
theyflysohigh.co.uk